DRESSING A TIGER

DRESSING A TIGER

By

Maggie San Miguel

Orchard Drive Press
Kyle, TX

Copyright © 2016 by Maggie San Miguel

All rights reserved by Orchard Drive Press. No part of this book may be reproduced without the publisher's written permission, except for brief quotations in reviews.

www.maggiesanmiguel.com

Printed in the United States of America
10 9 8 7 6 5 4 3 2 1

Cover design: Marie Carter

ISBN 978-0-9970360-0-8

Library of Congress PCN number: 2015918935

Our livelihood, our dwelling, our sustenance, even our success and fame, are the result of contributions made by innumerable fellow human beings. Whether directly or indirectly, countless others are involved in our survival—not to mention our happiness.

—The Dalai Lama, *An Open Heart*

For my son, Sage

Table of Contents

CHAPTER ONE
In Which We Are Introduced: Greenwich, Connecticut, 1967

CHAPTER TWO
In Which We See The Beginning and the Difference, Minneapolis, Minnesota, 1919

CHAPTER THREE
In Which People Come to Visit From Far Away and They Have A Bath, Greenwich, Connecticut, 1968

CHAPTER FOUR
In Which Some Souls Come, Some Go, and Some Reunite to Begin Another Journey Together, Minneapolis, Minnesota, 1929

CHAPTER FIVE
In Which the Dahlstroms Go to Washington and Flip Wilson Learns to Fly, Washington, D.C., 1969

CHAPTER SIX
In Which We Realize That Some Tales, No Matter How Great Our Intentions, Can Never Be Told Gently Enough, Innsbruck, Austria, New Year's Eve, 1969

CHAPTER SEVEN
In Which We Go Visiting and Deliver a Package, and a Sweet Old Grandmother Cooks Something That Smells of Home, Verona, Italy, January 3, 1970

CHAPTER EIGHT
In Which Plans Are Made and People Wait to Be Together, Hollywood Park Racetrack, California, 1942

CHAPTER NINE
In Which We Discover A Little Je Ne Sais Quoi, Greenwich, Connecticut, 1970

CHAPTER TEN
In Which Production Begins on a Project That Would Be Better Left Dead and the Teamsters Take a Chink Out of Hollywood's Armor, Greenwich, Connecticut, 1972

CHAPTER ELEVEN
In Which We Meet an Exceptionally Good Somebody, Greenwich, Connecticut, 1973

CHAPTER TWELVE
In Which We See That to Betray Certain Leagues of Men Is a Guarantee of Swift Revenge, Served Too Hot to Eat, Dallas, Texas, November 20, 1963

CHAPTER THIRTEEN
In Which Dinner is Nearly Ruined by a Crouton, Greenwich, Connecticut, 1975

CHAPTER FOURTEEN
In Which Treasured Memories And Coveted Secrets Are Wrapped in Paper and Packed in Boxes, Greenwich, Connecticut 1977

CHAPTER FIFTEEN
In Which We Grow Into Something Quite Different, St. Paul, Minnesota, 1978

CHAPTER SIXTEEN
In Which Wolves Line Their Cozy Den With the Soft, Trusting Down of the General Public, Dallas, Texas, November 22, 1963 - 11:20 am

CHAPTER SEVENTEEN
In Which Family Comes to Stay and a Package Arrives From Hoboken, St. Paul, Minnesota, 1979

CHAPTER EIGHTEEN
In Which We Reach an Emotional Summit, St. Paul, Minnesota, 1979

CHAPTER NINETEEN
In Which the Tiger Has Peeled Off His Fancy Clothes and Stands Naked in His Stripes, Present Day

CHAPTER TWENTY
In Which Camelot Crumbles and a Phone Call Is Made, Dallas, Texas, November 22, 1963 ~ 12:27 pm

CHAPTER TWENTY-ONE
In Which Most of the World Weeps While Others Simply Have Cocktails, Dallas, Texas, November 22, 1963 ~ 2:58 pm

Prelude to a Hit
Dallas, Texas, November 22, 1963 ~ 12:27 pm

The black Presidential convertible is moving slowly in the center of the motorcade. Security is thinner than Jack had anticipated. A flicker of bright pink moves at the back of the car like an unexpected wild flower blooming from a pile of coal.

Jack holds his breath waiting for the first shot. Nothing happens. They're late. They should have taken a shot by now. A deep, worried line creases between his eyes. He takes another look at the sewer opening across the street.

Then he hears it. One pop. Just loud enough for a few people in the crowd to turn their attention away from the President for a brief moment. Kennedy's head turns towards the sound.

CHAPTER ONE

*In Which We Are Introduced,
Greenwich, Connecticut, 1967*

The scream inside my head escaped as a feeble puff of air, which made me realize I'd never be good in a crisis, or maybe it was just too early in the morning for screaming.

When I opened my eyes this morning, it was right there – inches from my face – the Italian nose, broken from its fifteen years in the boxing ring. It would be distressing for anyone to awaken to this, but when the nose belongs to Jimmy Bruno, the thick and meaty bodyguard of an Under Boss, the ante is upped. This is not how a day should begin.

My usual greeting for Jimmy, when I'm awake and expecting him, is a half-slam half-hug, from which he pulls back and takes a boxer's stance, bringing his fists up in self defense as he enters our house. I mimic him, and we bounce around each other on the balls of our feet. He's taught me this sort of greeting, along with the Italian Chin Wave – the quick, confident tossing back of the head in a person's direction. Jimmy says that's what you do when your hands are full or you're in the middle of lunch.

As I wipe the sleep from my eyes, trying to make sense of this morning, Jimmy says, "Let's go for a ride, Sweetie."

Now, for the average American kid of five years old, these would be the sweet words of an impending adventure; a picnic, a scenic drive in the country to see the leaves turn in the fall and pick a few apples before the sun sets, or maybe a trip to the movies. In my house, they are cause for alarm.

Jimmy is holding a small green bowl under my chin. Jimmy is a potter and even owns his own kiln. He makes his pottery in the back of the garage he owns in Manhattan. It helps him relax, he says. Now I realize this bowl is meant to entice me out of bed, or to at least sit up and take notice, but instead, I look beyond Jimmy's hopeful face and his bowl and size up my father standing in my bedroom doorway. He smiles at me and tells me to get dressed. To Jimmy, he says, "Maggie will need some muscle today. Thanks, Jimmy." Dad is in a suit, which means he is on his way to work or to La Guardia to catch a flight. From here, I can tell he smells good – the way he always smells when he wears his suits. He has a routine that I've memorized: Before buttoning up his shirt collar and slipping a silk tie around his neck, he opens the medicine cabinet with the mirrored door and reaches for the bottle of pale blue liquid, pours a small bit into his left palm, rubs his hands together quickly, spilling a few drops into the sink, then splashes the aftershave on his jaw line and neck. I've spent many mornings perched on the closed toilet seat watching him, ready to assist him if needed. Before he replaces the bottle back inside the medicine cabinet, Dad grabs me by my face with both hands so that I smell as delicious as he does, and says, "Now you're ready for your day, too, Kiddo."

The scent of Dad in his suit can make me happy and sad at the same time. Happy because it smells of us spending time alone together and sad because it also smells of him going somewhere without me.

Jimmy is still holding the green bowl too close to my face as I study my father – trying to get a read on him and figure out what is happening. The light bulb in the hallway creates a shine on the top of his bald head. He fills my doorway, being so tall and broad-shouldered, and has two deep lines between his eyes that show even when he's smiling. My mother says the lines are from scowling for so much of one's life. Dad says they are evidence of many years of deep thought. I don't know which one is telling the truth.

The car smells like new leather and fear. I have no clue where we're going and I don't like the impending doom that's riding alongside me in the passenger seat of Jimmy's black Cadillac. A thick crucifix and a golden boxing glove hang from sturdy chains around his neck and his hair is black, slicked back. He's the sort of guy my brother, Sid, calls a Goombah. He's a tough one, with his thick New York accent and the pinkie ring on his right hand. They all wear them. Jimmy's has a small diamond set in the center. My father's has a ruby of bougainvillea pink, not red.

I watch Jimmy's right hand reach for the knob on the radio as he searches for a good station. The gold pinkie ring looks tight, making the skin around it swell. He's a gorilla in his shiny blue jacket with the Yankees emblem on the back, the steering wheel digging into his ample belly. I wonder if it's uncomfortable when he turns a corner. The radio garbles and halts and garbles again until he lands on a soft jazz station. I want to get out. I want to grab this metal door handle and pull it. I think I can manage it as he's taking the next turn. As the weight of the door swings it forward, I will throw myself out and roll away from the car, carefully landing in a ditch. Before he can pull over and put the Caddy in park, I will be gone.

As if reading my thoughts, he looks over at me and winks. I don't know whether this is meant to be comforting or it's a trick.

We drive through our neighborhood, which sits in the very middle of Greenwich, Connecticut. It should be a movie set with its winding roads lined with elm, maple and pine giants, and its stately mansions and manors framing the lake's shore, each one with an impeccable cobblestone drive winding up to its front door.

"Everything's gonna be okay, kid," he tells me as we approach downtown Greenwich. From my limited experience, when someone begins a scenario by saying everything is going to be okay, it usually isn't. My palms remain damp no matter how many times I run them across my lap. My stomach hurts. Maybe they're selling me to that Chinese lady with the black front tooth who works at the liquor store and smells of shrimp. She is always telling my father as he pays for my mother's vodka, "I take little girl home today. She come to live with me, okay?" She's inescapably creepy.

I know I'm not wanted – that I was *unexpected.* My mother often says that I arrived right alongside the Cuban Missile Crisis in 1962 and that I was a surprise. Not the sort of surprise where people jump out from behind the couch with paper hats on their heads, but the sort of surprise that occurs when you come home to find a disconnect notice from the gas company taped to your door or when you get clipped by a cab crossing W. 46th Street. Reminding me is unnecessary; it's something I feel. But I'm already here, so there's not much I can do to make my mother feel any better about my hanging around.

So maybe they finally came up with a solution. Maybe Jimmy's going to drop me off at an orphanage and give me the Italian Chin Wave as he pulls away in his car, heading happily back to his garage in New York to make another pot. I may never see the first grade in the fall.

We pass the First Presbyterian Church – our church – with its intimidating spires and murky stained glass, then my mother's favorite dress shop, then the Pink Poodle Lounge with the bright awning over the entrance where she vies for the window seat with the Kennedy clan – its windows are still dark, chairs stacked up on tables. The Cadillac is slowing down too much for my rolling-out-of-the-car-maneuver to have the same impact that it would have had a few minutes ago while we were flying up Putnam Avenue. Putnam Hill looked like a yellow cupcake with its hundreds of daffodils standing at attention. Entirely too late to escape now. I'm such a coward.

"Where are we going, Jimmy?" My voice comes out jerky.

He wipes his mouth with the back of his hand and doesn't answer. I'm going to throw up. I can't breathe. I force myself to look at his face. I can tell by the way his right eye (and presumably his left, but I can't see that) changes focus ever so slightly that he knows I'm looking.

"We're gonna go do a thing, and then after I'll take you to the Woolworth's down the block and we'll pick out something nice for you. Anything you want, okay?"

I don't want something nice, I want to go home. I want to run down to the lake, climb in my boat, and row out to the island where no one can get to me, where I won't be bothered with things like not knowing where someone is taking me. My pants are looking grimy from the sweat. I wipe my palms again anyway. A *thing*. What kind of a thing would entail me having to get up very early, be ushered into a car without a word and then necessitate a bribe of *something nice* from the Woolworth's? The jazz station has now decided on something loud and screechy – trumpet notes flying up and down and over and through – a noisy mess with no sense of order. This music is making me frantic.

Jimmy pulls into an alley between the Pizza Palace and Spiffy Dry Cleaners, which my mother says is run by bandits. We drive all the way through, coming out the other end by the train station. Jimmy stops the car. The sun finds us and beats through the windshield, making me feel exposed. We've arrived at the Catholic Church, which is much more intimidating then the First Presbyterian. I can imagine what's inside: people on their knees, rosaries wound around their fingers, nuns in black, rumbling organ music rising to the rafters like sorrowful smoke – I've seen it on TV. Depressing. Those Catholics take their religion seriously, like soldiers of God; heads bent down, up on their feet, down on their knees, open their hymnals, "Praise God," and up on their feet again, back in their seats – whatever command the Priest calls out. The congregation must be tired all the time.

Jimmy leads me up the wide stairway into the church with his beefy hand. His ring is cool against my skin as we pass a life-size statue of the Virgin Mary at the entrance. She holds her palm out to us as if she wants me to place something worthwhile in it.

Morning light filters through the stained glass murals high above, gathering in sharp angles, creating small spotlights of red and purple and yellow. Holy dust spirals in cascading beams as the light reaches the pews and the slate floor. I feel better now. What danger could possibly come to me here?

"Why are we going to church?" I whisper to Jimmy, hopeful for an answer more substantial than *a thing*.

Jimmy ignores my question and steps up to the holy water bowl at the entry of the cathedral. He dips two fingers in the water and then crosses himself, ending with a ripe kiss to his wet fingers. I reach for the bowl and his hand gently stops me.

"That's only for Catholics, Sweetie. C'mon over here," he says.

He takes my hand in his again as he swaggers up the wide center aisle. I feel like I'm an intruder in this club where I'm not a paying member. I don't belong here and I wonder if he's breaking some rule by bringing me here. As we move closer to the massive oak altar, I notice a woman sitting in a pew. She's wearing a silk scarf on her head, tied in a loose knot under her chin. She's the only other person in the church. Her hands are pressed together under the knot and her lips are moving as she pleads her case. I follow her eyes as Jimmy and I move along the smooth floor. Jesus. The sculptor – whoever the guy had been – hadn't left anything to the imagination. He's wearing almost nothing, only a loose piece of cloth on His waist, draped like some medieval diaper. Large nails are driven through His palms and into the cross. Deep red blood leaks from His wounds. He and the cross are enormous and His face is a mixture of despair and understanding. My mother has told me He died for our sins, but I had no idea about all of this. Who would volunteer for this? I want to go pull Him down. I want to rescue Him, release Him, bathe Him, hug Him and then take Him to Woolworth's and buy Him something nice. I want Him to live in my room with me. He's so thin and bloody. I've never seen a sight like this and it's disturbing beyond words. I had no idea this is what Catholics had to look at every time they come to worship. I can't look at His agony any longer, but I can't look away. Maybe the woman is thinking the same thing. Her lips are still moving.

As we reach big, bloody Jesus, Jimmy lets go of my hand and falls slowly to one knee. I don't know what to do. He crosses himself and stands again before I have to decide. I take a final glance back at the Savior as I follow Jimmy to an alcove filled with lit candles. I hope I never have to come back here again.

The flames cast a warm glow on Jimmy's face, turning him into an angel as he smiles down at me. This place must bring him peace. Shadows flutter on the low ceiling of the alcove, talking back and forth with the flames. He pulls a few bills from his wallet and stuffs them into a slot in a box that hangs on the wall, then reaches for a long, skinny stick and sets it afire from a candle that's already lit. I watch his steady hand move to three fresh candles as he lights them.

"This last one's for you," he tells me.

Maybe he's saying a prayer asking that I be raised properly in the orphanage.

"Is this the thing we're doing, Jimmy?" I ask, searching his face for answers.

"No. We're gonna go do the thing now."

Within five minutes' time, the jig is up. I'm standing out on the sidewalk, a half block from the church, in front of a medical building I know all too well, with my arms folded defiantly in front of me. I shake my head at Jimmy. I'd rather he drop me off at the stinky Chinese lady's house.

"Nope," I tell him.

"Look, kid. C'mon now, listen. This is only gonna take a few minutes, then we'll go have some fun."

"Nope, no way." I'm staring him down. This is not going to happen. I know I'm being difficult, but I feel tricked and resentful. Ambushed.

"Look here," he says, walking to the outside wall of the

building near the door, "See this?" he raps his knuckles against the metal plaque that hangs there, "O'Leary. He's a Mick – an Irishman. They're good at this sort of thing. They're good with people. Comes natural to 'em, like tending bar."

My guts are tangling up fast.

"Sweetie, look, your dad said we have to do this, so let's just do it."

I take a deep breath and look down at the sidewalk.

"Listen, when you're nervous about something, you never let 'em see it. What's your dad always tellin ya? Walk in like ya own the place."

Jimmy Bruno is a patient man and I will lose this stand-off eventually, I know this. No wonder my father calls him *Muscle;* he coaxes, he waits, then he springs the surprise on you at the last minute, forcing this *thing* on you, leaving no escape. Some protector *he* is. The tangles in my stomach are moving to my throat. It swells. My forehead is sweating. My fanny feels like it's sweating too as Jimmy opens the door to usher me inside. I go hollow.

My soul has just wiggled its way from my body, out through my spine and is now making haste down the sidewalk, back to the parked car to climb in the back seat and lock all the doors to wait until this is over. It's the smell that tipped it off: rubbing alcohol, enamel grinding to the brink of spark, laughing gas, the stale blue drool paper that will be fastened around my neck with the little alligator clip.

I can't believe Jimmy thought giving me an empty bowl would be incentive to follow him inside willingly. I'd rather have a crazy man walk up and shoot me in the temple than enter this den of Satan. I need to go back to the church and discuss this with Jesus.

Jimmy's standing in the open doorway expectantly. As I feel myself relent, the tears come. I reach up to hold my throat.

This is my fault. This is because of the last time when I'd out maneuvered them. I hadn't meant to be troublesome, but my parents had given me three days' notice. Three whole days to fret and worry and devise a plan. On the morning of the appointment with Dr. O'Leary, I snuck out the back door, down to the lake, hopped in my boat and rowed to out to middle of the water. I stayed there until I was sure I'd missed the appointment. Dad had paced back and forth on the shore for an hour; coaxing, negotiating, mildly threatening. I watched him without making a peep, oars in the water to steady my position. He wasn't used to this defiance and neither was I, being a child who most always behaved, but my gripping phobia was no match for mortal man, not even for a Teamsters negotiator. Even when my mother emerged from the house in her peach colored cigarette pants and flowered top to help my father wave me into shore, I did not go. She went from gentle persuasion to flailing her arms and wildly tugging her hair in a matter of minutes. And still I sat. Only after they'd gone back in the house and had been there for what seemed a long enough time did I row back to shore and my fate. Whatever punishment I received, I knew it would not be half as bad as going to visit the dentist.

So now I've been shanghaied. Dad employed Muscle to get the job done, and I never saw it coming.

"C'mon kiddo. It's okay. I'll be with you every step of the way," Jimmy says, still holding the front door open.

I move in jerky steps towards his outstretched hand, grab onto it and then step into my nightmare. He tells the girl at the front desk that we're here for our nine o'clock and then leads me to the waiting area. I sit next to my gorilla with my eyes closed. I can hear the dentist saying goodbye to someone and cover my eyes with my hands because I must be next. Except for us, the place is vacant.

"Breathe, honey. You're not breathing," Jimmy tells me as he flips through *Life* Magazine.

It seems only seconds before the girl behind the desk calls my name and we're on our way down the hallway to the room with its chair and the tray full of sharp metal instruments.

As we enter the room, Jimmy holds me back with his hand and takes in the scene. Dr. O'Leary fills the doorway. He is wearing black-framed glasses but this does not disguise the fact that he looks a bit like a badger. Sometimes he enters the room singing a song he made up about me, "Maggie Mag-A-Doo, how I love you." The song makes me feel clammy and faint.

Jimmy gestures to the tray and says, "Cover up those tools. A kid don't need to see that. What? This your first time doin' this or somethin'? C'mon, Doc."

Confusion sweeps over Dr. O.'s expression, but he takes a paper towel from the counter and covers the tools with it. Jimmy takes a seat in the corner. The dentist moves towards Jimmy and reaches to shake his hand, trying to make nice. He looks nervous; not something I want to see come over the guy who's about to rummage around inside my mouth with sharp things.

"I'm Richard O'Leary. Maggie's dentist. Some of my patients call me Dr. O."

"Nice to meet ya, Doc. This little girl was a little upset the last time you worked on her, and I'm here to make sure whatever happened the last time doesn't happen again."

Jimmy's not smiling. I feel the dentist beginning to dislike me more and more as the clock ticks the seconds away. I climb up into the chair to get this over with. Dr. O. takes a seat on his stool, rolls up close to me, swings the big light on the metal arm over my face and flicks it on. I watch Jimmy in the corner. He gives me the ever-assuring Italian Chin Wave. I want to climb out of this chair, walk over and kick him, and then go join my soul in the backseat of his car. The sharp metal hook makes its way to my mouth. I open as widely as I can, trying to make up for the rude introduction the dentist has just had. I grab onto the chair, bracing myself.

Jimmy stands up.

"Hold up, Doc. Wait a minute."

Dr. O'Leary stops short and recoils when he sees the

Muscle looming over his shoulder.

"Look at her. See how her knuckles are turning white? Look at her eyes. They just dilated. That's fear. That's exactly what I *don't* want to see here. So let's back up. Take it slow. Talk to her, tell her what you're gonna do before you do it. Make her feel safe." He takes his seat again back in the corner.

This could take all day. I should have dealt with it when I had that previous appointment. My breathing has stopped again, and the dentist looks shaken. He comes at me slower this time.

"Okay now, honey, let's just have a look in your mouth. I'm not going to hurt you," and he starts gently picking along the bottoms of my lower teeth.

I'm staring at the light, thinking of my boat, my lake, that bloody Jesus – anything but what's going on. He's being gentle – this is good. I begin to relax when he hits a nerve. Jimmy is up and out of his seat before the flinch seizes my face altogether.

"Whoa! Whoa, Stop! C'mere, Doc. Step out here for a minute."

Dr. O'Leary tosses the hook on the instrument tray, huffs a breath in my direction and follows Jimmy to the doorway behind me. I watch their reflection in the window across from me. The blue Yankees jacket leans in close to the white dental smock. The smock takes a step back until it hits the frame of the door.

"I assure you," he starts to tell Jimmy.

"No, Doc, I assure *you,* and you assure this little girl here. If you hurt her again in my presence, I'm gonna be doing a little dental work of my own." He leans in closer. "On you." I watch the Yankees jacket open up slowly. "With this. We good?" Without waiting for a response, Jimmy closes his jacket and returns to his seat in the corner.

Now the hook trembles as Dr. O. brings it up to my mouth. I can taste blood, but I'm not going to say a word about it, because when Jimmy sees this, he'll start shooting. I know what he carries inside his jacket.

Ingratiating myself to the dentist is fruitless at this point. I bet he won't even offer me one of those tin rings with the pretty stones from the velvet tray when I'm done, like he did the last time. I swallow the blood and open my mouth wide. He's barely touching me. This is much better but my body is still tense.

"She needs to spit. Let her spit," Jimmy tells him.

I sit up and spit in the little sink at my side. It's barely pink.

"Okay now, Maggie," the dentist's voice trembles, "I'm just going to put some paste on this spinning sponge and shine you up. We've done this before, right? You okay now?"

I nod at him and give him my most sheepish smile. My head hurts. He dabs the polisher into a small tub of blue paste and starts the spinning. He's looking more relaxed now and I know the worst is over since he hasn't mentioned any cavities.

As the drool bib is removed, calm envelops me. I make my way back down the hallway. Behind me, I hear Jimmy stop Dr. O'Leary before he moves on to the next exam room.

"Here. Why don't you take this and go out and buy yourself a bedside manner or somethin'." He stuffs a twenty dollar bill into the collar of the white dental smock.

We both order grilled cheese sandwiches and chocolate milkshakes from the bald man behind the counter in the back of the Woolworth's. The bald man jabs his thumb towards a clock on the wall and says it's not yet time for lunch, that it's barely 10:00 in the morning. Jimmy reaches for his wallet, pulls out a twenty and tosses it on the counter, glaring.

"Yeah? Here. What time is it now?"

I can feel my heart beat. I look over at Jimmy, who's just raised his eyebrows ever so slightly, which causes something to shift in the bald man's expression. I have a feeling he's about to go heat up the grill.

The man nods, wipes his hands on a rag, takes the money and goes back to the kitchen through the swinging doors. I'm glad he's decided this before the Yankees jacket has had to come open. I wonder what it's like to get whatever you want whenever you want it. There must be some lack of satisfaction in it, always knowing the outcome.

I know Jimmy means well. I've always been extra fond of him. And from what I learned last winter about what he does in the city, he takes good care of things such as looking after city cats during the colder months.

Every trip to New York is exciting. If the weather is pleasant, my parents and I will walk from our house to the path in the woods that runs along the lake and kicks out at Greenwich train station. We board the New Haven line, which takes us south through Westchester, then through Harlem, to Grand Central Station where I get to see the clock.

Mom sits in her seat by the window with her hands folded neatly in her lap. Her red hair is combed and sprayed in perfect order and there's a feeling coming off her that only happens on the train. It's not the feeling of her just having had a few cocktails – that's a different feeling and one I'm not particularly fond of, because that feeling is one that can change from happy and relaxed to miserable and out of control with no warning at all. The train makes her face glow, and sometimes she will smile down at me in the seat next to her and place her hand softly over mine for a moment. She becomes gentle on her way to Manhattan. I know it's not a permanent thing, but I enjoy it while I can.

After the train spills the three of us out into Grand Central, Mom inhales deeply, pausing on the platform. She breathes in the soot, coffee, hot bagels and the sizzling metallic scent of trains pulling into the station; we make our way through the river of travelers, passing the clock and as we exit onto the street we are greeted by the sounds of cabbies honking and hurling curses at each other in their tough Brooklyn and Jersey accents, sirens of the NYPD searing the night air, echoing and bouncing down alleys and through the thick forest of skyscrapers. We hurry along the sidewalk as if we're trying to catch up with something exciting like the beginnings of a parade, as a lone, haunting cry of a saxophone sails up a walkway and into the streets from somewhere deep in Central Park near the zoo. In all the chaos, my mother finds her calm, which makes the place a sanctuary for me, much like my island in the middle of Milbrook Lake. The city makes people feel like they're a part of something important. I'm pretty sure New York City is the center of the world. So that explains all the feelings.

My father feels important at Patsy's Restaurant on West 46th Street, where he is popular and fussed over by the man who takes his coat.

"Mr. Dahlstrom, good to see you again," the man says as he passes Dad's coat over a counter to the coat check girl.

"Evening, Joe. How's business?"

"Busy tonight. Mrs. Dahlstrom. You're looking beautiful as always," Joe says as he slips my mother's white mink coat from her shoulders. Mom glows at the compliment as the three of us are shown to a private table upstairs where the windows are covered with curtains. Dad doesn't care for sitting by windows or with his back to a door – Joe must know this. My father stops at tables along the way to pat backs and shake hands. People stop what they are doing when he enters a room. Conversations around tables quiet, cocktails pause in mid air. Men seem to want to know him. Women crane their necks to get a better look at him and some will bat their eyelashes in his direction. He walks a bit taller at Patsy's, and this makes me walk a bit taller at Patsy's.

On very cold mornings, my father drives in to work and leaves his pale yellow Lincoln Continental at Jimmy's garage in Midtown. By the afternoon, if it's warmed up enough, he takes the train back home so he can get some fresh air walking the path in the woods back to 88 Orchard Drive. He says he does his best thinking on the train and on the walk home, and he can relax because he knows Jimmy is watching his car overnight. I like to take the train in, so it's always good news if my father has left the car at Jimmy's.

My mother's high heels will start to pinch after an afternoon shopping at Bloomingdale's or a night walking the rough cobblestone streets of the theater district, which are worn smooth from decades of travelers, thespians, merchants and horses' hooves. When wet, the stones reflect flashing lights from the marquis. Bursts of steam fountain up from the sewers as if giant tea kettles live underneath.

"Oh for crying out loud, Jack, would you please slow down?"

"Patricia, I'm walking beside you, not dragging you behind me."

"Jack, Maggie and I are trying to keep up pace with you and these shoes aren't meant for that. I'm getting a blister."

I start to worry that another argument is going to break out once we arrive back home, but Dad stops on the sidewalk and reaches his hand out to my mother.

Mom doesn't like to be touched. It seems unnatural to me, but it's a rule in our house, and only on special occasions is anyone allowed to touch my mother and then only briefly. If you leave your hand too long, she stiffens up like a cat arching its back in the presence of a dog. I'm relieved when Mom accepts Dad's hand and allows him to guide her back to Jimmy's garage to pick up the car.

The Lincoln glows like a huge stick of butter under the vibrating overhead lights inside the garage. Dad tells me to stay out on the sidewalk with my mother while they get his car ready. I crane to watch as Jimmy's crew brings out the long metal poles with mirrors fixed to the ends. They sweep them back and forth under the car.

The first time I noticed the crew doing their prep work was last winter – the winter I started to see Jimmy in a different light – and I asked my father what the guys were looking for.

He put his fingers to his chin to think things over for a minute, then said, "They're looking for cats." My mother's hand pulled me back from the doorway when I asked him why. He said when the weather turns cold, cats will climb up inside to get warm near the engines. If you turn a car on with a cat up in there, things can get messy and the cats can get hurt.

It was then I realized that Jimmy Bruno and his crew helped everybody out. It also dawned on me why I'd never seen a cat on the streets of New York City. Now I knew where they'd been all along.

A chunky box sits on the lunch counter next to a metal napkin dispenser. When I open the lid, a dainty ballerina spins in front of a mirror. The lining is red velvet. Jimmy picked it out for me in the front of the store where we came in. He shows me how to wind it up – just so, not too tightly. The delicate ballerina dances to music that tinkles out into the air above the counter. It is something to cherish, although I'm not quite sure this was all worth it. At least my teeth are clean.

The bald man comes from the kitchen wearing an apron splattered with dried food. The grilled cheese is golden brown, a plump pickle on the side of each plate. I hope he hurries with the milk shakes before a threat needs to be issued – there's been enough of that today. I hear a bell ring overhead as the front door of the Woolworth's opens behind us, and Jimmy turns, on guard. I don't need to turn around, I know who it must be. It's my soul – the fair weather friend that it is – emerging from its hiding place in the car. It was the smell that tipped it off: melted cheese and pickles, with the promise of milkshakes. It knows it's safe to come out.

#

The Teamsters are coming to dinner and we should be getting ready, but things are going badly out in the garden. Something has set my mother off, and she is skulking around out there, hunched over and holding a can of Aqua Net in her hand, index finger on the trigger button. She's draped in mosquito netting, which forms a train behind her as it drags along the grass.

It's early morning, the day after doing *the thing* with Jimmy, and I'm still in my pajamas. I watch my mother through the window. She's developed a certain loathing for squirrels in recent months – something about keeping them off the bird feeders – but I suspect something more. Her arsenal of weapons, whether strategically or innocently placed throughout the house, has become a means to assist her in the annihilation of every last squirrel living in the Tri-State area; not with guns, not with explosives or poison, but with weapons meant to fool the squirrels – every day items meant to lull them into an unguarded state of fabricated immunity, as she puts it. A pepper grinder, yesterday's issue of *The New York Times,* a salad plate, a canned ham – anything handy and threatening. Once she hurled a copy of Dostoevsky's *The Idiot* at a squirrel sitting on a rock near the woods – luckily it was a paperback. The hair spray is new and I'm sure it will only result in some stickiness, but I'm still concerned. I step out the back door and address the situation.

"Mom, aren't we supposed to be getting ready for the dinner party?"

Startled, she turns towards me and shushes me from beneath her mosquito netting. Since I am only five years old, this situation is beyond my realm of expertise, so I go back in the house to find my father. I'm lucky he's home today.

My parents each have their own bedrooms located at opposite ends of the hallway upstairs so that there is very little chance they'll have to interact. I'm discouraged from entering my mother's pristine domain with its white carpet and the neatly organized flair pens of every color that sit in a cup on her desk, but

I have fairly unlimited access to Dad's space. He's in the shower. A warm waft of steam wraps its arms around me as I enter the humidity. His bathroom is much smaller than my mother's. I watch his distorted shape moving behind the frosted glass door.

"Dad?"

"Mag? That you?"

"Mom's out in the yard going after squirrels again. She looks funny."

"What's that?"

"It's Mom," I try a little louder, "she's going after squirrels. She has hairspray and – "

"Oh, Goddamnit."

A knob squeaks and the water stops. His hand reaches over the shower door and grabs a towel hanging from a peg on the wall. He says this a lot: *Goddamnit.* When things get really bad, he'll start with *Jesus Chriiiist!*, saying the Jesus part quietly and then, by the time he reaches the Chriiiist part, he's worked himself up into a full holler. It reminds me of the sound of a passing train. He steps out of the shower with the towel wrapped around his waist.

"I'll be down there in a minute. What's she doing anyway?" he asks as he slaps the fog off the mirrored medicine cabinet.

"She's going after squirrels, I think. She's covered in that net we keep down in the basement, by the fishing stuff?"

He looks at me and then slowly closes his eyes.

"Goddamnit. Alright, I'll take care of this. Let me get dressed first."

I turn to go.

"And Mag? Don't go outside until I come down."

"Okay."

I leave the comforting scent of Old Spice, shaving cream and mannish soap.

I'm changing out of my night clothes when I hear a door slam downstairs. And then, "Jesus Chriiiist!" I dress quickly and make my way to my father to see what could have gotten worse in the last few minutes.

"She's missing," he tells me.

This happens from time to time, this going missing. Sometimes there's a clue that it's coming, when she morphs into a fragile, yet threatening creature, walking down the hall towards her bedroom carrying a jug of vodka and a sleeve of Saltine crackers. She will hide herself away, sometimes for days. When you've worried enough, you will go to her door to find she's vanished. Sometimes there's no warning at all. But no matter what, she always seems to do this at the most inconvenient times. Or maybe it's just inconvenient in general when a mother goes missing, but either way it makes my father angry. He's glaring at the dogwood tree's pink buds just beyond the picture window in the den.

"All right. You go look for her in the back yard and I'll search the front. Goddamnit, I don't need this crap today."

I go.

I'm good at searching the back yard. I'm good at it because I know it so well. This is where I spend my time, where I build my secret forts; here in the yard and in the woods alongside our property. It is a large piece of land that slopes steeply down towards the shore of Milbrook Lower Lake. There is a Milbrook Upper Lake, which I'm not allowed to go near, says my father, but since he travels three weeks out of every month, and since my mother doesn't usually notice when I'm gone, I go to that lake sometimes, too, and sit near the bridge that connects the two bodies of water.

And I have the boat that God gave me. The boat that saved me from one dentist appointment, but not yesterday's. It's a white row boat with three bench seats and a slimy green rope for tying it up. It landed on our property during a flood, and we kept it. This single event opened up my world in ways I could not have imagined possible. The woods are great, as is our yard, but there is always the chance that I will get in my mother's way in those places when she's in a foul mood or hunting squirrels. On those days, there's a chance of me getting hit in the back of the head with a flying pepper grinder she's just hurled through the trees. So when the boat arrived, I found I was able to row it out to the island that I can see from my bedroom window. It stands in the middle of the lake and is the place I go to feel safe, a gift owing not only to the island's isolation but also from my mother's unrelenting fear of water and the obvious logistics of her not being able to get near me if I'm surrounded by it.

I'm poking the hedges along the back of the house with a long stick, trying to flush her out. I would like to have my brother or sister here with me, but they're both away at college. Jane is studying drama at SMU in Texas, and Sid is in Virginia studying English. They only come home on holidays now. Jane will take me walking in the woods or down along the shore of the lake. I watch the way her brown hair falls down her back and how she moves with the grace of a ballerina. She believes in fairies and tells me they live in the trees and if I'm very quiet they will let me hear their gentle songs and whisperings. Apparently, fairies hold all the secrets of the world and are willing to share these secrets if you behave in a certain way around them.

Sid is rough and tumbling. He plays his blues harmonica in the den after breakfast and teaches me to play chess – looking at me over his eye glasses in warning if I'm about to make a bad move. He smells like apricots and pipe tobacco. I like to sit close to him. Sometimes, if I sit too close for too long, he will grab me, ball up his fist and dig his knuckles into my neck – which is somehow excruciating and tickling at the same time. He stops just before I think I will die. I miss them both. I feel tired when they're not around.

Early morning is my favorite time to be out here, especially now, in the spring, when the fog billows in off the lake and makes its slow way to the woods to rest when the sun comes up, as if a giant's ghost has materialized in the dawn and now squats over our house. I'm missing the tranquility of early morning in our neighborhood right now because of this searching for my mother. Resentment is sneaking up and tailing me and I hope I find her before it's ruined my mood entirely. I move on to a forsythia bush and ram my stick into its center, listening carefully for any suspicious noises coming from within.

My father comes around the side of the house from the driveway. Looks like his knees are bothering him this morning. The way he walks on bowed legs makes him look like Anthony Quinn, but with less hair.

"Anything?"

I shake my head, still poking the bush.

"C'mon, let's go down to the lake and look," he says.

I follow him, holding my stick high in the air like I'm carrying a flag. Dad looks angry. We're on a schedule, and this hiding business can take some time to unravel once we find her. Sometimes we have to get her in the shower and she comes alive again, emerging from the steam a resilient and beautiful force, brightly lit from within, but other times it can be a mess if we've found Mom inexplicably covered in dirt or mud, hair matted, sobbing, mascara running down her face. When that's the case, it can take some scrubbing to set things right again. I wish she didn't feel the need to hide and that I knew her reasons for doing so. She's making bad choices today.

As the sun overpowers the morning mist, I'm watching our shadows as we walk down the hill toward the lake. My father's is tall and lumbering, looking like it's going somewhere it doesn't want to go. Mine is small, skinny and bouncy, not quite fitting with the seriousness of the situation. I harness the bounce. The stick's shadow looks like a weapon going into battle. My head is the problem; it's too big for the rest of my body. My brother, Sid, says I look like Tweety Bird because my skull grows sort of bulbous at the temples, gradually swelling up into my hair line as if someone placed a hose in my mouth and blew. I wish he hadn't told me this, because every time I see my reflection, this is what I notice.

The top layers of the lake are rippling towards the island, and a gang of mallards paddles along the shore. Dad stops and rests his hands on his hips, watching the ducks float up and waddle up the bank single file. Dad looks down at me and my stick and says, "Well, Mag, which way do you think she went?"

There is an important decision to be made and it rests on my shoulders, so I bring my fingers up to my chin the way he does when he's trying to figure something out. The woods are too thick to our right. She would have had trouble getting through there, so I point to the left. Dad starts walking again in that direction. I follow.

We are approaching the largest pine tree on the property. No one in my family is aware that underneath it, where the high bottom branches begin at the trunk three feet above my head and the tips hang down to the earth in a dark canopy, is my best fort. I keep my secret things inside: books wrapped in tin foil, some balls of twine, rocks with flecks of silver, and a stuffed owl to fool any mice who might be thinking of moving in. There could be a sleeve of Saltine crackers tucked safely between two branches as well, but I can't remember now.

Dad's breathing harder and looking frustrated. I follow him along the shore towards our property line. As we approach my pine tree fort, I eye it, looking for clues, listening for noises. I don't want her to be in there, in my sacred place. If she's in there now, being crazy or sad or angry, then it will feel completely different from now on. That's the thing about sacred places; you can't just barge in and be unpleasant in them. You have to walk in feeling good, otherwise you change the air, and then the person who built the fort in the first place has to abandon it and search the property for a new one, which takes a lot of time and makes the person doing all the work upset. As we pass it, I feel her. She's in there. I don't say a word because I don't want this to be true. I don't want her in there reading my books or touching my rocks or eating my Saltines without permission.

Small clouds, thin as fairy wings, are moving south, the same direction as the ripples on the lake. We are moving north. My father has been teaching me the four directions. I look back at my tree and decide I will wait until there are no places left to look before I tell my father where she is. Dad's not even looking for her anymore. He's just walking and breathing harder, watching the ground without hope.

We reach the beginning of the Lee's property and scan their back yard. It's a wide open space with a wooden jungle gym in the middle of it. I want to turn around now in case their son, Richard, comes out; I don't want him to know my mother is missing. My father reads my mind and turns back along the lake, heading south. The tree is coming closer and I have to do this. I lower my stick and point it at the tree.

"I think she's in there, Dad," I whisper.

"Where? Inside the tree?"

"Underneath it."

"What do you mean? Why would she – "

"I *feel* her in there. It's my fort."

I approach the tree, listening, trying to step lightly. I hunch over, hunting her. I pull back the branches at my *Getting-in Place* and hold them so my father can see inside. I don't want to look yet. I watch his expression instead – this will tell me everything.

His face falls. "Oh for Christ's sake!"

I take a deep breath and peer inside.

My mother should be kneeling in the garden, holding a hyacinth under her nose, filling her soul with its scent and saying it smells of Heaven, and the morning sun should be shining on her freckles and setting her red hair on soft fire, making her look like Marilyn Monroe before she went blond. Instead, she's sitting in a lawn chair with her hands folded on her lap underneath these branches. She is wearing the garden hose coiled into a ridiculous looking rubber turban on top of her head. But this is not the most disturbing part. After my eyes adjust to the darkness inside the fort, I can see a large piece of meat, possibly a pot roast, sitting at her feet on a piece of newspaper. It looks like it might be part of Dad's *Wall Street Journal*, which he likes to read while he has his coffee.

My fort is ruined now. It doesn't look as if she's disturbed any of my things, but still, this will force a rapid relocation and I'll have to explain it to myself later on – without getting embarrassed.

"Oh, there you are!" She's grinning at us.

Dad steps in closer, glaring down at the pot roast.

"Patricia, what the hell is going on here?"

She turns her head to look up at him and the garden hose slides off her head onto the ground. She's still smiling, not answering him.

"C'mon, let's get you inside. What the hell is wrong with you? I have people coming, remember? Stop messing around."

He goes to grab her arm and she slaps his hand away. I'm still holding the branches back, afraid to enter. I can tell by the way Dad is standing over her with his fists balled up at his sides that he's trying to keep control. Since I count on him to be the one who doesn't get angry, when he does, it frightens me. He reaches for her arm again and, more gently now, says, "Patricia, I need you to come up to the house and get ready. Maggie and I will help you in the kitchen. When the guys get here, we'll have some cocktails and show them your garden. Okay? How's that sound?"

She lets him help her out of the chair this time. I step back, holding the branches for them, when she stops and goes limp, collapsing on the ground next to the pot roast. Dad stops being gentle.

"Goddamnit, Pat. Get up! Maggie's watching you."

I avert my eyes and take a deep breath. This could take a

while. I hear movement from inside like a struggle is taking place. But it's my father storming out from under the tree with the pot roast in his arms. He's cussing under his breath as he rushes past me. I watch him take the meat to the edge of the lake. He raises it above his head and hurls it up and out over the water. It lands with a heavy plop and sinks to the bottom.

Mom has come out now and is standing by the tree with her arms folded in front of her, glaring at my father. He ignores her and heads back up the hill towards the house. I scurry after him. I don't know if she'll follow us. I can't worry about that now. I just need to get inside, find somewhere safe to sit and get my breathing right again.

I don't look back as Dad and I approach the garden. He pauses over the crumpled mosquito netting on the grass. I notice the fog has dissipated in the woods. A band of sunlight reaches down at a sharp angle over Dad, as if God is spot lighting him, finally giving him the floor. Maybe now is the time for him to say something to make her stop acting this way, to make this right, – to make her well. If he can fix a scraped knee with a kiss, a hole in my boat with some gunk or chase away uncertainty with a wink, then I wonder why he doesn't fix my mother with his words. As I wait for him to take his chance, he walks to the door and steps inside.

I have my nose pressed up against the front window waiting for the guys to show up. Every time I breathe out, a small ghost of fog shows up on the glass. It disappears again when I breathe in.

Mom's okay now. Dad put her in the shower and then gave her a glass of vodka and some chicken broth in a cup. She drank both. She's in the kitchen humming, which is a sure sign that she's happy again. Dad's in the den pouring himself a scotch, which is what he always does right before the guys arrive. He warns me for the hundredth time that I'm not allowed to go out in front of the house and that I can't even think about going back outside until they are gone again. This makes me want to go outside all the more, especially since Dad won't give me a good reason for not letting me out there. When normal visitors show up (folks that aren't the guys), I can run out the front door and down the slate steps to the driveway to greet them, hurrying them into the house as quickly as I can. Company takes the heat off me, but when the guys come, I have to follow different rules.

I don't ever have much warning when Dad's friends come to the house. It's always a surprise. Whenever I ask him when they'll be coming to visit again, he says it's important never to plan anything too far in advance because that's when you can get into trouble, so they call each other the morning of, or a few hours before they get together. When they leave, they say things like, "Okay, we'll see you down in Miami next month. I'll call you on the day."

Finally, as the sky falls pink and restful, a dark Town Car rolls up with its lights on. A familiar Italian man clutches the steering wheel as he delivers Lou Capalbo to our home. Lou is confident and slathered in a Dean Martin-esque charisma. He decorates his wife, Ruthie, in jewels and Chanel and never enters a gathering without a gift. He smells like the tailor shop where my father buys his suits, and on Saturdays he smells like fresh bread because that's the day of the week he stops in to check on his employees at Capalbo's Bakery in Midtown Manhattan. Lou is soft around the edges, but his charm disguises his pounds. He looks me in the eye; there's a quiet certainty in him that I can rely on. I am not yet aware that Lou is also a hit man for the Gambino crime family.

No one ever passes our house by accident because of the wooden plaque my father has nailed to a sturdy elm tree at the edge of our driveway. He has glued tiny reflectors to it that spell out the name, Dahlstrom, so that everyone knows not to keep driving once they see it. If they did, they'd find themselves right back where they started, as Orchard Drive is a long, wavy, oval loop. If seen from above, our street would look like a lasso tossed out too quickly. Neighborhood teenagers kept stealing our Dahlstrom sign from the tree before Dad grew tired of replacing it, yanked it out of the elm's side and took it to his work table in the garage. There, he drove nails into the wood, along the outer edges and very close together. Then he sawed the ends off the nails and filed the jagged edges down to needle-sharp points so that it looked like a dangerous flower. He painted the spikes black so they couldn't be seen at night. This took a very long time. As I watched him work, I saw a sour thrill wash over him. Sometimes he likes to walk to the end of our driveway to look at our name and check for blood.

The doors on Lou's Town Car open. I feel like a race horse, anxious behind the gate. I want to tear out the front door and hug him, although I'm no good at it; with Dad traveling so often, hugs are scarce and Mom prefers not to be touched, so without ample practice, I tend to be over zealous and just slam into people. Apparently, I startle.

The driver opens the trunk of the car while Lou hikes up his slacks, tucks his golf shirt in and lights a cigarette. I've seen the inside of this trunk before. There are assorted uniforms tucked neatly towards the back by the spare tire. Delivery man and mechanic's clothes, police blues, a bright yellow hard hat. Once I noticed a jumpsuit with the name *Larry* stitched over the breast pocket. When I asked about these outfits, he said they make it easier for him to gain access to places he would not otherwise be able to if he walked in looking like he usually looks. Like Dean Martin, I suppose is what he means.

My view is intermittently obscured by the fog I'm breathing onto the glass, so I hold my breath to get a better look. Lou holds the cigarette in his mouth while he gets a good hold of a large box with both arms and heads towards our house. The driver closes the trunk, leans his back against the car and narrows his eyes, which means he's just clocked in.

"Uncle Lou's here!" I call to the den.

Dad comes up the steps into the living room holding a cocktail and opens the door. As Lou glides in, I see the box contains Drambuie, Dad's favorite.

"Fall off the back a truck?" Dad says, eyeing the case of liquor.

"You know it," Lou says with wink.

He walks to the den and I follow. He sets the box down on the bar and notices me waiting patiently for his recognition.

"Hey Jack, who's this kid here?" he teases. I slam into his waist, deeply inhaling the scent of leather from his belt. He cups my cheeks and kisses the top of my head, then moves behind the bar to pour himself a drink.

A heavy car door shuts out in the driveway and I race back to my window, balancing on my toes. I know this is Paul Castellano by the license plate: DGZ 117. His driver slicks his black hair smooth with both hands as he greets Lou's driver. Paul stays in the car.

Sometimes he brings Carlo Gambino with him, but not today. If Carlo had come with him, the driver would be helping him out of the backseat and there would be a body guard hovering. I am under strict instructions to address Carlo as Mr. Gambino, because he is a boss. My father says he is *the* boss. This explains a lot: why he has the best shoes and why Dad doesn't clown around with him the way he does with his other friends; why the guys kiss him on both cheeks when they greet him; and why the soldiers keeping watch outside rarely address him at all. It also explains why I'm not supposed to slam into him or ask him a lot of questions about why he looks so worried all the time. His quiet, mysterious countenance draws me to him.

"Do you have a dog?" I ask him, placing my hand gently on his arm to make sure he notices me and my question. I get no response other than a thin smile. I stare him down and I try again.

"Would you rather have waffles or toast with jam for breakfast? Which is better?" I lick my lips and wait for his answer.

He smiles silently at me with his oily black eyes and starts digging in his pocket for loose change. He hands me a quarter.

"Once a squirrel got into our fireplace and ran into the living room and my dad threw a wad of tangled Christmas lights at him and he climbed up the curtains and tore them to shreds. Have you ever had a squirrel in your house?"

Carlo silently hands me another quarter. I keep my hand on his arm to make sure he knows I'm still talking to him.

"I have a boat and sometimes I make bologna sandwiches and take them to my island to have lunch. Do you like bologna sandwiches?"

He fishes in his pocket again and hands me two quarters. I take them and add them to the other quarters in my pocket.

"If you come down to the lake with me, I will wrap our sandwiches in wax paper. You wanna go with me? Since nothing's happening in here?"

He looks at me as if he's unsure how to respond or perhaps wondering why an adult hasn't come to drag me away already. Then I feel my mother's claw-like grip on my shoulder and am dragged away by the back of my shirt and ushered into the kitchen for a good talking-to.

In the kitchen I am called incorrigible, but I don't pay attention because I'm only thinking of what I will ask Carlo the next time I see him. The guy is a gold mine.

"He's out there playing his opera," Lou says from behind me, peering over my shoulder through the front window, "and got it turned up full volume, sounds like."

"Doesn't it hurt his ears?" I ask him.

"No. He's hard of hearing in one ear."

"Because he likes his music so loud?"

"No, I think it's loud because he wants to hear it. Makes him calm. Me, I can't stand it. I'm more of a Sinatra kind a guy. I like Elvis too." He puts his hand on top of my head. "What makes you calm, kid? Not Italian opera, I bet."

"Bologna sandwiches," I tell him, still watching the driveway.

Lou moves away from me chuckling softly.

The car door opens and Paul finally steps out and heads up the walkway.

The man is so tall and broad, he fills the entire doorway. His furrowed brow leads him into the house in search of my father and Lou. I stay at my window. Paul is jumpy, so I keep my distance and ask him fewer questions than I do the other guys. When I'm feeling especially adventurous, I ask if he likes to swim, if he's ever been to the Bronx Zoo, and if he knows that my mother was bitten by a llama there one summer. He either pretends not to hear me or gruffly hands me a quarter at Carlo's urging. On lucky nights, when he's short of loose change, he hands me a dollar, which should over joy me, but I sense it's just his way of getting me to go away – or like he's paying for four questions at one time. My father says Paul is a union leader, which I take to mean, he leads the union in a parade-like fashion to my father, who is the negotiator for the union. A negotiator, as it has been explained to me, is the man who gets people to do what they didn't know they wanted to do before he stepped up and told them to do it. I think my father should negotiate with my mother.

The humming in the kitchen has stopped, so I go to find out if it's because Mom has become unhinged again. The kitchen is empty. I run up the back staircase and look down the hall. Her door is closed, which means dinner is most likely canceled. I quietly tiptoe over the tan carpeting, passing the front staircase as Lou's laughter sails up and brushes the side of my face. The glass doorknob produces nothing when I turn it. I rest my ear against the door to listen for anything suspicious. It's quiet and the air feels peaceful, so I leave her alone and hope tomorrow is a better day.

This has turned into a *meeting* night instead of the intended *dinner party* night because the den doors are also now closed. I pause to listen. Paul talks of union, protection and territory. My father mentions contracts and beefs. Lou coughs, and someone's ice rattles in its glass. There is nothing here to keep me awake for long, other than what's on the rocking chair. It is Danger. Lou's leather shoulder strap hangs over the wooden back of the chair, where my mother sometimes reads her Dylan Thomas by the fireplace. The butt of his hand gun nests in its cradle. I want to touch it, feel its weight in my hand, but I am not as brave as this. At least, not tonight.

I take a final peek out the front window before heading up to bed, hoping in a small way, for one more car to pull up, for someone else to arrive, for something interesting to happen in this house with all its closed doors. I see only a cigarette's ember glowing in the dark as the drivers stand watch over 88 Orchard Drive and protect this place that I love. Next time I will hold the gun.

CHAPTER TWO

In Which We See the Beginning and the Difference,
Minneapolis, Minnesota, 1919

Edna Scott does not cry out when the pain comes. She closes her eyes and stoically pushes with everything she has, while her daughter, Bea, prays at the foot of the bed and speaks in soothing tones. Creamy light shines from the only lantern they own. Another contraction begins. Sweat breaks out on Edna's forehead despite the deep chill in the room. Breath plumes from her nostrils and forms brief clouds before her face. The boys have been sent out to find firewood in the dark but have already been gone an hour and the temperature seems to drop with each passing moment.

Pain comes again without a sound. Edna doesn't worry about raising one more as she steals a glance at the tattered, careworn Bible beside her. She knows God will bring the food and the firewood. This child is surely another gift brought here with a purpose. She pushes again. By now, bearing a child is like pulling a splinter. Eight mouths to feed, ten if she includes herself and her late husband's brother, which she must.

William went to Heaven in 1902, leaving Edna with five children, twelve dollars, forty cents and the rent due in a week. He'd gone to work that morning, like every other morning, with a smile on his face, a tip of his hat, a soft kiss to her cheek and had never returned. An explosion at the factory had taken him home to God and she'd carried on, surviving on the kindness of neighbors, taking in laundry and selling her sweet molasses bread when she had the flour. And this is where William's brother,

John, had stepped in; not out of loyalty or love for his brother, but because he needed a place to sleep, a good woman to cook for him and to keep him warm through a Minnesota night.

She does not love John Scott and never will, but she married him because of the children. That's what the Bible tells you to do. He refuses to work because he fancies himself a poet and enjoys entertaining the crowds from a Vaudeville stage. He rides the rails and drinks whiskey that he's stashed in her cupboard now that Prohibition is eight weeks under way. He rarely comes home with food or money; it's his wife's tender parts that he's interested in, staying just long enough to satisfy his craving before heading out again for new adventures, and that's only when he's short of coin for the whores of Wabasha Avenue. Edna has given him two children already: three-year-old Dee and five-year-old Jim, who stand in the doorway wrapped together in a blanket. Another will arrive before dawn.

The eviction had come two weeks after William's death, so Edna moved her family into this abandoned two-room basement. A basement with no house above. A tornado had swept it away long ago, leaving only the door to a stairwell leading down into the earth. The owner had offered it for almost nothing, hearing of her troubles and seeing her hungry, thin children. She took it gladly.

She pushes again as her hands, cracked raw from the washing, grip the sheets. She knows this will soon be over, and when that moment comes, she will allow herself to think of a treat. What she wouldn't give for a cup of the sweet, warm tea she and William used to share by the fire.

#

Paper shamrocks hang suspended in cigarette smoke from the ceiling of the saloon. It's John Scott's luck that this place has not been shut down yet, but they say it's coming any day. He drinks whiskey even though he has run out of money again and is risking another night in jail when his tab comes due and all he can offer the barkeep is a good old Irish song and the emerald green twinkle in his eye. Tonight he may get a break because this is St. Patty's Day, 1919. The year he has decided that he should have no troubles and for now he will sip his whiskey slowly and when he's done, he will seek the charitable warmth of Miss Lizzie Malone's ample breast over at Delta Blue's House of Ill Repute. She'll know he's good for the money, eventually.

#

Just before midnight, the boys return with six oak logs stolen from a neighbor's shed just as Edna's womb releases a baby with a full head of hair the color of embers and yams, like the seven before her. Bea decides on a name as she wipes the baby dry and wraps her in a moth-eaten woolen coat. In honor of the day, the infant shall be called Patricia – Pattie for short. The child's eyes open briefly and then squeeze tight against the world she has just found herself in, as if she knows her nights will be long and the inhospitable cold may always be too harsh to bare.

#

Four streets away and twelve brisk days later, Rube and Ruth Dahlstrom arrive home from the hospital with a spitfire bundle of baby boy. The brick house is solid, warm and smells of roast beef with gravy. They are greeted at the door by their young daughter, Mary Jane, in ringlets and lace. She has been waiting at the window all day with her nanny by her side, and, now that her brother has finally arrived, she cannot stop smiling for she has thoroughly fallen in love.

Ruth takes her place on the fainting couch by the crackling fire and sighs. Rube places a cool cloth on his wife's brow. He silently hopes Ruth will show more interest in this child than she has in Mary Jane. The bearing of children is a messy business and raising one is something she finds abrasive, to put it politely. If it weren't for the nanny, motherhood would be most inconvenient. Ruth would much rather be shopping or joining the ladies for a game of bridge and a cup of tea. Although Rube, family man that he is, will never consider leaving her side, he now accepts the truism that marrying a girl for her beauty alone leaves an emotional emptiness at the end of the day.

He met her coming over from Sweden when he was just seventeen. She had embarked at Norway and he had never seen a creature more stunning, with those searing blue eyes and button-up boots, the parasol shading her delicate frame. She'd seemed such a fragile thing at the time; innocent and fresh in her white lace gloves and long, creamy blue dress – a less highly maintained version of the woman he now knows her to be. He allows her these frailties because of the loss she refuses to relinquish, a treasure that serves her role as the ultimate victim and keeps any accountability at bay.

The tornado came a year after their ship slid up alongside the American shore and deposited them onto the land of promise and hope. Ruth had moved to a three-bedroom home with her parents and a young sister named Lea, just four blocks away from the house they now own. That afternoon, she'd been visiting with friends when the weather suddenly shifted. As the winds picked up and the skies grew threatening, she was hurried down steps into her neighbor's underground shelter, where they waited out the thundering funnel above. When quiet finally returned, the doors were pushed open and sunlight surprised them as they emerged to the devastation.

Ruth raced down the street and over three blocks, trying to navigate through nearly unrecognizable terrain. She passed overturned flower stands and barrels of feed at what had an hour before been the market place on the corner. Pieces of rubble and roof littered the streets. Trees that had been ripped from the earth reached out to her with raw, exposed roots. Piles of house upon house upon house confused her path and turned her around as she stepped over the fallen white steeple of the Lutheran Church.

When she arrived home, she found little Lea clutching the doorknob in her tenuous hand, frozen, her eyes vacant, the doorway miraculously untouched in its frame. The house had been ripped in half with exacting precision – completely, thoroughly cut through – and Ruth knew they were gone. She followed her sister's gaze beyond what had previously been the front parlor. Their mother was pinned to the wall in a standing position, impaled through the heart by a board, her arms limp against her blood soaked apron, face frozen in anguish. Her head hung down, neck bent at a peculiar angle. She found her father's legs broken and tangled in a bloody stew, intermixed with heaps of debris, one of his work boots still securely laced up for the day. They never did find the rest of him.

Ever since that tragic day, Lea sits by a dingy window in the corner of a room with a blanket folded neatly on her lap, staring lifelessly at her interminable future, trapped just beyond the glass. The nurses take her outside only when there is not the slightest breeze in the air.

Rube smiles down at his newborn son and cups the infant's head in his large Swedish palm. He counts his blessings as he considers how fortunate his children are to have a warm, safe home to grow up in. He thinks of the impoverished family that has taken up residence in the abandoned basement of his wife's childhood home, the pregnant woman who lives there with her throngs of red-headed children. The woman sells warm bread that smells of dark molasses and takes in his family's laundry with a tinge of shame.

They have named the boy Jack, a sturdy name for a stalwart young lad. It is the name of a fellow who will know who he is and won't take any guff from the world; a fellow who may achieve even more than his father has as the superintendent of this district's schools. This child is made for great things, Rube Dahlstrom feels without question, as his wife closes her eyes and sighs.

CHAPTER THREE

*In Which People Come to Visit From Far Away
and They Have a Bath,
Greenwich, Connecticut, 1968*

I'm supposed to be thinking of what I've done wrong, but instead I'm staring at my bedroom wall, rethinking the paint color. It had never occurred to me that a person could have too much red until Carlo Gambino stepped into my bedroom this afternoon with Uncle Lou and Jimmy Bruno and said in his watered down Sicilian accent, "So much red." After due consideration, I realize that there is an awful lot of it; the carpeting, the walls, my small table and chair, the plaid bedspread and pillows – it's all red. Red is strong, red is vibrant, I adore it. But now I know that some people can't handle it. I could have lived with that, but when Jimmy Bruno laughed and said, "Yeah, looks like a Scottish brothel, don't it?" self-doubt started tapping its bony finger on my shoulder. I don't know what a brothel is, but it sounds like an insult.

So many new words are being lobbed into my room at me today. *Catastrophic, Insolence, Mortified, Debacle.* These are words my mother has used to describe today's events. A debacle sounds like a sort of cake, a fussy looking thing that seems delicious from the outside but when you plunge your fork in, you find those dried cherries in the center and maybe some raisins and walnuts, and as the first bite sits politely on your tongue for a moment, you detect a good helping of rum in there too. There are so many things that don't belong in cake.

Mom believes in learning a new word every day and after

breakfast she breaks out her gigantic dictionary that is so heavy she can barely lift it. She opens it to a random place. I'm ordered to close my eyes and let my finger land on the page. Whichever word I land on, I must learn its meaning and use it correctly in three sentences that same day and also know how to spell it by the time she quizzes me at dinner. She says, "With those big, blue, innocent eyes of yours, people might think you're dumb, so you must have ten times the vocabulary that others your age do." The pages are thin and wispy, like those in a Bible, so many more words are crammed into our dictionary than in one with normal, thicker pages – enough words to ruin a kid's life entirely. It all feels like prejudice against blue eyes to me. *Prejudice.* I learned that word last month.

My only job had been to take the plate of cheese and crackers to the den while my mother finished getting ready and my father's train was delayed coming home from the city. Somehow I managed to ruin the day instead.

With Christmas right around the corner, I need cash. My mother had told me to make gifts for other people, but with only a few sheets of orange construction paper and a dried tub of Play-doh, my options were limited, so I ignored her advice. While the men arrived in their dark cars and the soldiers took their places in the driveway, I hurried around the house, dragging a kitchen chair behind me, climbing up quickly and removing as many paintings from their hooks as I could before the guys made it up the slate stairs and through our front door. I dragged the paintings upstairs one by one and set them up in a neat display against my red walls. I was going to auction them off to the highest bidder. My mother had once said that the William Merritt Chase in the living room was worth a fortune, so I was sure the rest of them were as well.

Making money the usual way was out of the question for me. I'd tried it before and learned that no one would hire a six-year-old for anything other than manual labor, and then grossly underpay, claiming "you young kids don't know the value of a dollar." This I learned from Old Man Skeen down the street, who last fall had me rake his entire yard before the first snowfall. It took me an hour and a half, and when I was done he handed me two dimes.

So when the guys came into the house this afternoon, I grabbed them and herded them up the stairs as quickly as I could. I had a little time, because I could still hear Mom's shower running and Dad had called from Grand Central to say his train was an hour behind.

I'm sure the men thought something had gone terribly wrong. I was frantic.

"C'mon! Hurry. Up here!"

And they all followed me.

My parents had taken me to an auction once before, but I wasn't quite sure how it worked. I had no practice in yelling numbers at lightning speed, so I simply began brow beating them out of their money. Uncle Lou and Jimmy were laughing throughout my sales pitch, which was annoying, but still I pressed on. Working quickly, I had just managed to sell Carlo a lovely painting of a pond surrounded by blurry cherry blossoms and some white geese for twenty-two bucks. I was in the middle of explaining to him that I'd have to see some proper identification in order to complete the paperwork, when my mother appeared in my doorway.

This is how I ended up in my rocking chair facing the wall.

"You have to think things through," my father said to me when he got home.

I was under the impression that I *had* thought it through.

"Maggie, that was blatantly disrespectful of you," Mom said.

When I tried to plead my case, her index finger whipped up and silenced me.

"You simply don't ask Carlo Gambino to come up to your

55

room and try to sell him our things! What's gotten into you?"

A smile had broken loose on my father's face as she hollered at me, and she caught it. "Jack, I'm glad you find this so amusing. You should have seen it! She had those three grown men lined up on her bed, with five of our paintings – including the William Merritt Chase, by the way – and she was demanding to see Carlo's driver's license!"

"Okay, Patricia, I get it. But you have to admit, it shows ingenuity. C'mon, let's go downstairs and join the party. Mag, you take a seat."

This is injustice, abuse even. I realize I'm not being beaten to death or chained to a pipe in the basement or harnessed to a plow in the baking sun, but this still isn't right. If I don't understand exactly what I've done wrong, then I'm likely to do some version of it again. This makes me sigh, because now I'm broke, vaguely confused, and in trouble. Worst of all, I feel I'm being set up. Someone needs to explain this to me.

Carlo has been taken away and it is my fault. Today he'd looked so content, without his usual worry, and I'd been glad I'd picked today to show him my surprise. But now he is gone. My father led him out of my room and down the stairs towards dinner before he had a chance to show me his driver's license or give me my twenty-two dollars. I've missed dinner, but I could hear them applaud when the platters of food were brought to the table. Jimmy and Lou have left also, and I can hear my parents discussing things downstairs in that parentally disappointed tone.

I'm reminded of the last time I landed myself in this chair facing the wall: it was the *Hannah the Cat Incident*. My sister had been home from college for a short visit and had brought her new black-and-white cat, Hannah, with her because there was no one in her dorm to cat-sit for her. She and our mother had gone downtown to shop, leaving me alone in the house. I wanted to row out to my island but then remembered my sister's instructions to watch over Hannah while they were gone. I'd never been in charge of a cat before. Jane was the cat person in our family; me, I'm prone to dogs, but after spending a good amount of time staring at Hannah, I concluded that she looked as bored as I was, so I picked her up, tucked her under my arm and took her down to the lake.

I soon discovered this cat was more afraid of water than my mother. As I was holding her over the boat, ready to drop her in, she took one look at the lake, scratched two deep gouges in my arm, and made a horrible noise very much like when a long string gets caught in the vacuum. She tore loose from me and raced back up to the house. That horrible creature was sitting on the back stoop, licking herself, when I got to her. By that time, I was embarrassed and bleeding and had already gotten excited about my boat ride. Since there's only one way to get excitement *out* of your system once it's *in* – and that's to go ahead with your plan– I picked Hannah up, carried her up the stairs and looked for a safe place to keep her until I got back from the island. She struggled a little, but I managed to stuff her neatly into my Easy Bake Oven. Then I went to the lake.

When Mom and Jane returned, we had a fashion show to see how Jane's new clothes looked on her and then we had a lunch of tuna fish sandwiches with slices of tomato on the side. I think we might have played Gin Rummy for a while, so logically, I forgot about Hannah. When the cat was heard meowing from inside the Easy Bake, and even though it is just a toy that bakes by the heat of a light bulb, I was ushered to this chair to face this red wall for a very long time. I should have known better; that oven never cooked anything but my goose. It'd put me in messes before, like the time Mom smelled meat cooking and found me roasting slices of cured ham in my room. I thought that was the entire point of having an oven in your bedroom.

"Well, Mag? Are you thinking?" my mother is saying behind me now.

I nod my head without turning around.

#

Since five days have passed, I expected to come home from school today and find my mother busy in the kitchen and for my punishment to be over. I expected her to ask me about my day and that we might spend some time picking up sticks in the back yard or raking crimson and honey-yellow leaves into piles so that I can dive into them and then wonder why I feel compelled to do that when I get dirt in my eyes and the landing is never as soft as I'd expected. What I hadn't expected was this.

Uneasiness seizes my insides because I'm once again very confused. My mother has the remnants of a bright red cocktail in her hand and she's smiling down at me as I set my Charlie Brown lunch box on the coffee table in the living room. There's so much to take in: all the bright colors, the faint smell of fish in the air, the giggles. I'm alarmed.

This is Friday, which means I have lake plans for tomorrow. By the look of things in the living room, those plans are about to be canceled. I'm searching my mother's face for an explanation but am only getting that expression she gets when you open a birthday present and you expected a Spiro Graph or an Etcho-Sketch or a Tonka truck, but it's a sweater. A sweater with big white snowflakes all over it and your Grandma Edna knitted this sweater for you in that creepy nursing home in Minnesota that smells of urine and overcooked peas, with the guy who always sits in the hallway in his wheelchair – the guy with no legs – and as you pass him, he calls out, "Look at all them legs!" and you walk a little closer to your mother, feeling guilty for having legs of your own. I *know* I'm supposed to cherish this sweater, to see it as some sort of heirloom to pass on to my children one day, but in the end, all I really wanted was the Etcho-Sketch. My mother is hoping I'll see things her way in a minute.

She pushes me gently between my shoulder blades and I lurch forward. I feel my face color.

I count five of them and wonder if there are more lurking somewhere in other rooms of the house. Five. All squished up together on the sofa in a colorful Japanese row of giggles. Even before my mother tells me, I know what they are because of the silk doll we have that's encased in glass, frozen in mid fan dance – the one I'm not allowed to touch. They are Geisha.

"Maggie, go say hello," and she gives me another shove. "Introduce yourself to these lovely ladies. They've come all the way from Japan and will be staying with us as our guests."

I look up at my mother, hoping there's more to the story as she slugs back the rest of her cocktail and smiles at them. She looks nervous, which makes me nervous, because when her nerves are shot, she very shortly thereafter will go missing. That means that I will be left alone in the house with five geisha. I take it all in: the kimonos, their pale, pale skin; some have teensy metal wind chimes stuck in their blue-black hair. They all giggle together, some smile behind their hands, one is showing me her tiny Japanese teeth, one is bobbing her head at me. It's too much. I catch movement out the corner of my eye, and I am further astonished that I recognize a woman sitting in the corner facing the geisha line-up on the couch.

This is Virginia Coopersmith Vanderoth. I like to refer to her as VCV because that name of hers is just too problematic. She lives two houses down, towards the path to the train station, in a dark little cottage that could be found in one of Aesop's fables. The roof is covered in moss and pigeons, and the house emits a constant hum of cooing. This would be charming if it weren't for the very mean black dog that lives beneath the pigeons. It's a standard poodle that spends its days testing the strength of its chain while beige froth showers the ground around him, his muzzle folded back into demonic snarls showing his teeth, changing him from a dog to a menacing ghoul. I've strategically avoided her and this dog for three years now. When I've passed her house on my way to one adventure or another, her dog locks eyes with me, and becomes instantly blood-thirsty. In response to the growl of warning, I cross to the other side of the road. If VCV happens to be out in her yard, she smiles and waves and threatens me with piano lessons. And here she sits, old and proper, behind horn-rimmed glasses with rhinestones around the edges and a loose gray bun of greasy hair. Her incredibly thick ankles sprout from a pair of corrective black shoes that are planted firmly on the carpet, hands clasped tightly in her lap. She has the posture of someone who used to dance.

Before my mother can give me another embarrassing shove, I move towards our guests. I'm feeling shy, an emotion I don't admire in myself; it makes me feel undercooked.

As if choreographed, the geisha rise in unison to a standing position as I approach the first in her paprika red kimono with white flowers embroidered along the hem. As she offers me a long narrow hand, palm down, I notice her skin; so pale, almost translucent, as if it's never seen the sun. Her fingernails are short and perfectly shaped like almonds. As she bows down to me, I catch a whiff of baby powder. Her face is serene with elegant, long features. I smile and bow back. We say nothing.

I move to the next. Wrapped in the color of salmon, she is less polished and much younger than the first. Her black, shoulder length hair is curled up and out at the ends. A white flower rests behind her ear. She bows three times and giggles nervously. Paprika leans in to her and whispers something in Japanese, which changes Salmon's face; her giggles pause, her face softens. I can see she's trying not to smile but there's a sparkle lurking in her eye that tells me to stay tuned for secret things to come. She's an imp, this one, and I like her right away.

Up close, the third girl is the most stunning. Her kimono is a bright yellow-green. A peacock with turquoises, greens and blues, fans its tail proudly across her lap as if competing with her beauty, yet knowing it will never win the crown. Her gaze is like warm, sweet milk, her mouth has been made in the most perfect shape of a heart, her nose is small like a porcelain doll's. As she bows deeply towards me, a blue-black wave of hair sweeps across her shoulder. It nearly touches my knees. The only smile she offers comes from behind her eyes. Her fragile hand cups me beneath my chin as she leans in and purrs, "Okuuura," into my face, making the hairs rise up on my neck. I will have to assume that this is her name. If it isn't, it oughta be.

Dark gray herons fly across the next girl's turquoise kimono. Her hair is pinned up behind bangs that showcase her long eyelashes. There is a tiny wind chime tucked in a tuft of her hair. As she bows to me, she says, "Hello, Moggy, so kind to meet you. My name is Kimi." Relief comes over me as she breaks the language barrier, even though she's petting my hair as if I'm a cat. I'm very tired all of a sudden and look forward to getting out of my school clothes as I reach the final geisha.

She's all smiles as I near her tangerine kimono. It has red and brown pinwheels sewn in overlapping positions from her waist to the floor. Her nose is flat. She is the least attractive of the five, but her genuine warmth makes up for her lack of beauty. The eyes become mere slits as the smile stretches across her face. She shows me a sliver of tooth as she bows.

"Yes! Happy, happy," she says.

A small wind chime sways at her temple. I smile and nod to her and then politely back away from the couch to go stand near my mother where I can examine them all from a safe distance, including VCV, who's just cleared her throat. I hope someone's about to tell me what's going on because this is too much like trying to find a light switch in the dark in a house I don't know.

"Patricia," VCV says to my mother, "the girls have very little English, except Kimi here, but of the four geisha at my house, there is one whose English is quite good. If you have any trouble at all, you have my telephone number? Townsend nine, thirty-three zero four?"

"I'm sure we won't have any trouble, Virginia. We're happy to accommodate, and I'm sure Maggie will enjoy spending time with them and learning about their culture."

Four more geisha at VCV's house. I am letting my mother's last comment worm its way into me. I hadn't expected to be learning about anyone's culture this weekend. I'd expected to wake up early in the morning, pack a lunch of bologna sandwiches and an apple and go down to the lake.

I think I will have to write all this down and sort it out, using the fat red pencil that our first grade teacher, Mrs. Ragland, decided was an easier writing instrument than the narrow, yellow #2s I'd thought we would use. I have two of these fat pencils in my room. They have an Indian chief stamped in gold near the eraser. I find them awkward, like writing with a banana, but Mom says I will get used to it. That's the problem. I know once I do get used to the fatness and the weight, by the time I reach second grade and am handed a normal, yellow #2, it will feel as though I'm writing with the bone from a bird's wing. Regardless, this is how I sometimes figure situations out, by writing them down. I'm wondering if I have anything other than that orange construction paper to write this story on when my father comes through the front door.

He's in his suit, his briefcase in hand. His ruby pinkie ring winks as he lifts his hand to remove his fedora. He takes in our new house guests and Virginia Coopersmith Vanderoth in the corner, her hands the size of Jimmy Bruno's.

"Whoa. What the hell is this?"

Knowing he's as surprised as I am makes me feel less alone. I am the one people keep things from, as if I'm not trusted with any vital information. I go stand by him as things are explained a little bit more. VCV eventually leaves us to entertain her geisha because it's time for her to go feed her very mean dog.

Supper is a lesson in cutlery for the girls. The one in Paprika watches my mother's fork and knife before she begins sawing at the meat on her plate. I don't think this is what geisha are meant to eat. After many trips to the bar in the den, my father is still trying to adjust to the situation. My mother's eyes are turning redder with each bite of her chicken and each sip of the vodka and cranberry, while Dad is attempting to understand Japanese as it squeaks and purrs its way around the table.

Because this chicken is slimy and my confusion is making me restless, I slide, as if boneless, from my chair and slip under the table to gain a different perspective. If dinner had been up to me, I would have served something worthy of these creatures; perhaps violets on a bed of soft greens, a soup the color of sunrise flavored with deep red rose buds, and for dessert, an angel food cake dyed the palest of blue and sprinkled on top with lavender sugar.

I still don't know why they're here, because I wasn't paying attention when things were explained to my father, but I'm mildly entertained. Silverware taps china, silk rustles. My escape goes unnoticed. I watch their very white socks with the split sections for their big toes, as if those toes each have a little sock of their own. It looks uncomfortable to me. I wonder where everyone's shoes have gone.

I think about my Uncle Jim, my mother's older brother by two years, because it is from him that I learned my hiding under the table trick. He'd done it once at a Christmas gathering, and I noticed that no one looked in his direction or bent down in their chairs to pick up the tablecloth with the poinsettias all around the edges, to see what he was doing – especially since dessert was about to happen. So I had slid down to join him. When I asked him what he was doing, he scratched his white beard in a thoughtful way with his densely freckled fingers, and, in a thick British accent – an accent I marvel at since he's never been more than a few hours from Mendota Heights, Minnesota, and my father says the closest Uncle Jim has ever been to anything English is while buttering a Thomas' Original English Muffin – he'd said, "Sometimes a chap just needs to find some peace and quiet amongst the chaos and the rioting." I stayed under that Christmas table with him listening to the conversation above until he dismissed me.

Now, I want to reach out and touch Kimi's turquoise kimono with the gray herons flying across the silk, but they may have forgotten I'm here, so I remain still and listen.

"We'll have to take you girls down to the Sound tomorrow. Maybe to Indian Harbor Yacht Club for a drink. Jack, what do you think?" I hear my mother say.

Dad clears his throat. I can hear him chewing.

"I think that's a fine idea, Patricia, and I'm pretty sure they can't understand a damned word you're saying."

Mom's sigh is loud enough for me to hear. I hope a fight doesn't break out in front of these geisha. It would seem cruel to put them through something like that; they may shatter into a million pieces and then sprinkle down like the last remnants of a fireworks display, landing on this soft yellow rug before disappearing entirely.

"Really, Pat. Watch. You don't understand a word I'm saying, do you, girls? Look there, see? Nothing. You could suggest that we line them up against the side of the house, blindfold them, put lit cigarettes in their mouths and gun them down, and they'd just smile and bow at you!"

Dad's laughing and chewing.

"Oh for God's sake, Jack," my mother says.

"Look, I have the guys coming over tonight, in about an hour, in fact, so you take these gals someplace else after they eat and keep them busy, or have Maggie do it."

"Jack! You did not tell me there would be a meeting tonight." Her voice is taught, shrill.

"Well, you didn't tell me I'd come home to the Japanese variety show either, Patricia. This isn't my fault. You just find something to do with them, or put them to bed. Stack them up in the guest room or something. Castellano's coming, Lou Capalbo, Bruno too. I need to talk to them, and the last thing I need is for them to be distracted by all of this."

Someone's fork has just been tossed on a plate in

exasperation. I find it a good time to slink back up to my chair in case I have to create a diversion so the geisha don't get scared. Too bad VCV has gone home; I don't think Dad would be this wound up if she were still here. Having her in a room feels like you're in the presence of a school's head mistress or a stern court judge, which makes a person want to behave. As I wiggle my way back up to my seat, I see that Mom's eyes have soured on Dad, and Dad's eyes have soured on his plate. These geisha seem to be well aware that tension is the next course being served. Maybe if I play it off, they'll think this is just a normal American dinner. I stretch my arms up above my head and fake a yawn, mimicking a casual mood, then smile at Okuura across the table from me. She's poking suspiciously at her chicken. The young one in the salmon kimono catches my eye and giggles. A few others join in. Dad rises up from the table with his empty glass, shaking his head. He goes to the den.

It's dark through my look-out window as I watch the cars roll up. I feel cool silk brush my elbow. When I turn, I'm surprised to see all five geisha peering out the window behind me. They move silently like vampires.

"Friends," I tell them, pointing at the driveway.

I go to the front door and open it before realizing I've just broken a rule. I'm just so happy to have English speaking people arriving. Uncle Lou and Jimmy Bruno come up the slate walkway. I notice cigarettes lighting up in the darkness, and Paul Castellano's tall frame is standing over the glowing tips. I'm relieved I don't see Carlo. Since I still haven't figured out exactly what I did wrong that day of the art auction, I'm not sure exactly how humiliated I should be, and I'd rather avoid him until I am sure. A fat ember rises from the back seat of the second car and singes the dark with the deep color of blood oranges, outranking the smaller cigarette fires around it.

Jimmy's smoothing out his pants in the glow of the porch light as he comes towards the house. Lou takes a long pull from his cigarette and flicks it into a small pile of yellow and brown leaves that have gathered in the driveway. I'm more excited to see Jimmy this time than I was the last because I know the dentist is closed at nighttime. He stops short on the path, making Lou bump into his backside. Jimmy's mouth is hanging open. I know he's staring at the geisha that are gathered behind me, and I'm secretly enjoying *his* being surprised for a change. Soft giggles sail out over my head as Dad walks up and tries to usher us away from the doorway.

Jimmy enters the door first and finds himself standing next to Okuura. He slowly eyes her from the long blue-black hair to the heart-shaped mouth to the thick sash of blue tied at her small waist and finally to the peacock.

"Holy Christ," he says, and then he blows air out of his mouth as if he's just walked a mile uphill.

Okuura seems aware of his eyes upon her even though she doesn't look at him. She places her delicate hand high on her neck, then slowly runs her fingers under her ear, down the side of her throat, stopping just at the collar of her kimono. Jimmy takes a handkerchief from his back pocket and wipes his forehead with it.

Lou steps into the house and raises his eyebrows. "What the hell is this?"

"Damned if I know, Lou. Ask my lovely wife. This is her mess. Want a drink?"

"At least," Lou says, following him to the bar, keeping a close eye on our visitors.

I take VCV's previous seat in the corner and watch these two cultures clash wildly in our house, trying to imagine how I will put this all down on paper so that I never forget it. Jimmy's still standing next to Okuura, as though he's trying to get his bearings. I've never seen him so emotionally disheveled before, which, for some reason, gives me a sense of tender revenge.

My father holds a brown drink near Jimmy's chest. Jimmy is wiping the back of his thick neck. He hasn't noticed my father, nor the drink, and may never.

Lou comes out of the den with a drink of his own and leans close to my father's ear. "Imagine it, Jack. A Wop that looks like a bulldog and a Jap broad that moves like an oriental panther? She'd eat him alive."

Dad's chuckling at the scene when Lou steps up between Okuura and Jimmy and smoothly steers her away from him. "Well, hello there. That's right, come with me, sweetheart. Let me teach you some Italian."

Paul Castellano is wearing expensive clothes tonight, and, since the weather has turned colder, he's brought out the cashmere coat and gray city hat, too. I watch him take inventory of the people in the house. His eyes move over the geisha with little expression. Paul's a hard one to read; like a closed treasure chest found under layers of dust, I have no idea what's inside and no key to open its lock. I only have my imagination to help me. There could be jewels and strands of pearls or crackling old maps with holes in the creases, leading to secret caves that no one has discovered. Or there might only be cobwebs and spiders spinning their tiny nets and crouching in corners. The lid of that chest may never be opened, which might be just fine by me as I think he may be too dusty to explore.

As Paul slips off his coat, I see an old friend from Texas come up behind him into the glowing light of the front porch. This is the man whose lap my mother likes to perch on. When she does that, it makes me want to look away for some reason.

His coat is long and black, and his cigar juts straight out from his teeth, pointing at our guests. He's biting on it like he thinks it might try to escape. I think it could snap in two. Because he's famous, this man is the only person allowed to stink up our house with his sickly sweet smoke. He immediately notices me in the corner and silently throws me a wink. I chin wave to him but don't attempt to move. I don't want to lose my seat because I know if I were to rise and weave myself into all these visitors, through their pant legs and silk flowing kimonos, I would get lost in a hurry. As it is, I'm in the position to experience the element of surprise with each person who enters; it's more fun when it's someone else who's being surprised and not me.

As if her celebrity radar has tipped her off, my mother appears at the bottom of the stairs. She has made a quick wardrobe change, entering the living room in a long leopard print dress that competes and almost wins against the geisha's shimmering embroidered silk. Her smile is bright, and I feel relief in her happiness. She's not wearing the garden hose as an accessory, she's not hiding beneath a tree, and she hasn't locked herself in her room, so I can watch without worry for a while. I sink into the overstuffed chair and make myself small.

My mother floats through our rooms offering something to snack on while the guests have their drinks and try to navigate through this affair. Hot cheese balls stuffed with green olives have stirred up Italian applause and Japanese nods. The geisha are paying appropriately demure attention to the mobsters, while the men jockey for position. Giggles and soft Japanese sounds mix together with loud laughter, Italian expletives, private jokes and the occasional smoker's hack. No matter how long I sit here, I know that these two groups of people will never blend into anything but a comedy of the most ridiculous kind. Eventually, when they have had too much to drink and they look around, remembering me, I will be ushered to bed by my mother. The night will begin to fade from my mind as I slip beneath my red plaid blankets in my deep red room.

Kimi and the young, unpolished geisha dressed in salmon have found Paul Castellano at the bar. I give them credit for trying to break through his gruff demeanor. He's trying to smile, to be polite, but I can tell he'd rather be out in his car with his opera than waste another minute with them. He's all business.

I want to take it all in because I know, as quickly and quietly as the girls appeared this afternoon, they will vanish one morning without explanation, as if I'd only invented them in a dream. This is how guests come and go from our house, like fireflies that fly too high over my head or go dark when I move too near.

Mom glides to the front of the room and greets our friend and his fat cigar, waving her hand through his smoke in mock disgust.

"Honestly, Henry, are you still smoking those vile things?"

"As many as humanly possible, my dear Pattie. How are ya?" Henry says, wrapping an arm around her waist and pulling her into him.

"I'm good," she tells him, patting his wide chest.

"It's a rare occurrence that I find anything surprises me at 88 Orchard Drive, but I've gotta ask. Have you opened a tea house? Formed an alliance with Japan? Learning judo maybe?"

"They're here to play a concert in New York with our neighbor, Virginia Coopersmith Vanderoth. She's very famous, Henry. A harpist and pianist from the Philharmonic. You met her last year at our Easter party."

He harrumphs as if he doesn't remember but takes her word for it.

This is Henry Wade – legal celeb and chain smoker. Mom has told me a boring story about him and something called Roe vs Wade. Until she spelled *Roe* for me, I'd assumed it was the only sort of *row* I know. I was certain this fame of his had something to do with a row boat and rowing somewhere much faster than someone else. But it's something about courts and being a lawyer and being brilliant, as she puts it. I just like that he pretends to be mad all the time and isn't. He's a man who masks his obvious satisfaction with himself behind a brittle bark, knowing all the while he is our family's hero. My sister, Jane, has told me a different story about Henry – one I wish she wouldn't tell me. Sometimes Dad retells his version to me as if he isn't aware that maybe I'm just too young to hear these horrible things.

I try to think of something else as I attempt to remain invisible here in my chair by the fireplace at 88 Orchard Drive but thoughts unravel without my permission about Sid's accident and how Henry Wade stepped in and took over, hunting down the drunk who'd sent Sid's Aston Martin careening into the side of a gas station like a cannon ball. Jane sometimes adds (and sometimes not, depending on the day) how our mother needed to be restrained so she wouldn't hurt herself when she lost her mind over it. Another detail I'd be happy to forget, but somehow cannot. Before the trial was over, according to my father's version of the tale, the defendant mishandled a Molotov cocktail while sleeping in his bed one night and burned to death. What a careless individual that man must have been.

Jane says my mother was finally untied from her bed and worked with Sid for months after his release from Parkland, braving his still swollen face, vacant gaze and half shaved skull marked with tracks made from the scalpel and chunky dents from the Mobil station's brick exterior. She taught him to read and write, to walk without a wobble. Life began to live in our house again.

When Sid is home on breaks from his studies at college, his harmonica wails the bluesy notes of a well practiced tune. His deep laugh permeates our kitchen while he watches my mother at the stove. He catches me as I walk by; bending me over, knuckles dug into my neck, and tickles me until I'm sure I will die. I let him continue the torture because I can endure anything as long as he's here. I know my family feels the same way; they covet his existence. It's a feeling that we've gotten away with something, have tricked the fates, because he speaks and he drives and he dates and he studies, he looks as he did before the accident except for that quirky eye. He lives. Perhaps all of that is why my mother likes to perch on Henry Wade's lap when he comes to call.

Someone has put a Tony Bennett record on the player and it makes Lou Capalbo sway, dancing with his glass of scotch in the corner as my mother shows the geisha upstairs.

The guys gather around the bar in the den, and I'm still in my chair as my father closes the double doors for their meeting. Water begins to run through the pipes in the upstairs bathroom, and I know the time is creeping close for me to be sent to bed.

I decide to risk it all. I rise from my invisible chair and move closer to the double doors.

"Paul, Jimmy took care of that job for us. You're not going to have a problem with that crew anymore. Isn't that right, Jimmy?" This is my father's voice.

"Problem solved," Jimmy says.

"You should have seen him," Lou says. "God, it was good! Jimmy, tell 'em. Tell 'em about his face."

"Nuthin' to tell. It was fast. The guy was scared, though. Problem solved, that's all." Jimmy sounds as if he's smiling while saying this.

"C'mon. You gotta tell em. Jack, listen to this: Jimmy has the guy leaning over a table, and I've got his hands tied up behind his back, right? So Jimmy walks up and goes around the table, looking at the guy. He's just walkin' around him like he's on a putting green trying to line up a shot. He takes a pair of work gloves and stuffs them both in the guy's mouth."

Lou's laughing a little while he speaks, and I hear my father start to laugh too. I wonder who they're talking about and if this is just another joke. They have so many.

Lou continues telling the story as I crouch by the crack in the doors.

"The guy's eyes are watering, and Jimmy starts going into this long, drawn out thing about how the fates have brought them together." Lou's having trouble getting his words out alongside his laughter. "And how isn't it interesting that the two of them are about the same age, and they had gone on about their lives and done their own thing and that now God has made their paths converge right there in the guy's lumber warehouse, that both of them had made decisions throughout their lives which landed them there together. Jimmy's giving him this big philosophical lesson like he's some Wop Guru."

Laughter has crescendoed from snickering chuckles to howling, and I want to go in so I can hear the rest of Lou's story more clearly.

"Okay, okay, so then Jimmy walks over to the trunk of the car," Lou continues. "We've pulled the car inside the warehouse, right? And Jimmy goes to the trunk and opens it. The guy's watching him with these wild eyes. He's frantic now. So Bruno digs in the trunk for a minute and pulls out a cattle prod. He's standing there now, in front of the guy bent over the table, and he says, 'I see you're considering the choices you've made and maybe you're thinking that it's time to be rethinking those choices. Am I right?' The guy's nodding his head. Then Jimmy gets all calm and says, 'Good. Okay, now, because I respect you, here's something that I usually don't do for people, I'm gonna give you a break this one time, and I'm gonna tell you what's coming before it gets here, just so you know what I'm trying to get across to you, to be considerate, to be respectful, because that's what I was taught as a young boy growing up, even though these are not things I'm sure you ever learned. So I'm gonna help you out some. Ya ready? Yeah? Good. Now listen up,' Then he walks around behind the guy and says, 'This is gonna hurt,' and he rams the prod through his pants and shoves it clean up the guy's ass! I'm tellin ya, he was surprised all right. Ha! *This is gonna hurt.* That was a good one. Hey, Jimmy, where'd you get that cattle prod from anyway?"

"From your mother," Jimmy answers.

"I met with that prick three months ago," Paul says. "It wasn't like he wasn't warned. I told him, 'You wanna keep building in Jersey? You wanna see another building permit again? Then you'll use our trucks, use our cement, use our guys. That's it.' He didn't want to listen."

"Don't worry, Paul," Lou says, "If he gives us any more trouble, I'll put a slug in him and toss him off the Triborough."

"He's been in thick with city officials for years, Paulie. He had it coming. We've got that territory covered from now on and --"

My mother's hand sends a tinny shock through my shoulder. When I look up at her standing over me, she points to the stairway without a word.

The sheets feel cool as I mull over the story I've just overheard in our den. I wish I hadn't listened, hadn't been so sneaky. I have to squeeze my eyes shut, thinking of Uncle Lou throwing a guy off the Triborough Bridge. And Jimmy is a protector, not a man who laughs as he crams things up people's back sides. He's supposed to be thoughtful and cuddly like a stuffed bear. I look over at the small green bowl he made for me on my night table. It makes my stomach hurt.

The bathroom door opens in the hall and all five geisha come out, one after the other, like candies spilling from a box, and I wonder how they all fit inside that tiny space together. As they pass my bedroom, they take no notice of me in the dark. I'm covered except for one ear and one eye, and I stay very still. They move toward the guest room, and their muffled giggles and melodic language soothes me. As I fight to keep my eyes from fluttering closed, I feel certain of one thing: if butterflies had voices, this would surely be their sound.

#

I haven't thought things through again, this I know. But none of this had been planned. I hadn't meant to upset the planet and everyone on it, and I certainly had nothing to do with the ceiling falling onto the dining room table. *Premeditated mischief* is what my mother has called it. I have to admit, she may be right about that. I guess I was feeling a little mischievous when this all began.

This red is definitely too red.

I hear the men cleaning up the mess down stairs, and wonder how long I will be sitting here waiting to be set free. My mother leaves my door open in order to pound my humiliation in further with every person who passes my room on their way to the toilet. I feel every one of their gazes on the back of my neck, hear them pause on the carpet. I try to guess who it is but am only able to recognize when it's my mother because weighty sighs accompany her footsteps. I don't turn around. I sit and I stare at this wall as instructed. *Reckless endangerment*. That term has also been used.

I wasn't aware that geisha can't swim. I guess it's like certain breeds of dog that are born without webbing between their toes. The result could have been tragic. It is tragic. I'm hungry. I'm alone.

The rain is washing my window with purpose, as if the sky itself is angry with me too. All I'd wanted was an adventure. An adventure that has now landed me in the precarious position of finding my way back into my mother's good graces, which was a prickly path even before all of this.

The guys returned to 88 Orchard Drive this morning and had taken their usual places in the den behind the doors. My beautiful mother gliding serenely through rooms in her leopard print gown had transformed again during the night. Her eyes were rimmed with red, trails of mascara running down her cheeks in long, inky streaks like some devastated clown, her red hair snarled and turbulent. I saw her out the window before breakfast but I told no one. Maybe that was my first mistake. I make so many these days, it's awfully hard to sort out.

I'd come down the back stairs smelling bacon burning on the stove when I noticed four holes the size of silver dollars in the sheet rock over the yellowish-gold telephone that hangs on the wall near the back door. The kitchen was empty; not a geisha nor goombah in sight. Black smoke rose from the frying pan, crackling with menace, so I turned off the burner, congratulating myself for being so clever.

I entered the dining room and passed the large windows flanked by their yellow curtains. I noticed movement outside, and that's when I spotted my mother. She was running at full sprint, down the steep hill towards the lake, still in her sheer, pale green nightgown, holding a very large bulletin board – the one that's supposed to be screwed into the wall over the yellowish-gold phone – above her head. I could see little scraps of paper flapping from their pins and I hoped they'd hang on; these are important phone numbers and emergency information that we keep on handy display. Just in case.

Thunder is rumbling and the rain hits the window. I wish this was one of those days you can do everything over; when you can go outside, pick some lilies of the valley for your mother, and that's all it takes to turn everything around and she loves you again. Instead, I'm surrounded by this catastrophe that lies in quivering, dying pieces on my blood red floor. I'm not allowed to read a book while I'm facing this wall, because if I'm reading, I'm not thinking about what I've done. It's not as unclear this time as it was with the art auction incident. Hindsight sits next to me shaking its head.

I should have knocked on the forbidden den doors when I'd seen her lower the bulletin board level with her waist in both hands. I'd noticed the two squirrels standing on hind legs, frozen, on alert, as my mother swung it back as if she was serving up a giant Frisbee. I should have called for Jimmy Bruno to make things right when she'd hurled the bulletin board towards the squirrels and they'd darted off in opposite directions. I should have knocked on the den doors and interrupted the meeting without care for myself or any punishment that would ensue. Instead, I watched it unfold. I watched the bulletin board sail effortlessly out of her hands, cut through the air and land hard against the bark of a tree. I watched her stomp on the ground with bare feet and cup her ears, shaking her head as if she were listening to something she refused to believe.

I haven't decided if my intentions were pure in those first few moments or not; if I was being heroic or just running away. There was no thinking it through. The plan had come to me as if it were a bolt of lightning sent down from the Gods when I saw them gathered in the kitchen a few moments later, all wearing the same kimonos from the day before, which was a relief because I'd still be able to tell them apart by what colors they wore.

The sky had still been overcast as my mother stormed into the house and up the back stairs without saying good morning. I knew there was only one place to go. After messy translations and too many hand gestures, I'd finally gotten the geisha into their high wooden sandals, which they call Obuki and look like tiny black tables, and led them outside. That's when freedom rang out, making me feel like a newly liberated creature with wings unfolding and spreading out to take some long-awaited flight.

As we trotted gracefully down the hill, geisha loyally following me one by one, I thought that if we were being watched from our house or from a seat in the sky, we must look like a bouncy blond kite with a colorful silk tail sailing behind it. I hoped the geisha would all make it down the hill safely and no one slipped on the green morning dew. That was my biggest concern at that point: not that my mother was now using larger weapons and might start driving Dad's pale yellow Lincoln through the back yards of Greenwich on a high-speed killing spree, but that one of my geisha would fall from her high Japanese shoes and go down on the lawn, sliding on slick silk toward the water. I thought of Uncle Lou and what he says when something ungraceful happens to something it shouldn't: It's like seeing a swan with the shits.

All the while, a small, itchy feeling was on my skin, telling me that transporting my Japanese contraband out to the island was a huge mistake, a message I'd ignored entirely. I should have stopped and turned back when Okuura arched a brow at the duck poo beneath her. It looked like she was going to resist, but then the four already in the boat called to her, offering assurance and thrill. After a tense moment, her heart-shaped mouth formed a coy smile and she melted flawlessly into the seat at the bow. The boat lowered ominously in the water with her weight. I eyed the water's edge as it threatened to spill up over the sides as the boat rocked in choppy dips. When their squeals rang out across the water, I gave them the international sign of shushing – index finger to pursed lips – pushed them off, hopped in and away we floated.

A strong breeze spun the scent of baby powder around us as a family of mallards paddled out of our way. The Connecticut Turnpike hummed faintly in the distance. We neared the island.

This is when I should have turned around for sure; this was the moment I had ample warning, when I could have avoided it all. A black wall of menacing clouds was creeping over the tree line, and with it came a giant invisible hand to push against the boat and fight me as I plunged my oars through the thickening lake, my feet coming off the bottom of the boat with every pull.

A burgundy canoe glided quickly through the water toward us. Mr. Blakely from down the road held his paddle suspended in the air, mouth slightly agape as he passed behind us. His golden retriever, Tim, cocked his head as he watched me row. I gave them the Italian chin wave and kept my steady course. The air pushed us back; with every lift of my oars from the water, we lost a few yards. A cold gust swept Okuura's beautiful black hair up in the air and laid it back down in a velvety waterfall against her back. I was afraid the wind would rip the tiny wind chimes and flowers from everyone's hair and send them sailing into the lake, but they were holding firm, so I carried on.

Hindsight snickers beside me. I wish it would leave but I know there's no better place for it to sit than beside me in smug satisfaction.

Paprika put her hand on my thigh – the next cue I ignored – and pointed back to the shore. My eyes followed the direction of her almond-shaped fingernail. I saw my mother cupping her hands in a large O at her mouth. Angry wind was whipping her red hair into snarls and stuffing her words back down her throat. Still I rowed. Even when I saw my father on determined bowed legs and Uncle Lou with a drink in his hand heading down to the lake, making big sweeping motions – lake to shore – coaxing us in, I refused to give in. Something primal was steering me away. Adrenaline-fueled panic took over when plump wet drops hit us cold, and Henry emerged from the house, the wind blasting puffs of smoke from his fat cigar into vapor. Soft squeals erupted when a sheet of rain swept across the water and hit the shore and the people waving us home. Water leeched up the kimonos' hems as it rose from the bottom of the boat. Finally, I knew it was time to let go of the oars and let the storm push us back in. And so I'd surrendered.

This was far less poetic an adventure than what I'd conjured up for myself this morning. In my version, there was no rain, no wind, no one panicking all around. In my mind, it was to be a soft autumn day with maybe a rippling of water carrying leaves the color of Moroccan spices on the lake, searching out an adventure of their own, and a gentle ride with the geisha to my island. I was Don Quixote brandishing a sword, taking my team of Oriental squires, who were brave and willing, ready to slay any windmills we might happen to find. This is my delusional, stubborn mind when it's wide awake and ready to go and I see nothing but my own goal in front of me. Tenacious to a fault when I find an idea, my mother says. Even a poor one. I'm beginning to understand what my Grandma Edna says about me: that getting me to see reason, once my mind is made up, is as useless a venture as keeping poets off a lawn.

It was the laughter that had given me hope, as my coward of a boat rushed itself back to shore on its own. Dad and Lou holding their hands high on their stomachs, Henry doubling over and staggering towards a maple tree.

A goombah had come down from the driveway, hearing the hollers and howls. He was holding his coat over my mother's head. As we floated swiftly in, I saw Virginia Coopersmith Vanderoth making her way through the woods along the shoreline, where the brush is thick and vines hang down from high branches forming tangled walls. She had an open umbrella that seemed to be getting stuck in the plants every few feet. I watched her struggle and pull and trudge in our direction with frantic gestures.

The moment I knew things had gone hopelessly south was when she hit the water. If she hadn't used so much force trying to pull her umbrella free of a bush, it wouldn't have happened. Her corrective black shoes and thick support hose would not have flipped up and out, landing her in the lake, holding the mangled umbrella up in the air over her head and making her hoot like some overturned owl. She should have known better.

"You've ruined everything for everybody today," Mom had told me on the way back up the saturated hill. And it's true. I've ruined Dad's meeting. I've ruined the geisha's rehearsal that they were too late and too wet to attend, five very expensive kimonos that I have no hope of replacing, unless I plan on raking Mr. Skeen's lawn for the next fifty years. And then there's the matter of Virginia Coopersmith Vanderoth's broken umbrella, torn support hose and the gash on her knee which bled on the white linen napkin I'd grabbed in an attempt to help. One of the six linen napkins my grandmother had embroidered with pansies and pale blue swirls around the edges and had given to my mother on her twentieth birthday three million years ago.

I sigh loudly and it doesn't help. The rain is letting up, leaving only a soft rhythmic drumming against the glass now. I can see the lake from my chair, and it gives me hope that a day will come when I can get out of this seat, climb into my boat and escape back to my island before they pack me up and ship me off to live with the black-toothed Chinese lady downtown who smells of shrimp.

I'm thinking of God and our guests in this house and am wondering, if God is looking down on us all right now and he should decide that we should all become a sandwich, what sort of sandwich would we be? The answer is obvious, of course. We are a BLT. My father's Italian men are the bacon; crisp, browned on the edges, its flavor overpowering – attendance not easily ignored. The geisha are the lettuce and tomato, bringing color and texture, a subtle compliment to it all. And I am sure that I am the mayonnaise – the ivory glue that becomes translucent against the warmth of the toast, almost undetectable, but something you'd miss if it wasn't there.

I'm not supposed to be thinking of sandwiches.

My hair is still damp, leaving me chilled. I wish I hadn't seen that final scene before my father ushered me up to my room. It was as if the house itself had turned on me too. After gathering all the towels and the blankets I could, I'd thought it was over, that it had all cooled down to a mere simmer. The geisha were stripped of their ruined kimonos and wore thin, white matching bathrobes. Their hair hung wet and tired around their faces, making them look like freshly plucked chickens, stripped of color. My mother sipped a tall glass of vodka with a towel wrapping her head. Henry Wade sat at the dining room table with a scotch and freshly lit cigarette, since he was out of cigars (thanks to me, I was sure). Jimmy slapped at the grass stains on his pants, which I also felt responsible for when my mother told me they'd never wash out. I'd tried to help when Jimmy slipped and fell down on his knees outside, but Uncle Lou told me not to bother a man while he was praying and pulled me away with a snicker.

When the ceiling caved in over the dining room table, a crackling moan came from above. All eyes looked up and followed large chunks of plaster raining down around us. No one had mentioned that the Japanese like to rinse off before they step into a bath. We didn't know that they'd gathered together – as the Japanese do – the night before and had pointed the shower head outside the tub, taking their turns to get clean before bathing, thus soaking the floor at their feet. That's why the ceiling is now downstairs.

"Jack, your house is falling apart in my God damned drink," Henry said as he lifted a shard of plaster from his glass.

#

It is inconceivable that a punishment can go on for this long. It's been weeks now and I see no end in sight. The snow squeaks under foot, tightly rubbing against itself with each step we take down Orchard Drive. I notice the post-snowfall quiet. Not a bird, not a car engine, not a bark. It's as if the world has had a blanket thrown over it and has become smaller somehow. This should be comforting, as it usually is, but it's not, for I'm being delivered somewhere by my father and Uncle Lou. As I walk between them, I think that if they were made of Play-Doh, I would smush them together and be able to make the perfect man. Dad, with his calm, heroic steadiness and expensive smells; Lou, with his suave, magnetic air and the protective, insulating feeling he has about him. I'm allowing them to remain my favorites despite where they're taking me.

My father and I should be testing the sled on the hill out back about now, me sitting up front with Dad's legs wrapped around me. We should be barreling down at break neck speed toward the frozen lake as my father's face pinkens and my eyes water, blurring the trail in front of me. He should be hollering, "Whoo hoo!" in my ear as we gain momentum, approaching the rock ledge of the shore, knowing that as soon as we hit air, there will be no time to pray for the ice to hold.

Instead, we're on our way to an apology and to begin the equivalent of a child's prison term with no hope of parole. I look back at our tracks on the street. Two sets of large ones flank small ones. Lou Capalbo's are straight and precise while my father's point outward. They each hold one of my mittened hands so I can't escape. I imagine what we look like from above – trudging against the winter wind, making these tracks, the three of us lacking any real color – the landscape shades of white and gray as in the most dismal scene from Dr. Zhivago. Bare branches stretch out overhead like fingers attempting to clasp together in prayer. It all makes me feel so Russian.

I give my father a worried look as we reach Virginia Coopersmith Vanderoth's stone cottage. The pigeons are gone. I wonder if she's finally had enough of their cooing keeping her awake at night and has had them all shot. The stake in the yard has a tall tuft of snow balanced on top and the chain makes an indent in the drifts. No dog attached.

"Well, kiddo, this should be interesting," Dad says.

I have nothing to say.

Virginia Coopersmith Vanderoth flings open the door. She is wearing rubber boots and a man's woolen coat. I want to turn back.

"Hellooo, hellooo. Come in, come in," she hoots.

I've never seen so many things in one place. Books, newspapers, jars of beads and buttons, everything coated in a thick layer of dust. There is too much furniture here, four overstuffed chairs and two velvety green sofas fighting for space with tables large and small, all stacked with more things. Three golden harps squat on an old Persian rug in the living room in front of a sleek, black, grand piano.

We follow her into her kitchen, which has more things than the living room. Metal shelving lines every available wall from floor to ceiling, holding empty bottles and jars, cookbooks and cookie tins, boxes of crackers, canisters of coffee, pots, pans, dirty rags crumpled, and one three-foot-tall statue of Saint Francis next to the oatmeal over the stove.

Dad slides his hands in his pockets and rocks back on his heels. Lou's shaking his head, smiling down at me. I say a silent prayer very quickly that they will not leave me here, that Lou and my father will sit politely in one of the many chairs and wait for this to be over, taking me home before long.

VCV offers tea and Lou suggests something stronger, so now I watch VCV pour Drambuie into masculine glasses. I think of what I've been told about this thick, steady woman; that she, at one time, played a command performance for the Queen of England. I wonder if she had to drag one of her gigantic gold harps through the streets of London, stuffing it into one of those old fashioned black taxis, and if she hooted like an owl when she entered the doors of Buckingham Palace.

"I was sorry to hear about John, Virginia," Dad tells her.

"Yes, you took the New Haven into the city together from time to time didn't you, Jack?"

"All the time. He was a good man."

"He was, he was. I hadn't expected him to go like that, so quickly. I suppose we thought we'd both live forever. We never discussed his wishes in the event of his death, but, nevertheless, he's up there now," she says, pointing upward.

I look up at the ceiling and find comfort in the thought that John Vanderoth no longer has to be around that nasty black dog, which makes me wonder where it's lurking. I hope Lou has brought his gun.

"I'm sure he is. As Patricia always says, 'Heaven should be so lucky,'" Dad adds.

"Oh. No, Jack. He's up there." She points upward again. "On the shelf, in the Hellman's jar. His remains, you know. I simply don't know what to do with him." Her laugh is filled with doubt and nerves.

The glass jar is filled with dirty white ash, coming nearly to the lid. The yellow and blue label is still on it. I hear Lou utter, "Aw jeeze," under his breath. I slip my hand into my father's warm, still gloved hand.

The three refill their drinks and we move to the living

room. I sense abandonment approaching. My muscles are tense, as is the lining of my stomach. I'm getting a headache. The room smells of creepiness and age. Virginia is explaining the people in the large portrait that hangs on a wall. She and her sisters sit in long gowns, each behind a different musical instrument. One at a piano, one with a violin cradled in her arm, and the third at a golden harp, her over-sized hands resting comfortably on vertical strings. The artist has given them each the same serene smile.

"My sister, at the piano there, is Rose. The one with the violin is Eve. Rose died at the age of twenty-four, shortly after this portrait was completed. Polio." She's gazing at her sister with dreamy eyes as I move closer to Dad's coat. "She didn't suffer long, thank the Lord. Eve was the one who suffered, I'm afraid. In and out of nervous hospitals all her life. It was such a shame; she was such a talented violinist. Played the Philharmonic for years. So much talent and life in that dear girl and then, just before my wedding day, Eve tied bricks to herself and walked out into the lake, here behind the house. Too late when we discovered her, of course."

The room is spinning, and I'm having trouble trying to focus. I was going to inquire about the dog, but I'm afraid if I bring him up, he'll materialize from the shadows and go for my throat.

They're going to leave me here, I know it. They're going to button their coats back up, slug back their cocktails, hand her their empty glasses and head out the door to a home that is warm and comforting, to sit beside the fire, to wait and see if I can survive on my own here. I feel the ghosts gathering around me, one after the other. My skin bumps up in rippling fear when my father and Lou Capalbo walk out of the living room, leaving me standing in my coat, my mittens and my boots, in this musical mausoleum. They'll be back in one hour, they say.

"Have fun, kid," Lou calls over his shoulder.

I can hear my father laughing as he and Lou walk towards

the soothing quiet of the cotton-white road. They make me sick.

Virginia Coopersmith Vanderoth closes the door against these traitors of mine, rubbing her large hands together to limber them up, in preparation, to make me pliable like a potter working her clay just before she slams it onto her wheel to create something beautiful from a formless lump of nothing.

And so begins the first of a series of punishments for me, a weekly penance disguised as piano lessons. I sit on the piano bench, perfectly aligned with the ivory middle C, as instructed, and VCV sits very close to me. When she leans over to turn a page of sheet music, the flab hanging from her upper arm brushes against me. It is gelid, flaccid and cool, like the underbelly of a very old reptile. I decide I will wear something with longer sleeves or maybe just keep my coat on for my next lesson.

I learned the whereabouts of that nasty black dog towards the end of my first piano lesson. VCV had taken him to Paris with her a few months back for a little rest and relaxation and some rich French food. Turns out he'd torn the face off a man in the hotel elevator somewhere between the fifth and sixth floors. The French authorities ordered he be put down.

CHAPTER FOUR

*In Which Some Souls Come, Some Go, and
Some Reunite to Begin Another Journey Together,
Minneapolis, Minnesota, 1929*

The kittens are frozen solid, their eyes squeezed tight against the cold as if the bitterness just happened. Pattie kneels before the potbellied stove's heat watching her mother mutter a soft prayer. One kitten is calico, one orange striped; two are black with patches of white on their paws and faces. Each fits in the palm of Edna's hand.

A baby brother came after Pattie two years ago. His name is Nathaniel Budd Scott; they call him Budd. His eyes hold the secrets of the world, and he guards them vigorously. What a sweet and loyal young brother he is, Pattie thinks. He watches from the doorway as their mother runs a warm palm over one kitten at a time, speaking in soothing, reviving tones. Pattie has never been extraordinarily fond of cats, but now, seeing these small creatures with fur that was once soft, eyes that were once moist and hungry, tiny pads on the base of their paws that once bounced and sprang and rolled in the grass, she is in love.

She prays with her mother, knowing that no one's faith is as strong as Edna Scott's. This is Edna's foundation – her faith in the Lord – the one thing she relies on to get them through the frigid, cruel winters and from one skeletal meal to the next. This Lord is also the rage behind the punishments, with her Holy Bible in one hand and a cracking belt in the other. A mere look in the wrong direction, a word spoken out of turn, and, once, for stealing an apple infested with worms from a tree; anything can bring Edna's wrath to life. Pattie thinks of the night she was beaten back into a corner until she prayed for God to take her home. The leather cut into her arms, sliced and bruised her neck, as she wrestled the screams back down to the seat of her soul, where they became nestling demons of shame.

Now, as she watches her mother stroke these dead kittens, holding them close to the flames so their fur can thaw and their limbs can bend, Pattie feels a twinge of jealousy for these tiny things. How she wishes her mother would stroke her and soothe her and keep her warm at night. Instead, with a rough box for a bed, the only warmth that ever comes is from her older brother and sister, Jim and Dee, and the rags that line the bottom. A grave liner meant for the dead. With so many children, this is all they have and they're lucky to have it. Her young brother, Budd, no longer fits in the drawer, and he will move to the rough box when Dee moves into her mother's bed tonight. For now, he's been curled up on the floor by the fire, wrapped in their father's old coat, which is partially burned after a drunken tirade landed John Scott in a fire by the railroad tracks. Tragically, he survived.

Nights are anguish for Pattie. Her sister, Dee, sleeps as soundly as the dead, even with an oatmeal paste coating her body, believed to remove her freckles. It dries and flakes into the box, making Pattie itch with insomnia. Jim, five years her senior, the brother who should be her protector by now, will not let Pattie sleep. He gropes and fondles her beneath her nightshirt, thrusting his hips, grinding against her, smothering her and finally releasing his young semen with a groan. She holds on to the sides of her rough box bed until she hears his soft snore and she can drift off to sleep in peace. She will sleep until her father comes home, when he will lift her from her siblings and place her on the floor; it is there that he will take his turn. He reeks of hooch and the well seasoned whores of Wabasha Avenue and she wonders why he didn't get his fill there. His nose is an angry pink from his love of the bottle. She has learned not to cry out when he enters the tender flesh between her legs. Her siblings sometimes watch the ramming, in the darkness, as she allows her essence to detach and rise above her body, joining the warmth of the fire that has nestled in the rafters and keeps a safe distance until morning.

A tiny, orange leg quivers under Edna's hand. The kitten bends its neck ever so slightly. One of the black ones with a patch on the tip of its tail opens an eye, then shuts it back tight. Pattie reaches for the calico, cradling it in her arms, bringing it close to the heat. It moves. A soft mewing comes from within. As life slowly returns to the creatures, Edna smiles down at her daughter and gives her a wink. Some things need not be spoken. A prayer of thanks is sent up to the heavens as Edna rises to warm their last precious cup of milk to offer to these small things squirming back to life. Pattie's skin tingles as she whispers to the calico that he is the luckiest thing in the world to have been discovered in the snow under a fallen gutter by Edna Scott, a woman of magic, a healer of incredible magnitude.

#

A pretty woman, a blue cloche hat sitting atop her dark, bobbed hair, enters the druggist's shop on the corner. Jack Dahlstrom is hanging with Bernie Botts and the boys on the stoop. They watch the back of her legs; one of them whistles. They've been arguing about the new building being erected in New York City. Some say it will never last, never stand that tall. It is only half way done, but Jackie knows the Chrysler Building will last, no matter what the boys say, because this is the age of miracles and of magic. Why, just look at the Georgia Peach playing for Detroit. And then there's Jack Dempsey – World Heavy Weight Champ. Magic is everywhere these days. So what about Wall Street? What's it to him? Sure, the banks locked their doors this year while angry crowds pounded on glass, demanding their money. It doesn't bother him, not in the least. He is untouchable. There's a lot of talk of New York City, even here in Minnesota, and he knows he will go there one day. He will be in charge of something there. He adjusts his newsboy cap low over his eyes and feels the piece of wrapped bubble gum in the pocket of his knickers, a treasure in the folds of the fabric next to the coin he flips in the air. The gum makes him think of his older sister, Mary Jane; she died of polio last year, leaving his mother even more useless than before. Ruth Dahlstrom now spends her time whimpering and sipping cooking sherry from the bottle. He used to surprise Mary Jane with small, wrapped pieces of pink gum, just to make her smile. He misses her terribly but never lets on. His mother has claimed the family's allotment of grief and refuses to share, because no one's suffering is greater than Ruth Dahlstrom's.

These buddies of his are hard boiled, rolling their cigarettes and tossing dice up against the curb, waiting for something to happen. And it always does.

President Hoover competes for headlines with the loud and sultry Mae West. Jackie knows he'd give her a run for her money if she came to town. He sees everything from his corner, and he runs the show. School will begin in one hour but he will not go. He can get away with murder since his father is the superintendent of the school district and quick to forgive.

But this coin in his pocket holds all the promise he needs for a bright future.

The man who gave it to him had come from Chicago six months ago on his way to a bootlegging hide-out across the river near St. Paul. As the sparkling green 1928 Cadillac sedan rolled up to the corner, Jack didn't know that the interior venetian blinds were made of quarter inch steel with slits above made to the exact dimensions of Tommy gun barrels. Jack watched this man as he stepped out of the back of the car in his impeccable suit and hat low on his brow.

In a month's time, on February 14, bullets will rip

through a garage and pepper their loathing into the bricks and the enemies. The St. Valentine's Day Massacre will slap headlines cold, replacing our outlandish Mae West. As future decades fall like toppled cards, the bricks will be auctioned off as pieces of mob Americana and will be said to curse the successful bidders for life.

Jackie remembers the soldiers flanking the man's sides, looking out for the numerous enemies this man had acquired along the way. Activity on the stoop ceased.

Jack was alert and ready to go. He leaned casually against the drug store railing and gave the gangster a sly smile.

This man was no dummy, he knew an apprentice when he saw one. He took the coin from his pants pocket and flipped it in Jackie's direction. It spun and turned, then hovered in the air for a moment, catching the sun. Jackie reached up and caught it as if expecting it all along. Al Capone narrowed his eyes and barked, "Watch the car for me, kid."

#

Pattie rose at five o'clock this morning to bake the molasses bread her mother will sell to their neighbors. Before she walks out in the cold, she takes one final look at the kittens curled up in the corner, breathing steadily, nourished and warm. She cradles her books from the library and worries about the bag she spotted on her mother's small bed before leaving. She was not foolish enough to ask, but she didn't need to anyway. She knew. Another trip *Out West* was coming, and Pattie would be left alone to care for her family, cooking and cleaning in between her studies and the incestuous thievery that plagues her nights. Edna's escapes come more often now that the children are older. She always leaves without warning.

"I'm going out west. I'll be back when I return." And with that, Edna Scott will pick up her bag and leave.

Three books are embraced in Pattie's arms as she steps out into the frigid day. When she reads them at night under the light of the lantern, she is always careful not to crease the pages. Each word is savored as though it were an individual treasure meant just for her. For Pattie, words are the wings that take her to lands that are safe and without want.

As she nears the corner of South Lowery and Penn, she thinks of the boys who hang around at the corner druggist. She despises every one, with their well-tailored clothes worn over their swollen egos. They tease her mercilessly, her dress, her shoes, the books in her hands. They are devils and savages. Pattie heads toward the corner, praying, *Please God, don't let them be there. Make them leave me alone, if just for today.*

#

Jack tosses his coin up in the air, taunting his buddies with its power, especially Bernie Botts, the chubby young bruiser. Bernie thinks he hides his envy of Jack, but Jack knows that Bernie would cut him for a dime. Sinister ideas come to the kid and when they do, something evil twitches high on his cheek just beneath his right eye. He wants all that Jack has. Bernie Botts is a friend to be watched.

Jack turns his head to spit on the sidewalk when something catches his eye. The clattering dice game rolls to a stop as the guys take notice.

"Attaboy! Give that redhead a squeeze, Jackie Boy!" Bernie Botts bellows.

The girl moves quickly past them, her chin hugging the tops of the books in her arms. Jackie holds a palm out to quiet his friends. He watches her move, licks his lips and feels her chill. What a doll. This poor little waif made of porcelain and rags who studies the sidewalk in fear. The collar of her coat is worn and her stockings sag as if they gave up on life long ago. The hair gleams like the setting sun but does not hang low enough to hide the dark circles that ring her eyes. Jack wonders what must keep her awake at night. Everyone knows she lives with a million red headed siblings in the ruins of Jack's mother's old house, the one she was raised in before it was blown to shreds by a tornado – the twister that impaled the grandmother he never knew through the heart and left his horrified Aunt Lea, the only witness to it all, a nervous ghoul who now sits by a window day after day drooling into her lap.

The redheaded doll's eyes cautiously lift and lock with Jackie's blues, and he feels something lurch in his soul, like trying to remember a wet dream. It's as if he's known her before. He can see she feels it too.

One day he will dress this doll in the palest of minks and emeralds that match her eyes. But for now he spits at her feet.

CHAPTER FIVE

*In Which the Dahlstroms Go to Washington
and Flip Wilson Learns to Fly,
Washington, DC, 1969*

"That's government property you're smudging up with your grimy hands, kid," my Uncle Budd says to me.

I ignore him. This is my mother's younger brother, standing puffed up with pride in the long driveway, trying to pull me gently away from the darkened windows of his Secret Service car. I'm trying to see the red phone in the console. My mother tells me it is a direct line to the President's desk. A phone in a car is astounding to me, much more so than being able to call the President at his desk.

Uncle Budd's freckled hand holds a side door open for us – my father, mother and me. I enter the place expecting some lunch. The hallways are decorated with splashes of Christmas and are filled with the aroma of leather bound books. It smells like the library here. I listen to my mother's heels click on the shiny floor and my uncle's tales of a secret city beneath it all with an entrance in the side of a mountain in Virginia. He says there are stores, restaurants and roads you can drive enormous trucks through that the public will never see. The way he says *public* – I sniff out disdain in the word.

There had been no warning about this trip, nor the one to follow. I shouldn't expect any, of course, but at times I'd like to voice my opinion about this not knowing of things before they happen. I could have prepared somehow.

There is a Blue room and a Red room and a China room. There are paintings of serious men with too much on their minds. Some of their eyes follow me, leaving a hollow longing in me to go back outside.

My parents and I arrived by train late last night. Budd's wife, Betty, stood out in the snow of their Virginia horse farm to greet us as the taxi's headlights fanned out over their sprawling front porch. Aunt Betty is a gentle soul with a fluttery soft voice that tinkles like rain. She is a talented painter and has traveled the world with my uncle, capturing people and villages on canvas in deep, earthen colors. Sometimes I catch myself staring at her creamy skin and the extra long eye lashes that frame her blue eyes, hoping that I will grow to be half as beautiful as she. Her features compliment Uncle Budd's rough Irish good looks and his ginger crew cut, which he has kept from his time in the war. The war that brought him here after he befriended the Supreme Commander of the Allied Forces in Europe – a man named Eisenhower – who was quick to laugh and walked with a determined grit that Budd admired, Mom has told me. When the man returned to Washington as Chief of Staff of the Army, Budd Scott's life followed, eventually landing him as a Secret Service Agent for this friend who had become President some time ago, but is now somewhere else. Now my father explains to me that LBJ is moving out and Richard Nixon is moving in. I don't tell him that I've already heard this news in school; besides, Carlo Gambino has also already tipped me off to this Nixon fellow. I don't tell my father that I'd cornered Carlo while he sat at the round table in our den by the window and asked a question while Dad and the guys were bringing very large wooden crates on rolling dollies into the house and jockeying them down the basement stairs.

"Mr. Gambino," I said, getting his attention by placing my hand gently on his upper arm, as usual. "I need to know how you feel about ducks. Do you like ducks?"

He began fishing in his pocket for money, so I continued.

"There are a lot of ducks in our back yard. How 'bout we go out back and see how you get along with them?" I lowered my voice to a whisper. "Knowing a duck can come in handy when you need a laugh."

Carlo, apparently out of cash that day, found a small white and blue button pin in his pocket and gave it to me instead of an answer. It was the size of a nickel and it said, in persuasive red lettering, NIXON NOW. I still have that button in my room back at home.

"I'm bringing Mom out from Minneapolis in May. I think she'll enjoy the trip...let her meet the boys in Washington. I'm sure she will tell them how to run the country," Uncle Budd tells my mother.

"She'll love that, won't she? I just hope the *boys* survive it," Mom replies.

They're talking about my Grandma, Edna Scott, as we roam the large building. She's the woman who gave them the trademark Scott twinkle in their eyes when they're feeling up to mischief. She's the grandmother who knits me red blankets and mittens to match my red room as she sits in a chair by the window at Sunrise of Edina Nursing Home. Her room is small and crammed with framed photographs of her thirty-two grandchildren. She came to Greenwich last year in the spring – the time she considers to be traveling weather. I had a fever of 103 that pulled my muscles so taut I was sure they would break loose from my body and scream out on their own. She sat in a chair at the side of my bed with an ancient Bible on her lap and placed a soothing hand on my forehead. Even through the heat of my fever, I could feel the warmth of her palm as it released me from my pain. In less than a minute, my fever had broken. I was sure this was some kind of magic. My mother watched from the hall with a look in her eyes that told me she was remembering something from long ago.

Grandma is nothing like my father's mother, Ruth

Dahlstrom, who insists on being called Grandmother and lives at the other end of the hall in the same nursing home. According to my mother, this proximity tests Edna Scott's reserves of compassion. Grandmother's fingernails are painted a deep red and her musky scent makes my head pound. She reminds me of a hound dog that used to be pretty but whose features are now lost in sags of skin and powder. I don't mind all of that, but the sighing makes my nerves raw. She sighs when we arrive and again when we leave. She sighs when my father bends down to kiss her cheek. I wonder if things can really be so bad. In contrast to Grandma's stories of travels and miracles and adventures afar, Grandmother has little to say. She likes candy and flowers, but only certain ones. Interest in anything else is hard to detect. My mother says we must try to find things to appreciate even in those who've never read a book or who bore us stiff.

My grandfathers both died long before I was born. I wish I'd met them because I'm told they were as opposite in character as my grandmothers are, which makes them great mysteries full of promise. Rube Dahlstrom was tall and Swedish, a gem and a peach, with never a negative thought. Nothing could get the man down. A friend to all. He liked to fish for northern pike in the lakes of Minnesota, and his legs bowed like my father's.

In sharp contrast, there was John Scott, my mother's father. What a drunken rascal he was. Riding the rails and performing vaudeville shows on makeshift stages put together by tramps in the woods. They say he was not a serious man about anything other than his self-absorption and the whiskey that pumped through his veins. A jester with the morals of a gypsy and sometimes a bandit of souls. My mother has described him this way; I wonder how powerful he must have been to be able to rob someone of their soul and what this means and if this made him dangerous.

A man on a tall ladder, changing a light bulb, pauses as we pass and gives us a nod.

"Afternoon, Clarence," Uncle Budd says to the man.

"Afternoon, sir."

As we make our way through these wide, desolate hallways, trying to keep up with my uncle's fast gait, I wonder at the empty feeling in the air. My mother pauses at a window, admiring the tall spike of a monument in the distance. I ask my father why it's there.

"They're trying to be impressive. They're under the illusion that they run things here," he answers.

"I beg to differ, Dahlstrom," Uncle Budd tells him with a smile.

"Yeah, that's usually the problem," Dad says.

"Now, now, fellas," Mom says.

We pass a busy woman sitting at a desk, listening into a telephone. She catches my uncle's eye and waves a quick hand in the direction of a creamy white door framed in thick molding. She appears to be the gatekeeper of this room.

I know I'm supposed to be impressed as Uncle Budd throws open the door, because my mother's breath stops and her hand rises to her chest as we enter, but I'm not. Two golden yellow sofas face each other in the center of the room. A large desk backs up to windows flanked by gold curtains. Two telephones sit on the left side of the desk, one is red – possibly the one attached to my uncle's dark car that I smudged up. I see the back of a large picture frame and wonder whose photo is inside. Two extra large flags stand at attention behind the leather desk chair. Beneath our feet is a rug with a gigantic midnight blue seal of the President of the United States. I wonder if we should be standing on it. I expect to feel great power in this room, but I don't, and I'm surprised. I've learned that power is such a palpable thing. It lives and breathes and lingers. In the presence of my father's friends, and after one of their meetings, it clings to the furniture in our den, leaves its scent in the curtains, the carpet. It stirs in Carlo Gambino's long coat, even after he's taken it off and handed it to someone to fold neatly over the back of a chair. Power rolls up the driveway just ahead of their black cars. Perhaps a more appropriate color for this house would have been black. That's always the color of the stallions ridden by the men who make the biggest impressions. It's the color of a wizard's hat, a magician's cape, and a priest's simple clothing. These are the men who have all the answers. White is never taken quite as seriously as black.

"So, where's your boss?" Dad asks Budd.

"In Hong Kong, as far as you commoners know."

My mother is staring up at the ceiling with her mouth hanging slightly open (another thing that surprises me, because in our house, one doesn't let one's mouth hang open because, as Mom says, it's a sure sign of illiteracy). The room really is oval, just like the books in school say. I lean on the back of one of the gold sofas, but my mother's firm hand on my shoulder immediately tells me this is a mistake. I hope we won't have to stand here much longer.

Things are more lively upstairs. I'm glad to be moving around and have someone interesting to meet. This office is dark and cozy despite its large size. My parents relax into the embrace of a man who speaks in a buttery southern drawl.

"Maggie, this is an old friend of mine, John Connally," my father says.

The man is large and calming, and I like him right away. He picks me up by my armpits and places me in the center of his desk on my feet.

"Stand right there, honey, just like that. Now look out this window. Very few people will ever see a view like this in their lives. Seat of the Nation. Beautiful, isn't it?"

I nod my head politely at him as I look out over the tour buses spilling people with cameras and shopping bags out onto the sidewalks. Large, pale buildings dot the scenery. Monuments with long lines of tourists snaking their way inside, waiting for a better look. This man is so pleasant I don't want to tell him that he should visit 88 Orchard Drive and see the view from my room: the steep back yard leading down to the lake, where ducks and Canadian Honkers live year round; my island; the woods beyond the garden, where fairies dwell at night. He seems so proud of his surroundings, and I like him too much to let him down. But I tell him anyway because I can't keep it on my insides.

"I have a boat," I tell him.

"A boat! What sort of boat do you have, Darlin'?"

"It's white." I know I'm bragging now, but I can't stop it.

"And do you fish from this white boat of yours?"

I feel as though I need to explain things, but in a whisper, so that he knows how important it really is. I lean in close to the side of his face. "It's not for fishing. It's for rowing to my island. It's where I go to be quiet."

"Oh, I see," he whispers back to me. "I sure would like to see that island for myself sometime. I like quiet places."

He lifts me up from his desk and gently replaces me back on the floor.

As I look out the window again at the tourists and my uncle explains this man to me and how glad he is that his friend survived a dangerous day, I decide that when John Connally comes to visit us in Greenwich, as my mother has requested, that I will take him to school for Show N Tell so I can show my classmates his bullet holes and tell them that this fine southern man was riding in Kennedy's car in Dallas that day someone killed our young President. The student with the most interesting and original things to show and tell always gets a Hershey's kiss from our teacher, Mrs. Ragland. These chocolate kisses are new to the world, and I think only teachers can buy them, so they're worth a king's ransom in my crowd. I'll have to be careful when I approach him about this matter. I can't let it go down the way it did the last time.

My father had been flipping through *The New York Times* at the kitchen table one morning and said to my mother, "Look here. Carlo's in the papers again." I leaned over his shoulder to get a better view of Carlo's picture. He was wearing his city hat with the brim flipped up, as he sometimes wore it when it wasn't too cold, a hint of a smile on his face. It was at that moment that I decided that, if

Carlo was interesting enough to be in the papers, then he should be interesting enough to drag into school so I could win the Hershey's Kiss.

"Mr. Gambino, Tuesday mornings are for Show N Tell, so I'll need you to --"

Before the proposition had been fully presented, I was pulled away from Carlo's side by the collar of my shirt and ushered to my room to face the red wall because, according to my mother, it's impolite to even entertain the thought of taking actual human beings in for Show N Tell as if they were some sort of freak show.

So I will give this some more thought before I approach John Connally when he comes to call.

Ignoring the scenery out the window, which wore out its intrigue at thirty seconds, I look down at John Connally's shoes as he exchanges small talk with my parents. Wingtips. I like these shoes; my father has two pair himself, one black, one dark brown. I used to polish them for him before important meetings, taking the small tins of polish out of the wooden box, checking the color was right, dipping the very old brush in and smearing the bristles with color before scrubbing the polish onto the shoes. Then he'd hand me a thin cotton strip of cloth so I could buff the shoes like the men did at Grand Central Station, slapping the tops at the end for good measure. When I was done, he'd always take the rag out of my hands, crumple it up in his palm, and hold it over my face, scrunching it into my skin until I became dizzy from the fumes. Then he'd thank me, stand up and leave without giving me my much anticipated tip. The last time I ever shined his shoes, I encountered Mom coming down the hallway as I was making my way to my bedroom. She noticed the black residue grimed up on my brow and across my nose and cheeks, and glared at me with her bloodshot eyes.

"I suppose you've joined a minstrel show now."

It occurred to me, as I hurried towards my room, that she must have a very harsh opinion of people who shine shoes. It made me think that it might not be worth doing them anymore. I must find out what a minstrel is and be careful not to join one of their shows if I find one.

#

Snarls. Tangles. Rat's nest. All such angry words. My mother is frantically ripping through my hair with Aunt Betty's wire brush like she's trying to put out a fire. I'm quite sure my scalp is bleeding. The pain is so severe that I consider this nothing short of torture. Tears roll freely down my cheeks and I pray she's almost done. The added embarrassment only makes the scene worse. They are all watching, my father, my aunt and uncle, and my new friend, John Connally.

It was the passport that caused all of this. If I hadn't asked to see it one more time, perhaps my mother wouldn't have noticed the state of my hair. But how could a person know what the back of their own head looks like? I've tried to look at the back of my own head in the mirror. It can't be done. I had been digging through Mom's purse when she took notice and cried out in disgust. I'd only been trying to create a diversion because of the incident that had occurred earlier outside by Uncle Budd's government car. I figured that taking another look at our shiny new passports would be a means of changing the subject.

I can actually hear the hairs being torn from my head, as my mother grunts and sighs from exhaustion. If I could only black out now I would be indebted to the angels forever; I seethe that not one of these people comes to my rescue.

It all started in this lovely room where we are gathered now. Dad, Budd and John Connally were gathered around the kitchen table having cocktails, and Aunt Betty was pulling a hot pie from the oven. I had been considering just how to ask to see the man's scars from the sniper's gun when something passed outside the window. It was John Connally who noticed it first and directed my father's attention to what was going on in Budd and

Betty's driveway. Everyone turned to see.

"Oh for Christ's sake," my father had said.

Uncle Budd hung his head down and shook it, staring at the floor.

"What's going on with Pat out there?" Betty asked.

My father stood up and put his fists on his hips. The mood tumbled downward from there. I could see Mom in her white mink coat and high heeled boots out in the snowy drive, making her way toward a cluster of bushes with a determined look on her face. In her hands, held high above her head, she carried Aunt Betty's black cat, Flip Wilson. His ears were pinned back against his head and all four of his legs were grasping frantically for something to latch on to. I'd never seen anyone – including my mother – throw a live animal at a squirrel before. It was difficult to watch. At least she'd had the forethought to snatch the most consistently upright of animals. I was glad it hadn't been a goat or a dog or a turtle she'd grabbed, because they would not have been certain to land on their feet. Flip Wilson sailed through the air like a furry black rocket in the direction of the bushes and a large group of squirrels scattered across Uncle Budd's horse farm in hysterics.

This farmhouse is filled with humiliation, mostly mine at the moment. I want to go home. I want to climb in my boat and float away from my mother and this sharp wire brush and my father's heavy breathing. He's glaring at the cocktail in his hand, and I'm no longer sure our new passports will take us to the great adventure I've been promised. It's four days before Christmas and I feel a serpent is making our travel plans.

CHAPTER SIX

In Which We Realize That Some Tales, No Matter How Great Our Intentions, Can Never Be Told Gently Enough, Innsbruck, Austria, New Year's Eve, 1969

There's blood in the water. I try not to notice how much more exquisite this makes my terror. I'm rocking, my arms tight around my knees. I hear fireworks booming and cheers ringing in the new year in the village below. These celebratory sounds clash with what's happening in here with me.

It had started with an innocent sleigh ride, just last night, when the snow began to fall. The Innsbruck Inn had seemed so empty, the only sound coming from a television hanging on the wall in the corner of the bar near the entrance. The German-speaking newscaster made the weather report sound like machine gun fire hitting flesh. Such a harsh language. An old brass elevator – a cage hanging from pulleys – groaned with our weight. I was glad to be going outside.

I clung to my father, trying to escape the cloud of foreboding that had settled over me back at my uncle's farm in Virginia, burying my face in his long city coat as we stood on a hill getting ready to go down to the peaceful, twinkling village below. It was like a miniature display placed beneath a Christmas tree, with its white rooftops and smoking chimneys rising stiffly above the gingerbread trim that framed eaves and doorways.

We had been joined by my father's childhood friend, Bernie Botts, and his wife, Eve, at the airport in Austria, who'd arrived the day before from Minneapolis. If I thought Lou and Jimmy were loud, I had another thing to learn when I met Bernie. He boomed and howled. His pock-marked cheeks bunched when he smiled, and he smiled at everyone he met from cabbies to beggars. Never had I seen such unbridled spirit, and I knew he would make this trip interesting. His wife wore a diamond the size of a penny on her right middle finger, a spotted fur coat, and false eyelashes that looked like feathers. She was as showy as her husband.

We were led around the corner of the Inn through the tightly packed snow to a sleigh driven by impatient brown horses stomping legs shaggy at the ankles as if they were wearing boots. Plumes of warm air streamed out of their velvety nostrils. The driver was unfolding and shaking dust from woolen blankets. He nodded a greeting to us as we arrived.

"So, I told him," my father said to Bernie, "'I have a couple of options: one, you get on a plane and you get out of town so I don't have to look at your face anymore. We had a deal and you broke it.' And this guy's pissed. He's inconvenienced, I can tell. Then I tell him, 'The other option is to introduce you to Lou Capalbo and let you two discuss the problem for a few minutes, throw what's left of you in a bag and toss you in the East River. Either way, our problem is solved. So how about you leave this meeting today and always be glad I didn't pick option number two?' You shoulda seen it. He stood up, there's not a drop of blood left in the guy's face, he throws his coat on, and he tells me he's headed straight for the airport."

"The art of persuasion, Jackie Boy! You always were good at that, weren't ya?" Bernie boomed.

"I should have mentioned that I could have his legs broken for $800.00 and that's cheap!"

"It's good to have options," Bernie said.

Their laughter echoed through the valley and hills of the village. As I watched Bernie's face, I noticed a twitch high on his cheek, just below his right eye. For a small moment, darkness passed over his gay expression – a darkness I wish I had had the foresight to warn my father about. While my mother and Eve discussed more civilized things a few feet way, we waited for the sleigh driver to give us the signal.

We bundled up cozy and warm beneath the red woolen blankets. I looked up at the clouds in the Austrian sky and waited for the snow to fall down in chunky, fat flakes. The horses' hooves tramping down on the snow covered trail made a deliciously soft squeaking sound: cloosh clush, cloosh clush. They trotted effortlessly towards the village, their manes bouncing in time with their steps through the night air. Sleigh bells jingled and leather harnesses creaked and rubbed together in a satisfying way.

When we entered the town, we saw strange black and white street signs, hats with feathers in their brims, chocolate shops, clock shops, bakeries and pubs. An old man in a doorway tinkered with the rubber tip of his cane, and two women passed him pushing children in strollers over cobblestones.

I tried to take in the scenery, but I was distracted by my mother, who had decided to move across the sleigh and onto Bernie's lap. He nuzzled his face into her neck and said something I couldn't make out. She blushed and slapped at his chest.

"You're shameless, Botts," my father said.

"I am shameless. Make no mistake about it! Just ask my wife!" Everybody laughed.

The blood in the water is thin and pink and I'm relieved it's not pouring out of me as one would expect. I'm not completely sure where it's coming from. I long to hear the jingle of the gold bracelets my mother put on tonight before they went out to the festival in the village. I want Jimmy Bruno to burst into the room with his gun fixed on the monster and whisk me away.

I shouldn't have complained that my throat was sore tonight. If I had listened to the angels that had been trying to warn me, I would be safe now. I would be holding my father's gloved hand and watching the fireworks exploding and shining against the snow.

The bottom of my footed pajamas are wet from the pink water. I keep my eye on the locked door, not knowing what I will do if I see that knob turn. I wish I could melt into this cream-colored tile and disappear into the wall. I am cornered. His heavy breath is just outside, and I see his menacing shadow moving slowly back and forth, blocking out the pale light that seeps under the door. Hindsight sits in the bathtub beside me, holding itself in the quarter inch of water leftover from someone's bath. It heaves frightened tears and rocks with me.

I should have ignored my fever and never said a word. When my father led me down the hallway with my book in my hand, I had sensed it all coming. When we entered the room, he'd been standing at the window with a drink in his hand. Something was different. I went to the bed and opened *Winnie The Pooh*, hoping it would take my mind off my throat, as so often a good story can do with things that hurt. My parents went down the hall, leaving me here with my book and this man.

Some time passed and he stayed by the window. I could feel his eyes on me. Piglet and Tigger sat suspended on the page that I could not bring myself to turn. My heart quickened as he eventually approached and stood beside the bed, not saying a word. I could smell the liquor and oily filth slithering out of his skin as he slowly removed the book from my hands and placed it on the bedside table beneath the reading lamp. He lifted a finger to his pursed, fat lips in quiet warning and he leaned in close. I felt his hot breath on my ear as he said, "Don't move." His usually boisterous voice had boiled down to a snarling, hoarse whisper. "If you say anything, I will kill your parents."

My body stiffened like the lake water that turns to ice and wraps itself around my island, squeezing tightly so it can't get away until spring. Then his large, ugly hand gripped my crotch with such force that my heart literally stopped beating for a moment or two. He inhaled deeply, loudly, and kept his grip on me. I clamped down on the sheets and squeezed my eyes shut. He leaned in close to my ear again, still latching on to me, and said, "No one needs to know what you and I did here tonight, Maggie. You don't want your parents hurt, do you? You want your daddy shot? Your mommy's head bashed in? That's what will happen if you ever tell anyone. Do you understand me?"

I forced my head to move as much as I could, to answer the monster with a rapid nod. This is when God left the room.

The monster backed away from my ear and let go of my crotch. I thought it was over, then he grabbed me by my ankles and yanked me with force to the foot of the bed in one fluid, angry motion. My body came off the bed as if I were being swept up in a tornado. Terror raced through me, rapid as lightning, and for a moment, I knew what it felt like to die a sudden death.

He stood at the foot of the bed, still holding my ankles high up in the air in front of him. I stifled the sobs that screamed to be let out as he dropped his pants and forced himself inside me.

The pain was so excruciating that it forced my eyes open for brief terrifying seconds. I memorized his pock-marked face. Ripping, stabbing, a devil tearing me apart with his blade. I saw a vision of it all taking place: My father with a bullet lodged between his beautiful blue eyes; my mother battered unrecognizable until her lovely skull was cracked in two. Hot tears rolled down into my ears as I heard myself make noises that sounded like screams trapped under water. I noticed his eyes rolled up inside his head as he rhythmically gouged my body. And after what seemed an eternity, with a guttural groan, he slowly turned my ankles loose.

When it was over, he went back to standing at the window. The glow from his cigarette burned against the night sky through the window. I saw the first fireworks burst behind him. The twitch high on his cheek winked at me, as his flaccid, gray penis hung thick from his open pants.

It seems hours before the party arrives back in the room. I hear my father's cheers and the gold bracelets jangle from my mother's drunken wrists as my parents and Eve return. I rise from my hiding place and leave the pink tinged water. I open the door and step into a new life without words. I am changed. I cannot name this thing that has just happened to me. I wonder what I will do now, without God in the room watching over me. I am only seven years old and I have a very long way to go without Him

CHAPTER SEVEN

In Which We Go Visiting and Deliver a Package, and
a Sweet Old Grandmother Cooks Something That Smells of Home,
Verona, Italy, January 3, 1970

It's Market Day, and I see my first piazza as we wind through long, narrow streets, passing one medieval door after another. I've decided it's safest to sit up front with the limousine driver and allow my parents, Bernie and Eve to sit in the back where the champagne and friendship is flowing. If I were back there, I would be required to speak and join in.

Thick winter vines fall gracefully from iron balconies. An ancient chapel stands like a beacon against a milk and lavender sky. Our driver's name is Heinz. He has little English, so he motions silently at what he might assume are points of interest. The market stalls are crowded this morning. Wheels of apricot colored cheese, misshapen loaves of rustic bread and bright splashes of fruit fill the bins, while Italian women with scarves framing their weathered faces count out change. People carrying pastries wrapped in paper and bouquets of winter vegetables weave through the bustle, passing plump green olives swimming in barrels. Young, dark haired lovers share a kiss near the edge of a fountain. These are the indelible images of an escape I so desperately need.

My words have been crushed deep down inside me. When they want to rise and scream out their anguish, I strangle them back. I don't think of my home or my island. I don't remember Jimmy's or Lou's smiles. I won't long for the days when my biggest worry was how long I would have to sit in my rocking chair staring at my bright red wall or the kimonos I ruined. I refuse all these thoughts because I am on that fragile cliff of terror and dread and if I let these thoughts of home enter my mind, I know I will shatter in two.

Our limousine passes a church spilling a wedding party out of old wooden doors. Rice sprays the air, and someone's mother, garnished in pearls, dabs her tears with a handkerchief.

My soul sees none of this. I've asked it not to come back. I won't be needing it now, maybe not ever. I look back through the partition glass at my father, and our eyes meet for a moment. His smile fades as a quiet concern passes over his face. I turn away quickly to watch Verona sail by.

#

My parents and I wait for someone to answer the bell. The shadows on the peeling green door exaggerate my father's hat and long coat. I experience only timid, temporary relief from the fact that we've dropped Bernie and Eve off at a touristy place for shopping and lunch. I haven't asked why we are visiting Lou's parents or what's in the large paper sack in my father's gloved hand. If this had happened five days ago, I would have been a hornets' nest of questions, relentless and insistent. None of it matters now.

The old couple squeezes together in the narrow doorway as they greet us. They resemble an Italian Santa and Mrs. Claus. They seem surprisingly small in stature to be Lou Capalbo's parents. The woman, in her navy blue apron, places an ancient hand under my chin and kisses me on the cheek.

"*Andiamo! Andiamo!*" the old man says, waving at us to follow him into the womb of his home.

When paint peels in Italy, it has the opposite effect that it would if it were peeling in America. Back at home, it would indicate a state of disrepair and poverty, but here in Italy, it suggests a swell of charm and graceful knowing, whispering secrets in your ear. The wooden planks of the floor give a bit with every step, and I wonder if treasures are buried beneath.

The rug is well worn. The windows in the back of the house are arched and give a serene view of the couple's garden, now blanketed in snow. A small metal table and chairs sit outside on a stone patio, the chairs facing west. I can tell it's a place they sit together when the weather is warm, sharing a loaf of bread or drinking a thimble of limoncello while they wait for the sun to set. This is a couple who have stayed strong through the ages, of this I'm sure. I hope, deep in my heart, that when old Mr. Capalbo takes his final breath, his wife will have someone to watch over her until she follows. I hope they've made the proper arrangements so that no one is kept in a mayonnaise jar until a decision is made.

Mrs. Capalbo leads my mother and me into a kitchen in the back of the house. There's a familiar smell in here, something that takes me back to our kitchen in Greenwich. The tender tug of homesickness is too much to bear just now. I slap the thought across the face and turn away from it. Images are prying into my thoughts. Flashes of Bernie, his greasy, pocked face; the whisper. He grips my ankles and holds them tightly in the air, breathing heavily. His words ring again in the mind. He will have my family killed. What sort of a man thinks such things? How could a person be this threatened by a child? I'd seen it for a mere flash of a moment, but it was unmistakable fear that stirred in that monster's eyes. Afterward, sitting on the floor of their bath, I'd heard the monster sing my name. Concentrate, I tell myself. Think of something else. I focus on a cat sitting outside the window on the old couple's patio, its black fur a loathsome warning to me.

A cyclone of omens had predicted this evil coming. There had been a crack in the ice on the lake before we headed to the train last week, and my foot had almost gone through. I'd seen an owl swoop past my window two times later that night. There was my mother slinging Flip Wilson at those innocent squirrels. Black cats bring bad luck and now here's another just a few feet away.

The signs had all been there. I feel as though I've been thrown into a pot of boiling water perched upon a fire made of sticks; Bernie's threat dances around me with a bone in its nose, its face painted black and yellow. It shows me its blood-stained teeth while drums beat a rhythmic call to supper.

My father hasn't seemed to notice my silence, but he should be grateful for it because his life depends upon it. I want to go to him now, to follow him into the small room he entered with the old man, that package in his hand.

Lou's mother places a plate of meatballs in front of me on the thick wooden table. That must have been the familiar smell. My mother can make these delicate balls. Lou taught her years ago from a recipe handed down through his family. They bleed with sauce and cheese; crumbled parsley is the secret inside. Usually I'd be ravenous for this, unable to wait for them to cool. But not today.

Dad always tells me that death is just a part of life. It's natural, like rain or a bee draining nectar from a trumpet flower. He hadn't even been upset when a neighborhood dog dragged a large femur bone up from the woods and dropped it at his feet one day when he was working out in the garage. I'd been there that day, sitting on a stool in the driveway, listening to my father whistle, and had pointed out that the leg bone looked human.

He had snickered a little, asking me, "Now, how in the world would you know what a human leg bone looks like? That's just a deer bone."

But for some reason, I knew.

A week went by and I'd forgotten about the bone until an odd stranger rang our doorbell. When my father answered, there stood an old man, a ghostly looking fellow with a long white beard and dirty clothes. This man didn't belong in Greenwich; all disheveled people, I was sure, were hurriedly ushered out of the town and deported back to Queens or Harlem or the Bronx, according to my mother. He held up a plastic bag and told my father he'd found the contents on our property, in our woods, where he'd camped a few nights on his way to somewhere mysterious. Inside the plastic bag was a human skull, a skull I was sure was part of a complete set, waiting somewhere in the woods, except for its missing femur. My father narrowed his eyes on the old hobo and sent me up to my room, with orders not to mention this to Mom, who was in bedroom-exile that morning because I'd insulted her cooking by sprinkling salt on my eggs.

I watched the woods through my window, waiting for the man to return to the scene and hint at where this body lay, but I never saw him again.

For months, I'd expected a skeleton to come hopping out of the trees on its one leg, but maybe the mess was cleaned up by one of the goombahs later on. Dad said someone had committed suicide down by the lake, but I didn't buy his story. The lake was my territory, as were the woods, and I'm sure I would have noticed an abandoned corpse or the smell of human rot. I would have felt that *knowing* that sidles up next to you and nudges you on the shoulder when something's up. I'd expected the police to come – despite the Never Call The Police rule in our house, because, according to Dad, calling the police is as futile as pissing up a rope, an expression I may never understand. I thought they would overrun our property with detectives wearing imitation London Fogs and badges clipped to their lapels, one of them lifting a revolver with a stick or gloved hand and dropping it into an evidence container. I'd expected a gurney and a body bag, maybe a guy from the *Greenwich Times* with a camera in his hand and a cigarette clutched between his teeth. Instead, we had lunch.

Mom and Mrs. Capalbo admire a bolt of lace in the corner of the kitchen while I keep my eyes on the closed doors for signs of my father. I can't bring myself to touch these meatballs anymore than I can push myself to wonder what's hiding in Dad's paper bag. White curtains hang over the glass of the doors, and shadows move over them in a ghostly waltz. I can hear my father's voice, and although nothing should surprise me at this point, I am taken aback when I hear my father's deep, confident voice speaking assuring words in fluent Italian, a language I didn't know he spoke.

CHAPTER EIGHT

In Which Plans Are Made and People Wait to Be Together, Hollywood Park Racetrack, California, 1942

Oxygen fills Jack Dahlstrom's lungs and clears his head as he watches the clouds bump lazily across the sky. Cumulonimbus. Winds mild, moving northeast. He inhales deeply a second time, holding the mask tightly to his face with a darkly tanned hand.

Jack has climbed to rank of Lieutenant, surpassing his Army Air Corps friends, here at Hollywood Park Racetrack in California, which has been transformed into a bomber training base and storage facility.

He yells out orders to the guys in the back, then safely glides the B24 Liberator towards home. This plane is a beast, with its bulging, pregnant belly meant to hold Jeeps, supplies, ammo, bombs and it takes a small fortune to get it off the ground. Whatever is needed to win this war. Jack sets her gently down. He breathes deeply again as he brings the plane to a stop, allowing the oxygen to chase away this bastard of a hangover he and the fellows brought home from The Derby last night.

The air in the cockpit is already warm at seven in the morning and his leather flight jacket does nothing to relieve him. A loud rap on the window makes him jump.

"Say there, sir, would you mind not hoggin' all the friggin air?" Private Lou Capalbo yells through the glass.

Jack's eyes crinkle into a smile as he takes one last inhale from the mask. Lou is his Italian friend from Brooklyn, the best looking fellow he knows with that black wavy hair and charisma that oozes from his being like a warm, smooth marinara. The girls flock to this man when they're out at the clubs, draping their arms around his neck and perching on his knee, lighting his cigarettes and listening to his stories of the old neighborhood. The guy's a dame magnet, which can lead to problems when you're supposed to be engaged, as both Jack and Lou are.

Jack hands the mask over to him and Lou pushes his flight goggles far back on top of his head. He breathes in the oxygen, shaking his head at the pounding last night's drinks have brought on. He rests his arm on the side of the plane waiting for relief to take over. "I think this might be why they have the rule: No drinking twelve hours from flying," Jack says.

Lou removes the oxygen mask, holding it a few inches from his face to say, "I believe that's: No drinking twelve *feet* from the plane, Dahlstrom."

"Yeah, that's right, twelve feet. Give me back that mask," Jack says.

"You heard from The Tomato this week?" Lou asks him, motioning to the pinup girl painted on the side of the plane. She wears a white top that shows off her bare midriff and a sassy green skirt that barely covers her fanny. One arm is bent back behind her head of rich, red hair while the other waves to Lou. Underneath the image it reads *Pregnant Pattie* at a sharp angle. She'd mentioned to Jack that painting those words might give the wrong impression, since they are barely engaged, but he'd assured her that the pregnant part was merely a nod towards the body of his plane and it's deep, swollen cargo womb.

"Nah, she's back home with the gals going through wedding dress patterns or some damned thing. She's got things to keep her busy until I can get back and nail her. The war effort, ya know."

Lou hands the mask back to Jack and laughs. They've grown to be close friends. They're alike, untouchable and suave. They've made a pact to reconnect after this mess is over, if it's ever over, and Lou will introduce Jack to his powerful connections back home, connections that will transport Jack back to the time of bootlegging days and Al Capone. He still has that magical coin he was tossed as a kid out in front of the druggist shop; he keeps it in an ashtray back home. Sam Giancana, a long time associate of Capone's and a helpful addition to the St. Valentine's Day Massacre through his connections and ability to organize a massive, flawless hit with the grace of a well-practiced tango, has become a friend and drinking buddy of Lou's through the years. Now the man is proving to be a conduit to fast money, casinos, movie stars and an easier way of life. He will be waiting back in Chicago, tucked safely in the bosom of his draft rejection after being deemed "a constitutional psychopath" because of his love of explosives and personal tastes. Jack likes the sounds of that and will be making the trek to Chicago for an introduction once the war is over. Lou will be heading out overseas in two months once his training is over but Jack isn't worried about his buddy. He'll be the one doing the killing and dropping the bombs. Then they will own the world together.

"I'll try my damnedest to be there, Jackie Boy," Lou tells him.

"When I nail her?"

"At the wedding, smart ass," Lou says, then turns to look around the nose of the aircraft. "Uh oh. Pop! goes the weasel."

Jack takes another deep inhale from the mask and sees Jack Rubenstein, their most unpopular mechanic approaching.

"Christ, what's he worked up about now?"

Rubenstein is huffing and scowling.

"He really changin' his name?" Lou asks.

"That's what he says. He thinks the fellows will stop razzin' him if he does. I didn't have the heart to tell him he could change his name to Rockefeller and it wouldn't change anything. He'll be hated for all of time," Jack says, snickering.

Jack knows that all Rubenstein has to do is cool down a bit. His temper has been a problem since the first day he showed up here on base after enlistment. He's been reprimanded, threatened and had the shit kicked out of him once or twice by the other enlisted men, but nothing will change the guy's bad attitude. On top of all that, he's just a crappy mechanic who is prone to tantrums. If this war is ever over, he'll surely wind up standing in a soup line or in prison, Jack thinks.

"What name is he leaning towards?" Lou asks Jack.

"Ruby."

"Jack Ruby," Lou says, trying the name out. "Has a ring to it, don't it? But it still don't change the fact he's a little weasel."

#

Pattie sits on a blanket spread out on the front lawn, flipping through the latest issue of *Vogue* until she reaches an article about Carol Lombard. A photo shows Lombard sitting in a chair and wearing beach pajama pants and a bare midriff top. A jar of paste rests on top of the scrapbook on the grass beside Pattie's blanket. The cover is bound in coffee colored leather and embossed at the bottom with, "My Stretch in the Service." She keeps everything Jack sends her; every newspaper article, matchbook and photograph to remind her down the road what all of this felt like. The longing, the excitement, the tension, the patriotic swell of emotion that everyone wears like a glorious cloak. She wonders if this feeling will last. War brings everyone closer in a common cause and a sense of hope. Maybe one day, years from now, someone will pick her scrapbook up and be interested in something pasted inside. An insignia button that reads "I Will Keep 'Em Shooting" is stuck to one of the pages. Alongside that is a picture from the newspaper of her friend Ted Schwandt tugging on a rope, a smile on his face. At the end of the rope hangs a caricature of Adolf Hitler. On a sign behind him, it says in large bold lettering, "Let's Hang Hitler High in August – Pull him up a notch every day. Keep 'Em Shooting!" Beneath the photo of Ted it reads, "HANG HITLER is the objective for Building 102 in August. Guard Corporal Ted Schwandt is seen here giving Herr Schicklegruber an extra tug for bad luck. Mussolini and Hirohito are in for the same treatment by TCOP workers in August."

Pattie almost enjoys going to work in the factory with her sister Bea and the gals from the neighborhood. They wear loose-fitting trousers and their hair tied up in back in chenille snoods. The pants are a thrill because when they wear them there's no need to draw a false stocking seam up the backs of their legs with charcoal pencil. She misses silk stockings.

They are required to carry Rumor Cards in their trouser pockets.

The cards read:

Kill That Rumor!
Test the story that you just told me against the following points:
Will it hurt the morale of the employees of this War Plant?
Does it make you distrust your Government or the Management?
Does such a rumor tend to discredit our Allies?
Who will benefit the most by spreading this story –
our enemies or the United States?
If this story won't pass this test, don't repeat it!
And the next time you hear one like it,
pass this card along – instead of the rumor. ~

Luckily, Pattie hasn't had to hand one to anyone yet. Every now and then, Bea hands one to her husband, Harold, just to shut him up.

Pattie's favorite piece of memorabilia is a longer than usual letter from Jack. She has read his sharp, angled handwriting a thousand times. The pages are already becoming tattered. She pulls it out of its envelope, which is affixed to a page in her scrapbook, and unfolds it gently. Her heart pumps nervously as she reads it.

My Dearest,

Things really popped today, didn't they? The odds certainly seem to be against us. I feel terrible about it Honey. I know you must feel worse. I won't have much time before I have to go to work so I'll just tell you I'm safe and sound. Capalbo and I went to see a show – they stopped the show and announced that all service men should report to their posts immediately – Pearl Harbor had just been bombed. We left and when we arrived back here, all planes were grounded – all trucks scattered and camouflaged.

We send weather balloons at 12:00 noon, 4pm, 8pm, midnight, 4am and 8 am. Things are really buzzing around here. There is a very good chance that we will stay posted in L.A. Don't worry about me, Pattie, please. I'll be safe. I didn't mind getting into war nearly as much as our putting our wedding off. As it stands now, all leaves and furloughs are canceled. It doesn't look very promising as to any change. I hate to think of our being separated for a longer time but it can't be anything else I guess.

I'll be true to you always, my Darling, as long as you want me. Something may come up so I can come home. I'll not send that money for a while. Xmas presents may be late or not at all – don't bother with mine until I'm stationed permanently. We will be moving constantly now in order to protect L.A.

I feel like having a good cry but I know it wouldn't do a bit of good. Keep your chin up, Honey. If you change your mind about marriage, let me know. Be sure to go out and have a good time and try to forget what a mess we're in. Please let the folks know I'm O.K. I'll try to write a more sensible letter later on. We're screwy here as you can no doubt tell. I love you, Darling. I always will. Don't worry about me. I'll be O.K.

All my love,
Jack

Bea sets a sweaty glass of iced tea down in front of Pattie and takes a seat in a lawn chair. It's Wednesday, their day off from the bullet factory, and Pattie's glad to be home with nothing to do. Their mother, Edna, is living with their brother, Jim, across town, which is a relief because their mother would never approve of this casual lounging around and flipping through fashion rags when there's surely something that needs cleaning.

Bea smacks a large mosquito on her shoulder.

"Only the females suck your blood," Pattie says, turning a page without looking up.

"They're nothing but winged devils," Bea says, wiping the blood away with a napkin from her apron pocket.

Harold comes out the front door and tosses the morning issue of the Minneapolis *Star Journal* on the blanket. He's a bit sour as a rule, but Pattie loves him. He drives the cable cars through the city. Sometimes, just to be cruel, when an old woman loaded down with packages or obviously suffering arthritis approaches, he pretends not to see her, slamming the doors shut just as she arrives and taking off down the track with a snicker.

"Look at that article on the bottom of the front page," he says, pointing at the newspaper. "'Hit By Train – Knee Hurt.' What sort of an idiot gets in the way of a train?"

"Harold, Pattie doesn't need to see stories like that. Take this away," Bea says, picking up the paper to sling it at her husband.

"Wait. Let me see," Pattie says and snatches it from Bea's hand.

She unfolds the paper and leans over the article with concentration.

"Says here, 'Charles Arnao, 21, Wayzata, was struck early today by a Northfield and Southern train as it was backing across Olson Memorial Highway. He suffered a knee injury and went to a private doctor for treatment.' Not quite front page news, is it?"

Pattie scans the other louder headlines, *Bataan Defenses Collapse; 36,853 U.S. Troops Trapped* and *Two British Cruisers Sunk; Battle Looms in Bengal Bay,* then she lifts the page and turns it carefully.

"Look there, Pattie, the April fabric sale at Powers. Maybe we should go there today and see what they have for your dress," Bea says, trying to change the subject from war and casualties.

"Let's see, they have printed rayon crepes and chiffons for 85 cents a yard, regularly one dollar a yard. They also have plaid and striped cotton seersucker for 78 cents a yard and novelty white sharkskin for 69 cents a yard. How about that? *The Bride wore a gown of novelty white sharkskin*...has a ring to it, doesn't it?" Pattie says with a wink.

"Sounds simply hideous," Bea says, "but why don't we go down and poke around today anyway?"

"Might as well."

Harold is standing on the lawn glaring at someone coming down the sidewalk. Pattie follows his gaze. The Western Union man is hurrying in their direction. Pattie's heart seizes every time she sees him coming. If the telegram is for her, she knows it will either thrill her or kill her dead. She saves every one of them and pastes them in her scrapbook. So far they've all been romantic messages of leave plans and love. Her brother Budd is overseas in the middle of the action, so a telegram could contain bad news about him just as easily as it could have exciting news from her fiancé.

"He's heading our way, Bea," Pattie says, rising up to meet him in her bare feet.

"I'm sure Jack is fine. He's in California, for God's sake, at a horse track, not hiding in some rice paddy or Nazi bunker, Patricia," Harold tells her. "I doubt anything diabolical can happen to him while he's mixing cocktails or getting a tan."

"Just because he's not off fighting on the front line doesn't mean he's not doing his patriotic duty," Bea says. "He's training bomber pilots. It's not like you saved the world when you enlisted a hundred years ago."

"I *was* on the front line! Dodging bullets, hiding in

foxholes through torrents of rain and blood."

"Harold, you made pancakes for the men who were actually doing the fighting. I don't think you get the Medal of Honor for that," Bea says.

Harold glares at his wife and then storms back into the house, muttering, "Six hundred pancakes a God damned day..."

It worries Patricia that her fiancé goes up in the air at all. People are meant to travel by ground. The Western Union man veers onto the lawn, approaching them. Pattie tries to picture Jack's glinting smile with the one slightly crooked front tooth and those blue, blue eyes that make her swoon. She hears his voice in her head one last time before the man nears her and asks, "Patricia Scott?" She nods to him and he hands her the telegram.

She rips the envelope open before the man can make it back to the sidewalk. Bea moves to her side and reads over her shoulder.

WESTERN UNION
KA11 9 TOUR=LOSANGELES CALIF APR 14 750P
MISS PAT SCOTT=
3830 SHERIDON AVE NORTH MPLS
DEAR PAT ARRIVING TUES AM ON UP CHALLENGER LOVE=
JACK.

"I guess we'd better get down to Powers right away. You'll need a new dress, my dear," Bea says, placing a comforting hand on her sister's shoulder. Pattie refolds the telegram and replaces it in its envelope and then bends down to tuck it safely into her scrapbook.

CHAPTER NINE

*In Which We Discover a Little Je Ne Sais Quoi,
Greenwich, Connecticut, 1970*

I watch the neighbors skate on the lake around the island, twirling and slinging one another in circles. Blades slice shallow trails in the ice on the lake. Sitting atop my overturned boat on the shore, I don't care that I'm more easily noticed now that the trees are bare and there's a backdrop of white to highlight my existence. A month ago I would have been anxious for the ice to thaw and for these skaters to leave me alone with my island, but now I see that no place is safe. Let them have it all. Let them stop to tighten their skates on the island's shore, let the teenagers stash their six packs of beer in the snow. I surrender it all to them. The thought crosses my mind that it might be a good idea to sit out here until I freeze solid. My ears are already stinging with the biting cold, my exposed legs feel as if a wolf is picking them clean. I wonder how long it takes to freeze a whole person.

Could you have fought back? my soul whispers at my back.

I close my eyes and ignore it for a moment, listening to the blades ticking across the ice. A young girl cries about not wanting to go inside; I envy her naiveté at thinking that this is the worst possible thing that could happen to her today.

I've seen you looking at their guns, my soul says as it takes a seat on the bottom of the boat beside me.

"I thought I told you to go away," I say.

My soul makes my head ache.

Remember when we first got back home and we were walking to school? And I came up beside you?

"You were limping," I remind it.

I was. And I mentioned you could have fought back. I reminded you of the lessons your father has taught you. I reminded you of the time the neighbor's dog barked all night and your father paid that neighbor a visit the next morning and oh so inventively proposed a solution, my soul says as it leans in to my shoulder.

"It wasn't exactly a proposition. He told the guy that he hadn't moved into a million dollar neighborhood to be kept up all night by some son of a bitch beagle. So he told the man he was buying his house—for an insultingly low price – and he'd better call the movers because he and his family would be moving by the end of the week."

And what happened?

"A Van Lines truck backed up in their driveway three days later and they were gone. Dad sold the house and said he made a good profit. He thought it was amusing. What's your point?"

I feel my attitude turning oily and my words come out sharp. Instantly I feel ashamed, but I don't show it.

People seem to get very nervous around my father. I have recently noticed that there's a darkness coiled up inside him that others fear and obey without question. A darkness with a pulse. I wonder why I never noticed this before.

My soul takes a deep breath and smiles beside me.

My point is that there is a solution to every problem. All you have to do is think creatively, think of something that hasn't occurred to you yet. Tell him what happened to you. Today is your chance. He'll be coming down the hill in a few minutes to look for you and you'll have him alone.

"I can't do that today. Things aren't going well up in the house," I tell my soul.

I know. I saw her.

The reason I'm sitting outside in this frigid air with my legs exposed is because of my mother. She's playing that game again. A game that now smacks of a cruelty I never before acknowledged, when she tells me I'm too delicate, too meek, that I should know a good joke when I see one.

I'd come downstairs expecting some toast and the gruesome reminder of my upcoming piano lesson on Monday, but what I found was my mother lying on her back underneath the dining room table. I presumed the reason she was holding a bouquet of taper candles clutched to her chest was because of the lack of flowers in our garden this time of year. Her eyes were closed and I couldn't see her breathing. I stood very still in the doorway and waited for signs of life. Usually, I would scream and run to her aid and shake her. Sometimes, if caught entirely off guard by the game, I would fall apart, sobbing at her side, pleading with her to be alive, to come back to me, that I would change, that I would behave and makes things right again. And sometimes she would open her eyes and smile. Sometimes she wouldn't and I would be forced to call a neighbor to come in to help. When she heard me lift the receiver to make the call, she would sit up, toss her flowers aside and accuse me of being too sensitive, too dramatic. This morning was different. There was almost a relief in her pseudo death, in the fact that there was one less murder for me to worry about, that the proverbial ax had finally fallen and she'd died naturally and not by the hand of Bernie Botts.

Worry holds me hostage now – worry, the least enthusiastic form of fear. I resent it. I suppose when I didn't react in the fashion she was hoping for, or anticipating, she felt the need to punish me. She rose from the rug and pointed the candles at me and, with a viscous sneer, ordered me to go up to my room and change into the lederhosen she'd bought me in Austria. I did what she wanted because she's right. I'm feeling fragile.

The lederhosen are a weird olive-gray suede with edelweiss and hearts embroidered on the bib. Every time she makes me put them on for company, I expect Julie Andrews to come twirling into the room, whip out her guitar and sing to me about some lonely goatherd or instruct me to climb every mountain. The lederhosen shattered the remainder of what little dignity I had left, for I had only been out in the driveway for two minutes, avoiding my mother, before a carload of teenage boys sailed up Orchard Drive and hollered, "Yodel Lay Hee Whooo!" in my direction. To think, I used to be such a cool kid.

So this is how I've ended up in the backyard, avoiding my mother and the general public, risking frostbite and talking to my soul.

Not only have I changed into something foreign and unappetizing, but so has everything and everyone else. Everything is painted with a heavy layer of distrust. My father's friends have changed. I watch their faces, I study them with this new need that insists I pay mindful attention so that I learn to read them, to know which ones are capable of becoming monsters when a door closes behind them. My silence has, I'm sure, come across as disrespect or petulance, but I've just gone somewhere else for a while.

I watch Paul Castellano most of all. His is the most distant and guarded demeanor. I sense something in him that wasn't there before Austria, a wanting greed in his expression when he's discussing business with my father and the others. A distrust stirs behind his eyes. It's fear, I think.

My new ability, if that's what it is, is creating a cavernous divide between me and the men. I have begun to think like my father. A slice of his spirit now resides in me, no matter how I try to suppress the ruffian that delivers fatal blows to what were once light and airy thoughts. It clings to me like a monarch butterfly clings to a blade of grass in high winds. I realize there is only one solution to this problem, to this threat against my loved ones' lives. The only way out of this tragic new world will be through Bernie Botts' death, or I will never be able to rest or smile or laugh again.

A squirrel hops through the snow in my direction. Before Austria, I would have tried to warn him, to chase him off our property before my mother noticed him. Now he will have to fend for himself. I have bigger problems to deal with, but this makes me feel selfish and sour. There's something not right about him. The fur on top of his head is coiffed into a severe point, like he's wearing an elf's cap. He has an extra white fluff around his neck like an ascot; it makes him look like he just hopped off the polo field, ready for cocktail hour. Flamboyant.

I glare at my father's shoes when I see him approach my seat on the overturned boat. He takes a pack of Marlboros from the inside of his coat and lights one. The squirrel rises to his hind legs to get a better look at my father's shoes.

"Mind if I take a seat?" Dad asks.

I shake my head, concentrating on the squirrel.

He wipes a pile of snow from the boat with a black leather glove and sits beside me.

"You don't feel like getting your skates on? The lake will be thawing soon. Might be your last chance this year," he says.

I shake my head again, but this time I force out a smile in his direction. I'm not ready to talk, and this feels like he's warming me up. Negotiations are about to begin.

Tell him. Do it now. This may be your last chance, my soul says under its breath.

"Got your lederhosen on, I see," Dad says.

I look down at my outfit. It feels like miniature prison garb with nothing but bad connotations woven into the stitching. These lederhosen have taken me to places I wish I'd never visited and make me want to do something terrible to myself. I don't like who I've become in them.

After the yodeling incident, I tried to take cover. With the pine tree fort having been infiltrated by Mom and her shenanigans, it wasn't a refuge any longer, so I made mournful tracks through the frosty woods along Orchard Drive, trying to figure out what to do next. I passed Mr. Skeen's house, secretly hoping he wouldn't be out front and decide that my outfit was perfect for shoveling his driveway in exchange for an intolerable wage. I found some thick brush to stand in two doors down. As I stood in some fairly nice cover, I noticed our hotsy totsy neighbor, Beth Gilleys. She is my mother's best friend. They golf at the club and lunch together at the Pink Poodle and take the train into the city to shop at Bloomingdale's. Beth meets Roger Mudd and the occasional Kennedy for drinks at the Plaza Hotel. At one point, she had some embarrassing run-in with Truman Capote when they attended Greenwich High School together. The details are fuzzy, but apparently he lived across the street from her, here on Orchard Drive. One day she caught him peeking through her bedroom window, wearing a feathered bathing cap. I don't know where he is now. My mother listens with happy attention to Beth's escapades and brushes with fame. Beth is a divorcee, which makes her a novelty. We don't get many of those here in Greenwich. I wonder who's killing spiders found in her shower, who's mowing her lawn and moving her heavy things. She inherited her house from her parents, and now she lives there wearing fabulous outfits and bleaching her hair.

  I stood watching from the trees, feeling a bit creepy, as she came out her front door with billowing layers of hot pink chiffon and sex appeal trailing behind her. She walked to the end of her driveway to fetch the *Greenwich Times*. An insulting wind whipped through the cover, stinging my legs, then a man followed her out the front door. He wore a long coat and was cupping his hat onto his head securely. I hoped it was someone famous and recognizable, maybe someone I'd seen on TV. With her, anyone and anything is possible – according to my mother – because Beth has that certain and undeniable *"Je ne sais quoi."* Beth scooped up the paper and turned to greet him with her arms open. He approached her quickly, grabbed her by her waist and, in one fluid movement, spun her, dipped her, then planted a long, syrupy kiss on her mouth. Her hands came up around the back of his neck. They stayed locked in their kiss for a full minute or more. I'd never seen such passion, not even on the movie screen, and I suddenly felt a voyeuristic thrill redden my face. The man placed her gently upright and tugged on the brim of his hat at just the right angle. He gave her a cute little salute and turned in my direction up the hill. I hunkered down between some thick vines for extra cover. I could understand why men had trouble resisting Beth Gilleys and why one would want to kiss her that way, why one would want to bask in her magnetic soup of sexiness and the way she tossed her head back and laughed with unbridled confidence. As the man walked up the hill, his features sharpened, and I saw that my mother's opinion of her dear friend was true: anything was most certainly possible concerning Beth Gilleys.

Mr. Je Ne Sais Quoi was my father.

My satchel of secrets is becoming heavy with burden as this day progresses. I can't tell my father what Bernie Botts did to me in that room in Austria, nor can I tell my mother that she'd better start allowing my father to touch her if she wants to stay in the running. I can't spill any details to Dad about Mom playing dead again, because it would certainly start an avalanche of rancid words and repercussions that I am not equipped to deal with any longer.

This brings me to my final secret: my plan to employ Jimmy Bruno to take care of my problem without anyone ever knowing. But first I must be shrewd and try to decide if I can trust him again, which is the difficult part because, although he says his job is to protect people close to him, the mere fact that Jimmy Bruno has a penis presents a new problem for me since I've recently learned that allowing your vulnerability to show in the presence of a penis can be the most dangerous arrangement of all.

"You'd tell me if something was wrong, wouldn't you, Mag?" my father asks.

His question jolts me back to present. I swallow hard and nod my head. He's watching the side of my face carefully.

"I have to tell ya, I'm a little worried about you. You haven't said ten words since we got back from our trip, so don't think I haven't noticed. Something has changed. So, you wanna talk about it?"

I yank the words that are lodged tightly in my gut to come up and out.

"I'm fine, Dad."

"You don't seem fine to me, kiddo," he says, putting his arm around my shoulder.

I stiffen under his grasp and instantly feel ashamed for my chilly response.

"If anyone ever hurt you or scared you, I'd take care of it. You know that, don't you?"

Before I can stop it, my head jerks towards him, catching his attention. I feel guilty and exposed. I catch myself and try to recover, scanning the skaters gliding over the ice across the lake.

"There's not a problem that can't be fixed, Mag, and you can tell your old man anything – because lucky for you, that's what I do – fix problems." He squeezes my shoulder, pulling me in closer to him. It makes a lump form in the base of my throat. "I can make just about anybody do what I want them to do, and I can stop people from doing what I don't want them to do. And if I can't, then I know people who can."

I know what's he's getting at. This is all supposed to make me feel better, but he has no idea what we're up against.

"So, like I say, if anyone ever hurt you..."

I'm not taking the bait. What he doesn't know is this: When the child inside you has died, and you're left open to all the harsh elements of a new and unsafe world, you can't pretend anymore. You can no longer enlist your imagination to take over at a moment's notice. Things come into focus with blinding clarity and emotions bump up against your insides but never truly emerge. You understand things that long ago could be disguised in innocent fantasy or fairytale. Before, you could ignore things that sent a chill up your back. But after the child has died – because God left the room at just the right moment – you see the truth, stripped bare of its mask, its identity revealed. You are no longer able to walk out your back door when things get tough and become Dorothy Gale from Kansas. When you push open that door, the one in the den that leads out to the garden, and you expect the black and white day to turn lush with color, it doesn't. And even though the witch may be locked away in her room with her Saltine crackers, swilling warm Smirnoff directly from the bottle, you are thoroughly aware that there are still flying monkeys perched in angry apple-hurling trees. There is still the threat that a carload of Lolly Pop Guild members will drive up the street to make fun of your lederhosen. And worst of all, there could be a charlatan in a circus wagon, somewhere on the edge of the woods, who will invite you inside to peer into his crystal ball as he unzips his pants and tells you your fortune.

An older boy falls on the ice a few yards from shore and grips his ankle with a grimace. My father chuckles, taking a long pull from his cigarette. I recognize that he finds entertainment in others' pain.

I think of all the closed doors in our house. How each one can mean a different thing. My mother's door, when closed, ekes out fear and loneliness through the keyhole. The den doors, when closed for my father's meetings, pulse with power and warning. When a guest bedroom door is closed, mystery and adventure seep into the hallway and onto the carpeting from underneath, whispering something exciting is stirring awake and will arrive in the coffee-scented kitchen before taking a train into the city or giving you a wrapped gift.

"Did you know I can have a man's legs broken for $800.00? Pretty cheap deal, really," Dad says.

It's not lost on me how wildly inappropriate this statement is. I know he's trying to impress me with his mobster discounts and that he considers himself a virtuoso in the art of getting things done, but I'm not falling for it because the other thing he doesn't know is that he's no longer my scarecrow, my trusty companion along the way. He's now become the Wizard, who would love for the world (and me) to believe that he holds the key to all problems. His suave smoke and mysterious mirrors are just that to me now, for I've been exposed to a heaping portion of what really goes on behind that curtain – a lot of spider-killing down the street at Beth's house. But I will not say a word.

My soul is making its way to the old pine tree fort. It stops before it tucks in between the low branches and points a cautious finger at me, letting me know this could be my final chance, then it tosses an Italian chin wave in my direction and disappears into the green.

CHAPTER TEN

In Which Production Begins On a Project That Would Be Better Left Dead and the Teamsters Take a Chink Out Of Hollywood's Armor, Greenwich, Connecticut, 1972

The Teamsters have made themselves essential in the making of the movie. They will build the sets, drive the trucks, furnish the supplies and get the shopkeepers to cooperate in allowing production to continue using their neighborhood storefronts and restaurants.

The Godfather has been shut down more times than has been made public. It's even been mentioned in my father's *Wall Street Journal* that the word *Mafia* will be eliminated from the script entirely, a non-negotiable suggestion that was offered by Paul Castellano.

When the guys arrive at our house, I hold very still in my new post, high in the branches of an old maple tree that hangs over the slate walkway to our front door. I was hopeful that my words would have reemerged by this point, but they have learned to come and go without much notice or stopping to rest at any particular place for too long. Like my father's friends, they cut through the silence, if they visit at all, with a mechanical motion, like sharks looking for supper.

There's a drizzle of rain landing on the dark cars, and Lou Capalbo holds an umbrella over Carlo Gambino in the driveway. Paul is here, as well as Jimmy Bruno. I wish I could feel excitement creep up my spine as it did in the good old days. But things have changed, and not just for me. Their meetings are different now;

they are more relaxed and informal; even the goombahs guarding the cars are on lower alert than before. My guess is that now that someone is making a movie about them, there are fewer reasons to be clandestine and shady. Their veil of secrecy has been pulled back just a tad, enough to give them a keen interest in the film, which they talk openly about. They are a coven of witches whose book of spells has been plagiarized, and they now have a new mission: To control it all. They've gone slightly Hollywood, I think, and business has been put on the back burner for now.

They don't always close the doors to the den these days, and I wonder if this is because, thanks to my new silence, there's less of a chance of my being an information leak, or because my mother has moved almost permanently to her bedroom. There are possibly just fewer reasons for them to take cover now.

Trying to rekindle my interest in these men, in anything, I have decided to take a seat outside the den doors later on, with a book in my hand, and make myself invisible and listen.

Dad is still trying to get me to spill the secret that has stolen my voice.

"Remember I told you about a guy who's making a movie about some of our friends?" Dad says.

I nod my head.

"I don't think it's going to be very good, but I was thinking, maybe you and I could go down to the Greenwich Theater and check it out sometime."

I say nothing.

"Maybe we'll recognize some of the characters. It started out as a book, but the guy who wrote it never met anyone in my crowd; he wrote the entire thing from doing research on Al Capone and the mob. I met Al Capone when I was a little kid, not much older than you are now."

He's been buttering me up so he can pry my secrets open. I smell it all over him.

Lou and Carlo move below me, as I clutch the thick branch

beneath my weight. I lay over the bark like a big jungle cat, my stomach, chest and chin melting into the maple. I wrap my arms and legs slightly tighter when I see the top of Carlo's head when the umbrella shifts. He's wearing his city hat and a new London Fog raincoat. Lou opens our front door and closes the umbrella as Carlo enters the house gingerly, his movements shaky. He's tired and his skin is the color of the underbelly of a snake. I think he's getting very old.

Paul comes up the walkway under my tree. He's wearing a suit, as usual, but he removed his coat when he stepped out of the car and threw it in the back seat. I'm glad to see Jimmy Bruno standing in the misty weather in his blue Yankees jacket, talking to the guys who will watch the cars. I've missed him. I've been discussing my plan with my soul, who has been following me around like a needy child. I haven't worked how exactly I will broach the subject of needing protection. It seems reckless to expose Jimmy to danger but I have an idea of how it all works now.

A few days ago, when Dad was trying to entice me to visit the movie theater with him to go see *The Godfather,* he must have been thinking about issuing threats. We were in the garage together and he was organizing his tool box.

"This is what has to happen: You have to be discreet. You greet the enemy with a hand shake. You lean in close to his ear as you're shaking his hand and you smile. You always smile. Then you whisper exactly what you plan to do to him, in detail, if he should ever cross you again. Then you smile a little brighter and you leave. Takes care of the whole mess usually. It's all about subtlety, my dear."

I would like to be there when Jimmy smiles and leans in close to Bernie's greasy ear. I would like to see the smirk melt away from Bernie's pocked cheeks as he listens. Issuing threats seems to be on my Dad's mind a lot these days. I have a strong feeling he's on to me.

As Jimmy makes his way up the slate walkway, he pauses directly beneath my branch. I freeze, hoping the rustling newborn maple leaves don't give me away.

"Hey kid." he cocks his head up at me with a warm smile. "Whatcha doin up there? C'mon down here. Let me see you up close."

This guy misses nothing. Reluctantly, I shimmy down the branches and into Jimmy Bruno's meaty arms. He pecks my forehead and places me down on the walkway.

"That's quite a hiding spot you got there. Who ya hiding from? You know you're not supposed to be out front of the house when the guys are watching the cars. You upset about somethin, kid?"

I shake my head, studying my sneakers.

"I was just resting."

"You sure been quiet the last couple of times I come over. Your dad's kinda worried about you, ya know. Makes me wonder if everything's okay. Somebody bothering you at school maybe?"

"I'm okay, Jimmy." I look up at him and offer a smile, wishing it was a more authentic one; you can fake the mouth but the eyes give things away. I've been practicing this in the mirror so that there are fewer questions. I can't keep telling everyone I'm fine and expect them to believe me without question. That isn't how these guys operate. They're experts on reading people, especially their eyes, and since Jimmy is well acquainted with fear, he requires a more enthusiastic performance on my part.

"Yeah? You're okay, huh? Listen to me." he squats down, which makes me a head taller than him. I feel unworthy, like a court jester might feel standing taller than a prince.

He places his hand on my forearm; the gold pinkie ring is cool from the spring air. "It's my job to keep you safe, remember that now. Remember when we took our trip to church and I lit a candle for you and everything turned out all right? I've been lighting candles for you again lately, because I can tell somethin's different with you."

The hair on the back of my head rustles to attention, and

my false smile slinks down my chin. I raise my eyes to look at his face, to judge whether this is the moment, whether I can trust him. I feel him reading me and wonder if I can tell the story with just this one look, without words. But if I don't say it now, I may never be able to. And if Jimmy doesn't get what he wants out of me, he'll start tossing $20s in my direction until he does, so I might as well find a way to make my request. He squeezes my arm. I'm about to open my mouth when my eyes betray me and begin to fill up with tears. Jimmy's face softens, and he pulls me into a bear hug. The front door opens and my father, a cocktail in his hand, says, "Bruno, what are you two doing out there in the rain? Get in here. Mag, what are you doing outside anyway? You know the rules."

Jimmy releases me and stands up straight again. I lower my head and quickly wipe my tears on the sleeve of my shirt.

"C'mon, kid, we'll talk later. Let's get you in the house. Your hair is getting wet," Jimmy says, patting my back as he guides me into the house.

The men gather in the den around the bar. I take a book from the shelf next to the fireplace and make myself comfortable in the rocking chair. I notice Lou has not left his shoulder strap and gun on the back of the chair today. He must still be wearing it, as Jimmy surely is wearing his inside that blue Yankees jacket. Even if I do get my hands on a gun, I'm not exactly sure how to use one, nor am I sure how many bullets it takes to kill a man the size of Bernie Botts, but I'm certain it will take more than Dad's eight-hundred-dollar-leg-breaking idea to fix this problem. I may need Jimmy's help after all.

"They are bringing unwanted attention to our business now," Carlo says to the men.

"They are, but the proceeds from their premiere should be going to the League, and we're manning the trucks and supplies for the filming. I sent Jimmy downtown to make sure the owners of all the businesses don't make it easy for them if they ignore even one of our demands," Paul says.

"Giancana says we have nothing to worry about. He and Colombo are dealing with them," my father adds. "They're a bunch of greedy bastards. They're making the movie thinking they'll be the ones who profit, but I guarantee you, the Union will bring in some good money from this. None of the bosses are going to be dishonored in the process. We've seen to it, Carlo."

"Jack's right," Paul says. "I'll be visiting the set when they're down in Little Italy tomorrow. They're gonna feel our presence. If they give us any trouble, we'll stop the trucks, and the shops won't let their crews into the neighborhood. I've been having Jimmy stop by and remind everybody to keep things straight for us and to call if there's a problem. My nephew's in the cast now, ya know, so I have no problem getting on a closed set."

"You wouldn't have a problem getting on the set regardless; that's one of our territories," Dad says.

"They got that Lenny Montana on the film," Jimmy says. "You know, that big dumb-ass wrestler? The prick that used to like to burn things up? Kinda retarded guy, used to be a bodyguard. Now he's Mr. Hollywood. I talked to him. He's playing a guy named Luca Brasi – a bodyguard, I think. Bet they don't know the guy probably can't even read. Hope he don't have too many lines." Jimmy laughs at the thought of it.

"This will bring us too much attention. I'm still not certain that Colombo has made the right decision, regardless of how much money it brings to us. He's been too bold with his threats. I'm afraid we will lose respect. It could weaken our position," Carlo says. "And Sam, he's too involved now."

"He's all right. I'm not worried, Carlo. Nothing will come of all this anyway. Who's gonna buy it? It's gonna hit the papers, be a big deal for a minute, then go down in flames," Dad tells him.

They discuss production. I try to stop listening so intently when Lou brings up a scene that has already been shot, where a horse's head is left in a movie executive's bed while the man sleeps. In the script, the executive is a stubborn connoisseur of thoroughbred racehorses and won't take the advice of the Godfather to hire an actor from Hoboken – a fellow modeled after Frank Sinatra. So late one night, they sneak into the man's barn, find his prize racer, cut its head off and slip it under the man's Egyptian cotton sheets and wait for him to change his mind.

"Funny thing is," Lou says, "that while they were consulting with real *made* guys, they got some advice to make the scene more authentic. Use a real head! They got a guy from the meat packers union to collect a fresh horse's head and exchange it for the fake one they'd had hanging around the set. It sent the actor who was playing the movie exec into hysterics when he lifted the sheets. Priceless. Don't think they're gonna tell the public about that at any premiere."

Paul mentions a phrase being used in the film, "Going to the mattresses," which is being misinterpreted as meaning going to war and fighting to the death. It bothers him, I can tell, as he's been acting as consultant with the film people and explaining to them that the phrase has a more literal meaning. When war breaks out among families and hits are being called on bosses and those directly in line for key positions, the targets are moved to safe houses where they sleep on makeshift beds or mattresses tossed on the floor.

"They're butchering a lot of it. This thing of ours – the organization – is something sacred. They're getting it all wrong and it's starting to keep me up at night. It's pissing me off," Paul says.

"They got the lingo all wrong," Jimmy adds.

"Yeah, the lingo," Lou says.

As I rock in the chair, holding the book open without reading the words, I think that I do not want to see this film now. I wonder why Lou thinks this horse's head business is so funny, and I worry about war being mentioned.

I notice that Carlo's voice has become slight over the past

year. His vocal chords sound as if they're taut, and he moves as if the life force is leaking from his frame. He spends some of his time in Miami now, and my father makes frequent flights with Lou to see him. Many of their meetings have been moved to Paul's house, so I see less of the men nowadays. Things are changing too quickly for me.

This Sam they keep mentioning, I've only met once. He is a favorite of my father's, and if I was how I used to be I'm sure he'd be one of mine too. I was very small the night Sam Giancana came to a party with an entourage of gangster types flanking him. Dad had asked him how his house hunting was going in Mexico, so I figured he must be a very brave and exciting man to want to go live in another country.

I was instructed to call him Mr. Giancana, because he is a boss like Carlo, but it turned out I never had the opportunity to call him anything. He had nothing to say to me, and I had no questions to ask. There was no mystery about him, unlike the others. When he entered the house, he took notice of his surroundings and beamed as though he knew the answers to every riddle. He walked straight to the kitchen like he owned the place. He made himself at home, removed my mother's apron from her waist, wrapped it around his own, and began stirring the sauce that simmered on the stove. He leaned into the wooden spoon and tasted without blowing, which indeed meant he was a very brave man. He asked my mother to rummage in the pantry for more tomato paste to give it some legs. I watched from the kitchen table. He was how I wanted to be, oozing confidence, fearless in every regard. Mom stood with her hands on her hips, enjoying having an authentic Italian tweaking her sauce. Sam ordered my father to bring him another drink from the den and asked why there was no music playing. "Sinatra now, Jack! It's time for Frank! Is this a party or what?"

I was sure if I pricked his finger, he would bleed movie stars and fireworks. I wanted to be his friend.

Uncle Budd and Aunt Betty were there that night. They'd pulled into the driveway in Budd's dark government car with the red phone in the console. Sam Giancana and Budd seemed to be friends, laughing and telling stories, resting their arms on each others' shoulders, so I naturally assume that members of the mob and government men are well acquainted. After observing John Connally, it seems to be adding up that way.

Now I long for those happy and innocent times when I would assault Carlo with my relentless questions, make-believe box with Jimmy, wait for Sam to bleed movie stars, but mostly for the days when Beth Gilleys came sailing into a party and she was just my mother's best friend and not my father's lover; when Dad handed her a cocktail and she handed him her coat – an exchange of effortless grace, as if they were dancing – the reason was that he was just a great host, and not that he knew what she would want even before she entered the door or that they knew how to move around each other in such comfortable ways.

There are so many things I would love to erase, things that now churn in my stomach and incinerate my emotions to ash. I sense a finale approaching, something sad and lost from memory. I pay attention to these feelings now. They are my only protection. I need to snap out of this.

CHAPTER ELEVEN

In Which We Meet an Exceptionally Good Somebody,
Greenwich, Connecticut, 1973

My sneaker makes a suction sound as I pull it from the mud at the rim of my island, so I put my foot back in the mud and pull it out just to hear it again. I like this sound. There's something satisfying about it like the clush cloosh sound horses' hooves make in packed snow.

I hear voices carry across the water in my direction and I see Dad standing on the shore in our yard with his legs bowed and his hands on his hips, watching me. Then I notice Uncle Lou, wearing a lavender colored golf shirt, making his way down the hill towards my father, trying to light a cigarette as he navigates the hill. Jimmy is trailing behind Lou, holding a yellow helium balloon up in the air by its ribbon.

"Mag! Come on!" Dad yells, "The guys are here!" He makes a sweeping motion, persuading me to come off my island and row home.

I untie my boat, make one final suction noise with my sneaker, hop in and begin to row across the lake. I feel the familiar surge of excitement ramp its way through my body like it used to when the guys came over. I've been working things out in my mind lately, trying to get myself together. I know I've lost my charms since Austria and being charmless, after a while, becomes a rotten place to live and one becomes sick of oneself in no time. I recently realized I need to grow up – I turned twelve last month – and that's when my soul finally showed up again. It gave me a good talking-to about focusing on happy thoughts; on remembering the past is only something that used to be, it's not happening now. My soul reminded me there's no need to be scared anymore; the threat issued in Austria – the one that tossed me in the pot of boiling water over the fire made of sticks and danced around me with the bone in its nose to the beat of black drums – is gone and it feels safe to come out. It felt safe a while ago but I somehow missed it.

Sometimes I need to remind myself that Bernie Botts has never come to visit us (and if he does, I will simply go to the island until he goes away) and nobody has been shot dead, no one's skull has been crushed and no one's tossed me in a pot of boiling water to cook me for supper. My soul says when I think my fear has returned and is about to grab hold of my ankles again, I should turn it into one of those shooting stars that streaks across the night sky, commanding all of our attention for a second, making us gasp momentarily and then, without warning, fizzles out completely, leaving only the vague memory that something unusual has just happened to us. It feels better in my stomach to deal with it this way.

Thirty-odd feet from shore, I wonder about the balloon Jimmy is holding. It's not my birthday and I wonder where he got it and why he's brought it with him. It must be for me as I'm the only kid here. And then it hits me: The only other time Jimmy ever brought me a gift was the morning he woke me up with the small green bowl, shanghaied me and delivered me to Dr. O's office in his Caddy. And I stop rowing. I gently lower one oar in the water and spin the boat slowly around to look at the three of them, to eyeball them good and hard. I narrow my eyes at my father who's now close enough to see my expression and, hopefully, my suspicion.

Jimmy gives me the ever-assuring Italian Chin Wave. I give him my *nice try, pal* look and steady my boat.

"C'mon, Kid! We're taking you out today! What are you

doin' out there?" Lou says.

"Taking me out?"

"Yeah, row on over here, Sweetie," Jimmy adds as he steps closer to shore.

"Are we going to church again?" I focus my question on Jimmy.

He laughs, "No, not this time. C'mon! Let's go."

"Are we going downtown?"

"Nope," he says grinning.

"What's with the balloon?"

"It's a hint. C'mon, now. Let's get you up on shore."

"Does this have something to do with taking me to Woolworth's to buy me something *nice* again?" I scowl, giving each of them, one at a time, an individual and stern warning with my face – which is a very difficult thing to keep on my face without cracking a smile because I'm so fond of them.

"It's alright, Mag," Dad says, "You're not going to the dentist today. This is a fun outing. Now, let's go." Dad turns and heads back up to the house, losing his patience with my distrust, while Lou and Jimmy wait for me. I work the oars backwards through the water so I can face them as I slowly, cautiously, make my way towards this surprise they have up their sleeves. This way, if anything changes in their expressions in the next few strokes, I can quickly make my escape.

"Toss me that rope, kid," Lou says as my boat bumps into the shore.

I throw the green, slimy rope to him and he catches it on the first try. As I lift the oars out of the water Jimmy grabs the front of my boat, pulls it up and out of the water and slides it gracefully onto land with one hand. As we make our way up the hill towards the house, Lou takes my hand. Jimmy hands me the string of the balloon and with my goombahs flanking me, we head in the direction of a surprise.

#

Jimmy's car smells like comfort and faintly of popcorn. I'm in the front seat between the guys. The radio is off. Lou whistles *That's Amore* while we travel out of Greenwich and towards Cos Cob and sometimes when Jimmy turns a corner too sharply, the caddy leans me into Lou and I can feel his gun tucked into its halter, like an old, reliable guard dog nuzzled against his ribs.

"Capalbo, what are your plans for New Year's Eve anyway?" Jimmy asks as he makes another turn, steering wheel digging into his belly.

"New Year's Eve?! What the hell are you talkin about? It's the dead of summer! What are you talkin New Year's Eve for?" Lou says too loudly.

"I know it's summer! I want to know what your plans are. I was just thinkin about it, is all."

"Jesus, Jimmy. What? You have something planned for me? I'm not going to your mother's house again if that's what you're thinkin."

"What's wrong with my mother's house? I thought you had a good time over there. Hell, you ate about thirty of her cannoli that night and that was *before* anyone got there! And my mother was not pleased about that, by the way."

"Oh yeah? Well I wasn't pleased that I found one of your mother's mustache hairs in my drink. How bout that? You'd think she'd have shaved before a big holiday like that!" Lou's laughing at himself.

As Jimmy tries to think of a clever comeback, off in the distance on a gently sloping hill, I see a Ferris wheel rising up like a gigantic, spinning monument. I point at it through the windshield, hoping that's where we're going.

"Hey! Look at that!" Lou says.

"Did you know the first Ferris wheel was put up at the Chicago World's Fair in the late 1800s? It was 80 meters high," Jimmy says, matter-of-factly.

"80 *meters*," Lou comes back, "Bruno. *Meters*? What are

you? British, all of a sudden?"

"80 meters," Jimmy repeats.

"Feet, Jimmy, feet. We're in America, remember?"

"Meters," Jimmy is trying to suppress a smile. He's taunting Lou now. I like it when he does that.

"Hey! Henry the Eighth, I think you were supposed to turn off back there," Lou yells.

"Oh. Sorry, I was distracted."

"Yeah, you were planning your upcoming tea party in the UK. Hey! Maybe that's what we could do for New Year's – go to Buckingham Palace, visit the queen. She's your type. She actually looks like your mother a little…except for the mustache."

Jimmy's ignoring him now. Lou's gun is jiggling against my arm as he laughs. The Ferris wheel looms large against slow, puffy clouds as we pull into a parking lot at the edge of a carnival that looks out of place, as if it's a new and strange variety of mechanical flower that has sprung up in the middle of a graceful Connecticut field. A rumbling excitement gathers momentum in my tummy as we exit Jimmy's Caddy.

"Let's go have some fun, kid," Lou says to me, ushering me out of the car, "Jimmy! Maybe we can find something to eat. I'm starvin."

"Maybe they have cannoli here for ya," Jimmy tells Lou, "About fifty of them. Think that would tide you over?"

"Maybe you can find yourself some tea and crumpets, Nancy. What do you think about that, huh?"

"I told you not to call me that," Jimmy says, giving Lou a narrow eye.

"Sorry, Betty. My apologies."

The metallic sound of gears propelling the carnival rides becomes louder as we approach the midway. A small crowd of patrons is gathered in line at a tiny ticket booth. We pass the booth completely, making me think Jimmy and Lou either bought tickets in advance when the yellow balloon (which is now tied embarrassingly to my wrist – thanks to Jimmy – like I'm a two year old who can't manage a balloon properly) or men like them just don't require tickets. A heavy waft of cotton candy, fried treats and hot dogs hits me in the face. The smell is overwhelming at first, sickeningly sweet and it makes my stomach lurch momentarily, but then it creates an excitement somewhere deep, down inside, bringing a familiar spring back in my step. Something good is about to happen.

"Lou, where do they keep that Scrambler ride?" Jimmy slows his gait to survey the midway.

"You're gonna take her on that?"

"Yeah! Why not? It's a good one. I always liked it," Jimmy says, giving me a wink.

"You do know there's a weight limit on some of these rides, don't ya?" Lou tells him, "You could crush her to death if your Scrambler gets out of control."

Jimmy ignores the dig, searching the area, "Where the hell is it? I know it's here somewhere, kid." He grabs my hand and pulls me away from Lou and in the direction of the Ferris wheel.

"Yeah," Lou calls after us, "try that way…about *80 meters* to your left, Bruno," Lou's laughter sails through the carnival, trailing us in our Scrambler search.

Jimmy and I find the flying swings first and settle into plastic seats fixed to the ends of gigantic wheel spokes above. I feel as if we're the dangling pieces of an oversized wind chime. Lou has caught up to us but sits this ride out as he leans on a makeshift fence lighting a cigarette. The thought occurs to me that I haven't asked why they've brought me here and if this is the *thing* we're doing or if it's just a preview to the *thing* we're really doing. As the ride starts up, gently lifting us off the ground and around in a circular motion, I glance up at the chains holding Jimmy's swing to the steel spokes, hoping they're going to hold him and not come loose, suddenly catapulting him back in the direction we came from and into the middle of downtown Greenwich with a thud. The ride gains momentum and kicks us out at an angle. The carnival spins wildly and every now and then I catch sight of Lou below us as we sail above his head and his cigarette smoke. Flying like this, spinning ever so slightly in this swing, I feel free and scared at the same time. Powerful, even. I smile over at Jimmy and he looks like he's having a bit less fun than I am and perhaps a little pale. I hope he doesn't get sick all over Lou down on the ground. I close my eyes and feel myself give in to the whirling lack of gravity, of being weightless and free and I let myself forget about why the guys have brought me here or if this is just a prelude to the real *thing* and I let myself giggle out loud.

#

Lou's cigarette isn't even half way smoked by the time our ride stops but I can tell he's ready to move on to something more exciting. Jimmy seems slightly unsteady as we walk away from our swings. He's blowing air out of his mouth the way I do when I'm trying not to throw up.

"Ok, Sweetie, what's next?" Jimmy asks me, slicking his hair back with both hands.

I don't answer yet. There's too much to take in and we could move in any direction and find an adventure, so I let him decide. Lou's not coming up with an answer for us either, so the three of us start to wander in the direction of the game booths. There are five or six different booths to choose from. Jimmy stops to eye one of the games. A grungy looking man is guarding a table stacked with milk bottles. He holds a baseball out to us and yells, "C'mon folks! Win the little girl a stuffed bear today!"

"Nah, nah, nah…Jimmy. Let's go find more rides. I can't stand to be around these barkers. They drive me nuts," Lou protests while he lights another cigarette.

Jimmy ignores him and steps closer to the booth.

"How much?" Jimmy asks.

"For you? Five dollars for three throws! That's a deal. I usually charge five for one throw," the barker barks.

"Yeah, sure he does," Lou says, "Maggie doesn't want one of these crap bears, Jimmy. Let's go."

"Hold on, now. Let me give it a try. She should have a souvenir."

Jimmy decidedly pulls a wad of cash from his pants pocket, sifts through the bills, finds a five and tosses it at the man. I don't remind him that I started this day with a souvenir that I left tied to the fence by the flying swings. If he does win me a bear, I'm pretty sure he won't feel the need to tie it to my wrist. I'm far too old to have things tied to me.

The barker places a shallow basket holding three dirty baseballs in front of Jimmy and steps back to give him space. Jimmy picks the first ball up and bounces it in his palm to test its weight. He rears back like a pitcher, shifting to his back leg, front leg coming up slightly and hurls the ball towards a stack of bottles. And he misses completely. Lou snorts a muffled laugh, taking a pull from his smoke.

"This could take all day, kid," Lou says, winking at me.

Jimmy tries again with the second ball and hits one of the bottles on the bottom of the stack this time. The bottles don't budge.

"You got those bottles nailed down to the table or somethin?" Jimmy growls.

The barker, looking smugly at Jimmy, smacks another stack of bottles with the back of his hand without answering and they all tumble over. Jimmy slicks his hair back, glaring at the guy.

"Want me to shoot him for doin that?" Lou asks Jimmy, chuckling.

Jimmy ignores him. My palms are sweating. Last ball. Jimmy repeats his pitcher's stance and lets out a grunt as he releases the ball into the stack of bottles. It's a direct hit. The bottles tumble. The man looks preoccupied – as if we've just become invisible to him now that the game is over – as he yanks a stuffed brown bear down from the frame of his booth and tosses it at me without even looking in my direction.

"Okay if we move on now, Mickey Mantle?"

"The game's rigged, is all," Jimmy says, hiking up his pants, "You like your bear, sweetie?" I nod up at him and thank him for his efforts.

"Good. Now where's that damned scrambler? Let's try over this way."

The three of us wander through the now thickening crowd. The late afternoon sky is ushering in the evening, drawing in more people as the carnival seems to brighten and become more alive against the changing light.

We discover there is no scrambler here so we settle for a gentler version of the same – the tea cup ride. This is fine by me as no one ever got crushed in a tea cup as far as I know. To my surprise and delight, Lou joins us this time. The guys look ridiculous sitting in this giant, pale green tea cup and the best part is that they're completely unaware that they look ridiculous. Lou is still running the world, legs spread out, elbows resting back on the edge of the cup, surveying the crowd. Jimmy is eye-balling people in a watchful way as they walk the midway, ready to toss twenties at anyone who steps out of line.

"Give me your bear, sweetie. You should be holding this," Jimmy says, pointing to the steel wheel attached to a pole in the center of our cup.

I hand him my bear and latch on to the wheel which moves slightly, making the cup swivel easily despite the weight of its contents.

"Bruno, if that's not a sight, I don't know what is. Look at yourself," Lou says, shaking his head.

"What?"

"Look at you. Never thought I'd see the day. Jimmy Bruno sitting in a tea cup with a teddy bear in his lap. This is one for the books."

"Excuse me, but shut up. Aren't you sittin in a cup?"

"Yeah, but I can pull it off," Lou smirks at him, "Seriously, though. You look good, Nancy. This is perfect. Your very own giant tea party."

Jimmy gives Lou the Italian chin wave, but spices it up with the threatening gesture of biting the side of his own hand. Lou takes a cigarette out of his pack and sticks it in his mouth, searching for his lighter in his pants pocket.

The ride operator sitting at the gears notices and calls out, "Sir, no smoking on the rides."

Lou finds his lighter, raises his eyebrows at the operator and lights up.

"Why you smokin so much anyway?" Jimmy asks him.

Lou ignores the question.

The ride lurches and as we begin to move I notice a small thrill come over the two of them and I think the guys are having a better time than they'll ever admit to anyone or to each other, but I see it. As the cup spins round, lights from the midway dance around us; tinny music fades in and out as our cup changes position and the guys hold back their smiles, as if enjoying this would ruin their reputation. I like to see them have fun. The ride seems short to me when it ends and Jimmy's color has changed again.

As we disembark our cup, we head towards the back of the midway. The Ferris wheel looms over us and I can only assume that is our next stop. I don't mention my displeasure with heights or that I'm sure I used up most of my courage on those flying swings because I don't want to spoil their adventure (or mine). I hope they don't see my hands shake once we get to the top.

"Let me take her this time, Bruno," Lou says, grabbing my hand and leading me to the vacant carriage that has just come to rest at the bottom of the wheel, "With your girth, one of these babies could come unhinged and the two of you could plummet to your deaths."

Jimmy humphs under his breath but gives me the *go ahead, I'll follow in the next carriage* look. Lou's words hang in the artificially lit air, *plummet to your deaths.*

We're rocked far too much for my liking as our seat lifts off and moves up a space, allowing Jimmy to embark behind and below us. Lou puts his heavy arm around my shoulders and pulls me close. I'm glad his gun is on the other side so I can squeeze into him as we climb higher. I turn around, keeping a constant eye on Jimmy, when the Ferris wheel affords me the opportunity. Watching him takes my mind off how incredibly high we're going. We reach the very top of the Ferris wheel, which places Jimmy in front of and slightly below us. Lou is laughing at the back of his head, pointing, when Jimmy turns around to smile at us and his smile quickly sours on Lou.

"Why don't you light another cigarette and mind your business?"

"He's so sensitive," Lou whispers.

"Why are we stopping for so long this time?" I ask Lou.

"They're just letting other folks on down below. Take a look over the side."

I can't look. I nuzzle closer to Lou and pray that this contraption hasn't broken down and we're not going to have to wait for the Cos Cob Fire Department to rescue us. This is a different sort of feeling than the swings and the freeing, powerful thrill I felt; this is the *I'm at the mercy of a complete stranger who didn't seem to be too thrilled about his job down below as he was working the big lever or to be paying too much attention to the racket the ride was making when we boarded our carriage and this ride probably hasn't had maintenance in years and we could very easily die here* sort of feeling. I want to get off. I always want to get off a Ferris wheel when I'm just sitting at the top, being helpless.

This ride seems too long after only a couple of rotations and just when I think I'm about to get a headache about it, we reach the bottom and are set free on safe and solid ground. The sun has set without me noticing it and the carnival is buzzing with people. We discuss finding snacks and in our search, Jimmy stops at a young, blonde woman, dressed in a skimpy purple dress, standing next to a large scale who wants to guess Jimmy's weight for three dollars.

"Don't waste your money, Bruno," Lou says, "I can guess your weight for nothin."

Jimmy ignores him and saunters up to the woman to begin negotiations. Behind the large scale there are rows of boxes stacked up higher than Lou's head, stamped with the words *PAPER CUPS*. It looks like a storage section which robs this area of any intended carnival magic. As I survey the boxes, trying not to become impatient while waiting for Jimmy to be weighed, I catch movement near the farthest stack of boxes. A black bowler hat rolls out from behind the stack and settles in the dirt a few feet away from me.

I glance over at Jimmy and Lou to see if they've seen the hat. They haven't, being completely engrossed in the skimpy girl and her sales pitch. I move closer to the hat. It's very old fashioned, a hat only seen in black and white movies these days and the person belonging to this hat might prove to be very old fashioned himself and therefore, very old, and therefore again, very interesting because old people have the best stories. I take a step closer. It just sits there looking inviting like it wants me to pick it up and try it on. I take another step and bend over for a better look, when a small flash of something blackish-brown whips out from behind the boxes, runs to the hat, grabs it and disappears in the shadows where it came from. The moment nearly knocks me back and I let out a sharp squeak. I have to blink my eyes for a moment to get my bearings, to help my mind adjust to what I've just seen and as I do, a man who looks to be about a hundred years old comes out from behind the boxes, wearing the hat. In one hand he holds an empty metal crate and in the other he cradles a small blackish-brown monkey.

The man doesn't seem to notice me. He turns around,

monkey in hand and goes back behind the boxes. As I'm taking a cautious step in their direction they reemerge again and I stop, not sure what to do. The monkey spots me and scrambles ably up the old man's arm and perches on his shoulder. Making eye contact with a monkey at such a close range makes my breath catch. It's nothing like seeing a monkey at the Bronx Zoo. This is different, more intimate, like it means something. I take a step closer and this time the old man sees me.

"Oh! Well, oh my. Hello, there, my dear." he says, politely tipping his bowler hat with his index finger. He's dressed in black and his clothes seem to be as old as he is, tattered with frays at his shirt collar and a noticeable sag in the hem of his pants.

"Hello," I say.

"Mr. Natale, it appears we have a visitor," he says to the monkey.

The monkey watches me, lifting his eyebrows, scanning me quickly from head to toe, as if to give me the once over. I take a step closer, a bigger, bolder one this time. The man picks up the metal crate and turns it upside down and pats it, inviting me to sit, then goes back into the shadows for a moment. He returns with another crate.

"Go ahead; take a seat beside me, my dear. Mr. Natale likes visitors."

I'm transfixed as I watch the monkey's tiny hands grasp the old man's neck for support as he sits. I take a seat beside them.

"How rude of me...we haven't formally introduced ourselves, have we? I am Bertram McSweeney. My friends call me Mac, so please feel free to address me as such," he extends his very old, arthritic hand in my direction and I take it gently as it looks tender, "and this handsome fellow is my superior, Mr. Babbo Natale."

The monkey begins to climb down off the man's shoulder and, as if on cue, stands tall on hind legs in the center of Mr. McSweeney's lap and extends a miniature hand to me. I take it in mine and marvel at the sensation. His skin is warm and slightly leathery and his little fingernails are shaped like perfectly manicured rectangles and before I can get a better look, he pulls his hand away and blows a tiny kiss in my direction.

Naturally, the first place my mind goes is taking this monkey to Show N Tell, but our class has outgrown that ritual, plus, there was the Carlo Gambino and the John Connally incidents where my mother scolded me for trying to put actual humans on display for Show N Tell (and monkeys are close enough to humans to get me in trouble), and we're on summer break anyway, so the next place my mind goes is my boat and rowing this monkey and Mr. McSweeney out to my island, but then I remember Hannah the Cat and, of course, the geisha incident and then the next place my mind goes, naturally, is having the two of them come to live with me in my room, the way I wanted big bloody Jesus to do years ago. But I stay quiet about these ideas as I'm practicing not getting into so much trouble these days.

"I'm Maggie. How old is Mr...,"

"Natale, dear. Mr. Babbo Natale. The name means Santa Claus in Italian. He was born on Christmas Eve, according to some. I call him by his formal name, Mr. Natale, for respectability purposes, you know. He turned thirty years old recently but we call it twenty-nine; makes him feel younger."

"Where is he from?"

"Detroit, originally," Mac says.

Not really what I meant, but I leave it alone. Mr. Natale shows me his teeth in a rather taunting smile; small, very white fangs on either side.

"What kind of monkey is he?"

"An exceptionally good one," Mac says, giving Mr. Natale a nod.

Again, not really what I meant.

"We met back in '55, long before you were born. I was traveling on a circus caravan through the Great Midwest – I was a Joey."

I feel my forehead wrinkle up the way it does when I'm confused about something and he must have seen it because now he looks confused himself.

"Well, oh dear...I'm sorry, my dear, I sometimes forget I'm not always talking to the carnies around here. They have their own language – Carnie Talk – different words from what regular folks use; sometimes you'll hear them speak a sort of Pig Latin too – to keep the patrons from knowing what they're really saying. Keeps the mystery alive, ya know. Well, anyway, I'm rambling on now...a clown, my dear. I was a clown."

I widen my eyes at him and smile because I want to know more. I've never met a clown before. Now that I know this, it should have been obvious to me. He looks like a clown naturally, even without make up or a rubber nose, deep laugh lines creased into his cheeks from decades of being happy and large, green eyes infused with a permanent twinkle – even if they do look quite sad around the edges.

"And Mr. Natale, here, was an entertainer with the Rodeo circuit that was traveling through the same area. His handler was retiring; was a clown himself – a rodeo clown – very dangerous job, that, and we struck up a friendship. Mr. Natale was far too young to retire so I agreed to let him take care of me for a few years and well, here we still are today. Eighteen years together, for better or worse."

The monkey sticks his tongue out and wags it before showing me his teeth again.

Mac looks lost in their history for a moment, then perks up again as if he's regained his train of thought.

"Mr. Natale had quite a following back in the early years. Children from all over the country were his loyal fans and he still has a few pen pals he keeps up with. How would you like an autographed photo of him? He could send you one once we get back to base camp. He could use a new friend; I'm afraid I bore him at times now that I move a might slower these days."

"I would like that."

He pats his shirt pocket and fishes out a golf pencil, then looks around behind him for, I assume, something to write on.

"Mr. Natale, a sheet of paper, if you would be so kind," Mac says and with that, the monkey scampers off quickly, disappearing behind the boxes.

I hear Lou cough behind me and when I turn to look up at him, I see he's eyeing the old man on the crate. I introduce them and as they're shaking hands, Jimmy joins us. He's holding a large, soft pretzel with a glob of mustard smeared across the top of it. Before I can make this second introduction Mr. Natale runs back to Mac's lap clutching a small piece of paper in his little hand. Mac accepts it with a bow of his head and looks at me expectantly, golf pencil poised over the paper.

"It's Maggie Dahlstrom. 88 Orchard Dri—," I begin.

"Whoa, whoa…what's happenin here, kid?" Lou interrupts, "Why are you giving out your address?"

"Uncle, Lou, this is Babbo Natale and he's going to send me an autographed picture of himself once he gets back to base camp. We're going to be pen pals!"

Lou eyes the monkey, "Oh. Well, alright. Go ahead. We need to get you back home though, so let's wrap this up, ok?"

I nod at Lou and return to focusing on Mac and his pencil, "So, that's 88 Orchard Drive," I wait until I see he has the street name spelled properly and then give him the rest of my address.

He carefully folds the piece of paper in half and tucks it in his shirt pocket. The monkey pats the pocket and climbs up on Mac's shoulder, watching Jimmy and the pretzel.

"My dear, it was an honor meeting you and your friends," Mac says, placing his gnarled hand on the top of my head. Mr. Natale kisses his own little monkey hand and flings it out in my direction to say goodbye. I return the gesture, hoping my address isn't lost in all the carnival hustle and bustle and that I receive mail from him very soon.

As we head to Jimmy's Caddy, he stuffs the remainder of his pretzel in his mouth and licks some mustard from the back of his hand.

"You know," he says, smacking his lips loudly, "that was a capuchin back there."

"What?" Lou asks.

"The monkey. It was a capuchin. They're from South America," he swallows the rest of the pretzel down hard, "named after an order of friars – the Capuchins – in the 1400s cuz they look like they're wearing hooded robes. Ya know, that darker fur on the backs and coming up over the top of their heads?"

Lou is standing at the passenger door of the car, looking impatient with his hands on his hips.

"They can use tools, like humans," Jimmy continues, "and they're supposedly the smartest kind of monkey. They really look like people too, don't they?"

"Hey, Mr. Britannica, could you please unlock the friggin door here? We need to get back to the house. I'm starvin, and by the way, did you think of buying anyone else a pretzel? No, you didn't. So, open the friggin door."

Jimmy smiles as he very slowly takes his keys out of his pocket, and even more slowly puts the key in the door lock, smirking at Lou over the roof of the Caddy. I take one more glance at the lighted midway, grateful for the adventure the guys have given me and excited over the anticipation of mail coming from a new friend, but my feet are tired and I wish Jimmy would quit fooling around. I'm thinking about putting my hands on my hips.

#

As the Caddy winds slowly through the Milbrook streets, I finally ask my question, knowing that we really are on the way back to my house and the carnival wasn't just a trick to get me into the car to go do a *thing* that could have turned out to be unpleasant.

"So, why did you guys take me to the carnival, anyway?"

"Cuz you're a good kid. That reason enough?" Lou says.

"And you seemed to need a little fun, Sweetie. Everyone needs a little fun to bring them back to life sometimes," Jimmy adds.

Mom is already in her room by the time we arrive back at the house but Dad is waiting in the den. I recount our day for him in as much detail as possible (purposefully leaving out the yellow balloon I abandoned) before being pointed in the direction of bedtime. As I reach the top of the stairs with my bear in my hand, I hear the comforting sounds of banter start up below me.

"Jack, bad news: Jimmy paid a brawd twenty bucks to tell him he's fat," Lou says.

"What? Bruno, is that true?" Dad says, "Could have spent your money on a hooker and come out better."

"Not if the hooker charges by the pound!" Lou yells out.

Laughter fills the house and sails up the staircase, trailing me to my room. I pause at my door, wanting to hear just a little bit more before going to bed, making the day last just a bit longer.

"That's just the hookers you know, Capalbo," Jimmy comes back.

"Glass of scotch, boys?" Dad asks.

"Yeah, I'll pour," Jimmy says.

"How much do hookers charge per pound these days anyway, Jimmy?" Lou asks.

"I dunno, how bout we call your mother and ask her?"

After slipping into my pajamas and in between my sheets, I feel sleep try to take me under and away from the low rumble of the guys' voices downstairs – the voices that have once again become my very own private and protective lullaby.

My soul slips into bed beside me and whispers in my ear, *I think you're doing great. You giggled today. Your voice has come back. It did take quite a while though, didn't it?*

I nod my head.

Did I help at all?

"You did," I say, trying to reassure it.

Who knew how much mending could come from a few carnival rides with the guys and a yellow balloon?

"And a monkey," I whisper back.

CHAPTER TWELVE

In Which We See That to Betray Certain Leagues of Men is a Guarantee of Swift Revenge, Served Too Hot to Eat, Dallas, Texas, 1963

It's the last slice of summer of 1963. The Dahltroms are living in Dallas, Texas, in a modest house on Classen Drive. Patricia cuts fresh lemons to add to a glass pitcher of lemonade before the guests arrive. Sixteen-year-old Jane folds paper napkins at the kitchen table while Jack is out by the pool, firing up the grill. Patricia hums quietly to herself to calm her nerves. Something is wrong – she just doesn't know what. This feeling overcame her about an hour ago and she can't shake it. Her insides feel tangled in knots and she has a slight headache. She sighs loudly as she drops the lemon slices into the pitcher.

"Mom, you okay?" Jane asks, noticing the worried expression.

"Sure, honey. I'm just not myself today. We probably shouldn't have invited that Beverly woman – the one who bought the Gibson's old house. I don't think the other neighbors are very fond of her; she's a little flashy. When is your brother coming home?"

"He said he was going to drop by Marty's house to pick up some money he owes him and then get some gas for the lawnmower at the Mobil station."

"Marty Thompson is the last person Sid should be lending money to – he'll never see it again. That boy hasn't worked a day in his life; probably never will either."

Jack stomps in through the back door. "Patricia, is that meat ready yet?"

"I've been a little busy in here, in case you haven't noticed. Why are you yelling? And close that door. You've been letting flies into the house all day."

"All right, all right! What's wrong with you now?" Jack closes the back door with a slam.

Patricia whips a wooden spoon out of a drawer and rapidly stirs the lemonade, glaring at Jack. Jane averts her eyes and studies her pile of folded napkins. The phone hanging on the kitchen wall blares, halting the uncomfortable storm that's brewing.

"Hello," Patricia says into the mouthpiece. She hopes it's not one of the guests calling to cancel at the last minute.

"I need to speak to Mr. or Mrs. Dahlstrom. This is the Emergency Room at Parkland Memorial Hospital."

"This is Mrs. Dahlstrom," Patricia's voice comes out in a hoarse whisper. She turns to Jack, making frantic eye contact, grabbing the countertop to steady herself.

"Your son has been in a serious accident."

Jack moves closer to Jane, trying to decipher what's just made his wife go completely pale.

"Serious," Patricia repeats.

"We need you to come to the hospital right away."

"Jack?" Patricia's face morphs into an anguished grimace as she holds the phone out to her husband.

Jack hurries around the counter and takes the phone from her.

"This is Jack Dahlstrom. Who is this?"

As he listens into the receiver, his face falls more with each passing moment.

Jack hangs up the phone.

Jane rises from the table, clutching the napkins in her hand. "What's happened?" Her eyes fill up with tears before anyone can answer her.

"Sid's been in an accident. Watch the baby. We need to go to Parkland now."

The corridor leading them to the Intensive Care Unit seems unending. Jack and Patricia follow the nurse to a doorway. They can hear noisy machines inside the room making rhythmic bumps and beeps. Patricia grabs Jack's arm, trying her hardest to remain standing.

"We're trying to stabilize your son," the nurse says in a hushed tone. "Dr. Clark has called in some brain specialists and is on his way to talk with you. The injuries are quite serious, so I just want you to be aware before you see him."

Patricia gently pushes the nurse out of the doorway and walks into the room. What she sees stops her cold. An oxygen mask covers Sid's mouth and nose. There is blood on the pillow. Two nurses in surgical scrubs are leaning over his body, adjusting tubes, checking the machines that churn beside the bed. Patricia's not sure this is even her son. Maybe a mistake has been made.

She takes a step closer as the two nurses back away, giving her room. She hears Jack make a deep gasping sound from behind her.

Sid's head is swollen on one side, making it jut out as if someone has tucked a cantaloupe up under his scalp. Patches of deep, red blood clot his hair. His eyes are both bruised and already swollen shut.

Patricia reaches out and touches her son's hand. It's cold. She feels Jack's hands grip her shoulders. For once, she doesn't tense up from the touch. He says nothing but she can hear his erratic breath behind her. Jack turns when he hears someone coming in behind them.

Dr. Clark enters the room in his white coat and looks gravely around the room. They know him from their ten years in the First Presbyterian congregation. They have shared polite small talk at church functions and cocktail parties. On occasion, Patricia bumps into his wife, Alicia, in the A&P. Dr. Clark has watched this family grow; has witnessed Sid rushing up the aisle towards the Dahlstrom pew, late for church as usual, toting Maggie by the hand in such a hurry that he lifts her completely off the ground, sometimes losing a tiny, red Mary Jane shoe in the aisle. The recognition and familiarity should make this moment feel a bit more hopeful, as if this personal connection with the doctor can give them some kind of edge. But the look on the doctor's face shows nothing but terrible news is coming. He leans over Sid's body momentarily and scans the monitors beside the bed.

"Jack, Pat, I've called in some help from Houston. There's a lot of swelling in the brain and I don't feel confident about operating just yet. Sid's not stable enough to be put under. We're doing the best we can at this point. I'm very sorry. We have a long road ahead of us, I'm afraid."

Dr. Clark reaches a quick, professional hand out and pats Jack's upper arm. The gesture leaves Patricia with a fresh sense of dread.

Three long weeks into Sid's coma, Jack sits in the uncomfortable chair he's come to know too well. A bottle of scotch sits on the floor between his feet from which he pours himself a belt every time he realizes that Sid isn't going to make it out of this. Patricia kneels at Sid's bedside, holding onto the metal railing. Jack wonders if she's praying or simply catatonic, as she seems to have been for days now. Patricia can no longer bear an anguish this demanding. Jack sees this clearly. The doctors haven't allowed Jane to come up to Parkland yet. Sid's appearance is still too disturbing. Instead, they have left Jane in charge of caring for Maggie at home, hoping the baby will be a good distraction.

A nurse steps into the room and says Dr. Clark needs a word with them. Jack rises from his chair and helps Patricia to her feet.

Under the insulting, harsh lights, doctors gather in the hallway, their heads bent down in conference.

Dr. Clark says, "Jack, the situation is very bleak. We don't expect Sid will survive this. If by some miracle he does, he'll never be the same again." Sid is 18 years old.

Jack holds Patricia up by her arms as they listen. Jack realizes Sid will never again help his father tinker with a car engine or pluck a tune from his Goya guitar. He will never again be capable of teasing Jane for being a mere junior in high school or of threatening her suitors. If he survives, his brain will never be able to string together a thought or send the message to his arms that it is time to tickle his one-year-old sister while waiting for dinner to come out of the oven. He will never read a book, take a walk or recognize his tribe as his own.

Patricia collapses in the hallway, hitting the cold cream-colored tile floor. Her howling fills the Intensive Care Unit. She grabs her enchanting red hair in both hands and rips two large chunks out by the roots. The doctors and Jack scramble to restrain her but she overpowers them. Patricia rolls onto her back and begins violently kicking and throwing punches, trying to get the men away from her. Dr. Clark catches her left wrist and holds it tightly, yelling at a nurse coming out of one of the rooms, "Get a tranq over here now!"

Patricia lets out a battle cry and with her free hand, digs her fingernails into the right side of her face, raking deep gouges into her flesh from her eyelid to her jaw bone, then down and across her throat.

The hospital staff is finally able to get the tranquilizer into her system while Jack stands back and catches his breath. The needle jabs her flesh like a bayonet.

Patricia has exhausted herself. She sits in a metal chair in the hallway outside of Sid's room. She stares at the floor, unfocused, still clutching a large nest of tangled red hair in her left hand.

During the next four black weeks of Sid's coma, Jack has no choice but to call in assistance. Lou Capalbo and one of his buddies from Brooklyn arrive in Dallas to take over at the house. If the situation was lighter, Jack would think it comical to see two rotund, chain-smoking Italians transform into baby-talking nannies who fight over who gets to give Maggie her bottle; to see Capalbo with an apron tied to his waist, washing dishes at the kitchen sink and arguing over whose turn it is to go check the restraints that keep Patricia tied down to the mattress.

But nothing is funny here. His life has lost all color as he sits by his son's hospital bed, listening to the machines that keep Sid alive and rob the room of all dignity with their insistent reminder that all the noise they're making is just a vain attempt to save his son.

It's day forty-eight at Parkland. At times Sid's eyes will involuntarily flutter open, the right one, dislodged ever so slightly from its socket, moves independently from the other, when it moves at all. At first, Jack found hope in these signs. Now, Jack doesn't respond when this happens. It means nothing. Patricia hasn't been to visit Sid in weeks now. She's so heavily medicated that Jack wonders if she even knows she has a son anymore. He takes another swig from his bottle of Scotch. No matter how much he drinks, his mind won't give him the slightest peace. What he wouldn't give to be blind drunk during all of this.

Jack is awakened by the phone on the fiftieth day of Sid's coma. He snaps on the light at the bedside table, noticing Patricia is still in a dead sleep.

"Yes," he answers.

"Jack. He's awake." Dr. Clark sounds as if he's choking back tears.

By the time Jack arrives up at Parkland, Sid is wailing in horror, as if wrestling invisible demons with all the fury he can muster. He's trying to rise from the bed while professional hands press him back down to the sheets. Jack enters the room in a panic. Somehow he thought that if this day ever came, it would come with a calm gentleness. He's glad he left Pat back home under the watchful eye of Lou Capalbo.

"Sid, it's all right. I'm here, son."

He can tell Sid is fighting to speak, to break free of his swollen, sluggish brain in a desperate attempt to communicate. Dr. Clark and two nurses struggle to hold Sid on the bed, trying to be tender.

Finally, the words come a few at a time, wrenching thickly out of Sid's mouth between angry sobs.

"My sister...where is she? She's in the car," he cries out. His moans stretch out and haunt the polished halls of Parkland Memorial, pleading that someone, anyone, understand.

"The baby...I killed my baby sister."

Now Jack understands; Maggie was so often his traveling companion as he toted her around like a sidekick or mascot. They had been inseparable before this.

"I think you need to bring Maggie up here, Jack," Dr. Clark whispers. "It might be the very thing that keeps him here with us."

Jack summons Lou to deliver the baby to the hospital. He worries momentarily if Maggie will be traumatized by Sid's appearance, but he has no choice; he has to reassure his son that she wasn't in the car the day of the crash.

Lou makes fast time getting up to the hospital. He's still wearing his apron and the baby's nightshirt and the left side of her forehead appear to be covered in grape jelly. He hands Maggie to Jack.

"Got here as fast as I could. Jane's watching over Pat at the house," Lou turns his attention on Sid, who is trying to focus on him. "Hey Buddy, you're awake! So good to see you."

A nurse raises the head of the bed slowly, moving Sid to a reclining position. Jack approaches him and gently places Maggie in his son's lap. Dr. Clark clutches his mouth, waiting to see what happens. Sid bends his head down and looks at the baby with his good eye. A distorted smile writhes up his wrecked face, then a primal groan rises from his throat as the onlookers in the room realize this is a laugh. Sid raises his hand as if trying to find something in the dark and holds it swaying over Maggie's head, and then pats her as only a big brother can.

#

Budd Scott appears to be casually glancing around the room looking for a good table. His head tilts back ever so slightly, his arms fold, his eyes narrow. After eighteen seconds he's memorized details an average man would miss being in this place half the night.

A man at a corner table is wearing work boots with two different colored laces.

The hooker two tables from the door has her arm draped over the shoulder of a man who smokes camels and is wearing a wedding ring; he cut himself shaving this morning.

The fire extinguisher on the wall near the stage sits a bit off center. There appears to be a bullet hole through the wall just above it.

A group of four young men lean into their drinks – three beers and a water, no ice. One of them smokes with his left hand, flicking the ashes to the floor, ignoring the ashtray. Eight dollars and seven cents sits in the center of the table.

This attention to detail is so deeply ingrained in Budd now, he can't help it. As a veteran of the Secret Service, he's sure this talent will ride alongside him wherever he goes, no matter the occasion. In a place like this, it could definitely come in handy, but sometimes he'd like to turn it off.

"Budd, c'mon over here," his brother-in-law says to him as he walks toward a table with four empty chairs in the back of the club. Budd follows him.

A few heads turn to acknowledge Jack Dahlstrom. He nods to the man with the hooker as he takes a seat at the table, making sure his back is not to the door.

The Carousel Club is thick with smoke and the music is on fire. On stage under smoky lights a brunette dressed in a skimpy sailor suit dances for the thin crowd. Dahlstrom likes coming in here on Wednesdays when Trudy dances. She smells of fresh air even when the Carousel smells like grime and desperation. He avoids Tuesdays because it's "Precinct Night" and he can't stand to watch Jack Ruby's nervous, greedy hovering near the cops of the Dallas Police Department. He owns the Carousel and is under the impression that people come in here to see him, but the truth of the matter is that they only patronize this place more than others because he gives discounts to certain patrons and brings donuts to the police station every Monday morning. He makes it a point to know everyone.

Ruby enters the club from the back room and stops to take in the crowd. He slips his hands inside the pockets of his slacks and watches Trudy as she adjusts the strap on her low-cut dress while she bats her lashes at the bartender washing a glass. Ruby watches her with a territorial pride. He notices Jack Dahlstrom and makes his way to their table in the back of the lounge.

"Fellas! Good to see you tonight. What'll ya have?"

"Two glasses of scotch, no ice," Dahlstrom says. "Ruby, when are you gonna start serving Drambuie in this dive anyway?"

"When you start paying for your drinks," Ruby says, smiling and resting a welcoming palm on Dahlstrom's shoulder.

"You remember my brother-in-law? Budd Scott, Patricia's brother," Jack says.

"Good to see you again," Ruby says.

Budd nods his head, barely turning his eyes away from Trudy's ass at the bar. Ruby walks off to fetch the drinks, looking nervous, wringing his hands.

"He's a squirrelly son of a bitch," Budd says.

Jack chuckles, watching Ruby at the bar. "He wants to be your friend, Buddy Boy."

"The guy's an asshole. Look at him, he's like a jackal. Nervous, sniveling. I can't see his pupils. Who doesn't have pupils?"

"I can't see your pupils either," Jack says, smiling over the table at him.

"Had 'em removed when I started working for the government, so I don't register emotion."

Dahlstrom laughs out loud. Ruby struts back to their table with two drinks in his hand. He places them down on the table and pulls a handkerchief out of his pocket, wiping his hands dry. He waits for recognition, like a lap dog wanting a pat on the head.

"You get the flowers I sent to the house?" Ruby asks Jack.

"Yes, thank you. Patricia loved them."

"Sid doing okay now? I hear he's back at home."

"He's recovering nicely. Patricia is working with him every day. He's getting better all the time." Dahlstrom gives Ruby a polite nod and a look that tells him he's ready to stop talking about his son, the accident.

"Horrible thing, drunks," Ruby says, turning to watch the hooker whispering secrets in her customer's ear.

"You hear from Candy Barr lately?" Dahlstrom asks him, changing the subject.

Ruby brightens. "She'll be up here in a couple of days. A shame she can't work; girl has such talent, but I s'pose she's happy. Says she's living the clean life."

He lays a hand on Budd's shoulder and says, "Fellas, I gotta go see about a delivery. Be back in a minute." Budd glares at the hand. Ruby removes it quickly and heads toward the bar.

"Be his pal, Budd. He likes men of your caliber." Jack says.

"He's an asshole." Budd takes a large slug from his glass.

"He used to do hits for the guys up in Chicago, Detroit sometimes. He likes to think of himself as retired, but he's still in as thick as he used to be. Now he just kisses police ass and pays them off so he can do business without being bothered too much. He's not so bad really," Jack says.

"No, not for a prick, he's not," Budd swallows another sip of scotch, "Candy Barr was Ruby's headliner. He'll go to pieces without her," Budd says.

"He misses that girl, but Judge's orders – no dancing. She's being a homemaker and raising her kids, I think."

"Does she wear pasties when she's vacuuming?"

"I believe she does, Budd. I believe she does."

Candy Barr said she'd been set up by the cops for the marijuana charge that landed her some time in Huntsville Prison. Jack Dahlstrom knows her fairly well, almost as well as he'd like to know his wife, but Patricia lost her mind when Sid was hit by the drunk driver and lay in his coma, so they haven't been intimate in a damned long time. She'd started drinking too much and flying into hysterics with no warning. Jack had always thought of her as having deep reserves of strength and stoicism, but with the accident came an avalanche of crazy that Jack wasn't equipped to deal with. He had too much going on at the time: a teenage daughter, Jane; a one year old, Maggie, still in diapers; Sid's coma and trips back and forth to Parkland Memorial to check on his condition, and all the while Patricia becoming increasingly unhinged. Eventually he called in some assistance. He also fashioned a belt system to tie her down to the bed, just to stop her from clawing at her own face and ripping her red hair out of her head.

He is exhausted. To top it all off, he's been dealing with the arrival of the President in a couple of days and a lot of meetings with his associates. They're all worked up, which is not how these men usually operate. For the most part, they are cool and calm, especially in times of upheaval. But this is big. Kennedy has taken a wrong turn and pissed everyone off – the CIA and Sam Giancana, and the other mob bosses. That's the thing with politicians: you get them elected and then their own agenda becomes more important than the promises they made to the men who got them there in the first place.

Jack knows that Kennedy wouldn't have had a chance at being elected had it not been for the president's father, Joe Kennedy, an old time bootlegger and friend of Al Capone, asking Giancana for a favor. Sam has a lot of persuasive clout and when he wants something taken care of, it gets taken care of and quickly. It was Joe Kennedy who made all the promises on behalf of his son, and Sam had expected his old friend to make sure the President tightened the collar on his insidious little brother, Bobby, and demand that the Attorney General kill the Organized Crime Program and leave things as they should be. Things are screwed up in Cuba – Castro kicked the casinos out and millions of the organization's dollars have gone down the toilet because of it. JFK was behind it in his attempt to restore relations with Cuba while bringing financial strain to certain mob boss casino owners at the same time – which pisses Sam and the others off even further. Jack longs for it all to end. And it will end...in two short days. In the meantime, he's worried about keeping his family away from downtown on the day JFK is due to arrive. It would be too dangerous for them to be anywhere in the area. He plans on visiting the high school to make sure Jane is made to sit in her classroom while the rest of the school is let out to watch the motorcade come through. Baby Maggie, Sid, and Patricia will be less of a problem. Sid is in no shape to go anywhere and Patricia should be home juggling caring for him and the baby.

"Oh, Jesus, here he comes again," Budd says, glaring into his glass.

Ruby is making his way to their table. Dahlstrom slips a hand inside his suit coat and pulls out an envelope. He waves a finger to Ruby to hurry it up.

"I need you to take this down to City Hall in the morning. We had a logistics problem," Jack tells Ruby.

Ruby turns the sealed envelope over in his hands and eyes the flap.

"Don't open it and don't get all nerved up now. Just give it to them and tell them things have been switched around. Take it in the morning."

Ruby nods, tucks the envelope into his pants pocket, and walks away.

"I'm tellin ya...that guy's an asshole," Budd says, monitoring Ruby moving through the smoky club.

Dahlstrom tilts back the rest of his scotch. He has doubts as to whether this will all go down as planned. It's a big hit, the largest to date, and there's not a doubt in his mind or the minds of everyone else he knows that it needs to happen. The thing is, no one actually enjoys a hit. Not really. At least the contents of the envelope will make it go more smoothly.

Jack knows this operation will not only make him rich – the millionaire and Jaguar sort of rich – but will very likely change the world altogether. He likes being part of making history, even if the circumstances are somewhat unappetizing.

District Attorney Henry Wade appears in front of their table, a smirk on his face. Jack and Budd raise their eyes to meet his. Henry has the demeanor of a bulldog; he always looks as if he's just about to take a chunk out of a person's neck. He's wearing a good suit, his tie is loosened after a long day in court. He looks like he could use a belt of whiskey. Wade pulls a fat cigar from the inside of his coat and places it in his mouth without lighting it, scowling at Jack and Budd.

"Dahlstrom. Drinking with government men again, I see. Think that's wise? Considering their lack of scruples?" Henry says, clenching down hard on the cigar. He glares at Budd Scott.

"I have no choice. The guy's my wife's brother. I'm stuck with him now," Jack says.

Henry harrumphs as Budd rises from his chair and stands close to him. They size each other up for a second, then Budd grabs him by the scruff of the neck and pulls him in close.

"Wade, you old son of a bitch, how are you?"

Henry wraps his arms around Budd in a gruff manner, tilting his head back to protect his cigar from Budd's shoulder.

"I'm good, Budd. What about you? You in town for any special occasion or are you just here to fund Ruby's dynasty?"

"I'm not funding anyone, especially that fuck. Anyway, I don't have any money; you know who I work for," Budd says.

"Here, take a seat Wade," Dahlstrom says, pulling a chair from the table. "You look like shit. When's the last time you slept?"

"1951, I believe it was." Henry takes the seat and turns in his chair. "Who's waiting tables tonight?"

"Ruby will be over here in a minute, I'm sure," Budd says, returning to his seat. "He's got a bat's sonar, can tell when someone comes in that he thinks he needs to impress. Just watch, he'll come scurrying over here any – oh look, here he comes now."

Jack snickers as Ruby actually does scurry in their direction through the thickening crowd of patrons.

A burlesque beat crackles through the club. A girl wearing a magician's cape and high heels comes out on stage.

"How's Sid doing?" Wade asks Jack.

"Coming along slowly. Think it's gonna take a while."

The accident is always a conversation stopper but everyone always has to ask. Jack wishes he could turn back time and stop Sid from getting in the car, wishes he had some kind of sixth sense about things like this. The drunk driver had gone into hiding once he learned who the victim's father was. He didn't leave Dallas though; he'd been hunkering down in a variety of seedy motels off the Interstate for weeks. Henry Wade had tracked him down, then had him watched for a few days. The guy only came out to walk two doors down to a liquor store and then promptly returned to Room 27 to sit in the dark and worry. That is, until Wade called Jack and told him where to find the bastard.

Lou Capalbo had enlisted the help of a friend from Brooklyn, a young kid named Jimmy Bruno, who was sure footed and lacked sentimentality when it came to killing, especially killing drunks. His father had been a brutal alcoholic himself and had spent years going after the backs of Jimmy's legs with a pipe and burning his wife with his Zippo lighter when dinner was late. His upbringing had made him perfect for his line of work.

Jack had wanted to do the job himself, wanted to watch the fear in the man's eyes as his life leaked out onto the cheap wall-to-wall carpeting of Room 27, but Lou had advised against it. When it came to circumstances that involved family and emotional investment, it was always better to let someone else do the dirty work. Jack reluctantly agreed. He didn't need to be seen beating the guy to death and wind up in another legal battle or in jail. His fragile wife couldn't have handled another wave of grief or worry. He was sure a strong wind would be enough to provoke her to wriggle out of her restraints, walk to the kitchen, take a butcher knife from the drawer by the sink, and plunge it into her own temple. So he let Lou take care of the whole thing, although he insisted on watching. He wanting to make sure no family ever had to suffer pain like this again by the hands of this asshole.

On the day, Jack and Lou sat waiting in the front seat of Lou's rental car while Jimmy did his thing in the back seat. He was a good kid, a tough Italian from the old neighborhood with a surprisingly calm disposition. He'd been respectful and polite when he'd asked Jack how he'd like the situation taken care of.

"What are my choices?" Jack had asked.

"Bullet in the head, or you can start with bullets in the feet and work your way up slowly. Set him on fire. Take him for a ride to the outskirts of town and chain him to the back of the car and drag him, but that takes a lot of space. Not sure you wanna go that route. Drowning. Breaking his neck. Hang him upside down from a roof for a while before letting go. Really, it's up to you. I'd recommended getting him early in the morning, when he's hungover and hating life. That way, the last thing he considers is that maybe the drinking life wasn't all it was cracked up to be."

Jack tapped his chin while he considered his options, "He likes drinking so much, let's serve him one final drink."

So Jimmy sat in the back seat of the rental car the next day, in the early morning hours, putting the Molotov cocktail together with care and precision. When it was time, and the flat horizon was turning the Dallas sky the color of a ripe peach, Jimmy opened the back door and casually made his way to the window of Room 27. Lou glanced over at Jack in the passenger seat and nodded with a wink, assuring him that this was the way to go. Take care of things yourself, no need to wait for the justice system. Jack felt his heart beat speed up slightly. He'd long since lost any shred of compassion he might have had for the pathetic bastard. Jimmy took his lighter from his pocket and lit the rag sticking out from the neck of the bottle. He lunged back into a pitcher's stance and hurled the cocktail through the cheap glass window. Then he pulled his gun from his shoulder strap and held it down at his side. Through the parting of the curtains, Jack saw a fast inferno rising inside the room. Jimmy stood calmly waiting for his cue. Jack saw the outline of a person rising from the bed, flailing arms and bending wildly back and forth at the waist, fire clinging greedily to most of his body already. He was amazed at how quickly the fire consumed him. The curtains caught fire as Jimmy sauntered back to the rental car. Jack and Lou kept an eye on the motel and the parking lot until Jimmy opened the back door of the car and slid into the seat, slicking his black hair back with his hands.

"What about we go get some breakfast, huh? I need to eat," Jimmy said.

Lou put the car in gear and they headed out onto Interstate 35 in search of an open diner.

CHAPTER THIRTEEN

In Which Dinner is Nearly Ruined by a Crouton,

Greenwich, Connecticut, 1974

Mom reminds me to stomp the snow and slush off my boots before we enter the front door, so I do. We've just come from Caldor's at the edge of town to return some Christmas gifts that didn't work out and I'm glad to be back home and away from the senseless rule: *If you ask for it, you can't have it.* Never will I understand this logic of hers. If I don't point out what I want from Caldor's, then how will she know I want it? It's very much like the warning she likes to sling at me when I've weighed my options carefully before embarking on a big adventure and have decided that yes, I'm about to have a really good time: *Be careful, there. You're laughing now Maggie, but you'll be crying later.* What possible help could this be to a kid? I should understand her by now; I'll be thirteen in six months – I've had plenty of time. But I don't.

So right in the middle of thinking I'm glad to be back home, coming through the door, smelling the comforting scent of our Christmas tree which is standing near the fireplace, looking a bit lonesome now with its tree skirt empty except for a few scraps of wrapping and an abandoned red ribbon curled up beneath it, I think that New Year's Eve is the worst possible time to be a Christmas tree – no preening; no more oohing and aahing going on; no more perfectly wrapped gifts crowded and stacked around its base in nearly maddening anticipation; and more often than not, someone always forgets to turn on the lights after Christmas, leaving it to look like a large, hulking form propped up in the corner with some crap hanging from it. And soon, the only attention it will get will be someone bitching about its mere existence and "all the damned needles are stuck in the carpet and they've ruined the vacuum again, Jack!"

In trying to forget the post-Christmas depression that's here, I'm immediately reminded why I'm glad to be back home when I see, sitting peacefully in her wheelchair, next to the old tree, my Grandma, Edna Scott. She arrived last night by plane from Minnesota, telling me she has packages in her suitcase that she still has to wrap and distribute, so Christmas is not as completely over as I'd thought.

I run to my Grandma, bend down and hug her, wrapping my mittens around her tightly. Her white hair, combed neatly into a bun smells like freshly baked bread and now, two seconds later, the last lingering fragments of Christmas shatter and fall to the ground like ducks being shot from the sky by hillbillies covered in leaves. The reason for this has just cleared its throat and is sitting in the other chair we keep in the corner on the other side of the fireplace.

Virginia Coopersmith Vanderoth. Extra large hands clasped so seriously in her lap; thick ankles tucked into black snow boots with fur trim (unusually fancy for VCV); horn-rimmed glasses. I let out an audible sigh. Nothing good ever came from a visit with VCV – nothing except my geisha, of course. Other than that one Japanese fluke it has been endless weekly piano lessons; her ferocious black mongrel dog (dead or alive, I'm still afraid of it); the arm flab; those two dead sisters of hers; her owlish splash into Milbrook Lake and I could go on if I had to, but there's no use in continuing the list in my head because I'm sure she's come here with some sort of diabolical plan to add more to the list. I nod a meek greeting towards her while Grandma wraps a comforting arm around my waist.

"Virginia!" my mother addresses her, smiling, "I'm sorry, were we expecting you? Maggie and I decided to run some errands in town while Mom took a nap."

"No! No! You weren't expecting me at all. I just walked over to deliver that literature I promised you," VCV says, waving a large envelope in the air with her giant hand.

"Oh, thank you very much. I'll look it over tonight with Jack. Can I make you a cup of tea, then? Mom? Would you like some tea?"

"Tea would be nice, Pattie," Grandma says, squeezing me a bit tighter.

"No, thank you," VCV says, standing up, fishing a pair of gloves from her coat pocket and snapping them open, "I have a million things to do this afternoon – preparing for a gallery opening in Manhattan this evening. Have to catch the New Haven by six."

Mom kisses VCV on the cheek as she exits our house and says, "Virginia, what about those fantastic boots? New?"

"Oh! Yes! Treated myself, you know. Fox trimming! It wouldn't do, wearing my husband's old galoshes to all the events I have to attend this season."

I eye her fur trimmed boots and that familiar old feeling of relief dumps over me as she leaves, just the way it does when Dr. O removes the alligator clip from around my neck. Fox fur. Vanderoth's gone Hollywood. I'm disgusted.

VCV waves her gloved hand at my Grandma and me and turns to go, hooting something I can't make out all the way down the slate walkway. Mom closes the door and sighs, smiling at me. Grandma gives me another squeeze and whispers, "We just need to say a prayer for those who unsettle us, my dear. Remember that. They need it the most."

I follow my mother into the kitchen and sit at the table, waiting for the tea to be ready so I can deliver it to Grandma. VCV's envelope sits on the table in front of me. The large print on the front reads GREENWICH ACADEMY. I say nothing about this because Mom has taught me that a lot of things just simply aren't my business and this is probably one of them. I know of this Academy and secretly hope that they're thinking of sending me there one day – with its grand buildings set up like a college campus; its large duck pond which is swept clean by the long, draping branches of weeping willows; its students who get to wear the prestigious, dark green wool shirts with corresponding cashmere cardigans. Attending that school would make me feel much more grown up than my stinky old public school ever could with its dirty hallways; noisy, crowded lunchroom filled with mayhem and the constant threat that some bully is about to make fun of me or rob me of my bologna sandwich. I'm excited, yet still unsettled, so I decide it's okay for me to say a silent prayer for myself as Mom pours Grandma's tea into a cup and gingerly hands it to me to deliver.

    Since Dad's not home yet, Mom is the one who pokes the glowing logs around in the fireplace, sending sparks up the flue. Then she carefully adds a fresh log and pulls the metal screen curtain closed so Grandma doesn't catch on fire in her wheelchair. I drag the rocking chair over to sit close to Grandma, thinking about the envelope on the kitchen table. She sips her tea quietly and I can see her shoulders drop a bit as she swallows the calm. I watch her hands wrap around the warm cup and remember my mother saying those hands held healing secrets and could bring things back from the dead. If these hands were gigantic and belonged to VCV, this would creep me out but because they're Grandma's hands it feels like something magical.
    As if knowing what I'm thinking about, she lowers her cup, smiles at me and says, "There's life there, in that fire, Maggie. It's one of the elements given to us by God. That's why people stare into the flames – we're mystified by the mere sight of it and we must know, somehow, that there's magic there."

#

The fire has died down, making Grandma chilly so I help her slowly down the stairs on fragile footing and into the den while Mom relocates the wheelchair to a sunny spot by the large picture window that overlooks the lake.

"Mag, go upstairs to the guest room and get Grandma's blanket, please. The blue and green one," Mom says.

I race through the living room, turn sharply and then head up the staircase.

"And my Bible, please, dear," Grandma adds.

Taking three steps at a time, my speed is too much for me to keep up with, so I allow my weight to propel me forward, letting my hands land on the carpet and I scramble upstairs on all fours.

"And her Bible!" Mom yells, breaking one of her own rules – knowing I'm probably already near the top of the staircase, so yelling is now required and permissible indoors.

By the time I retrieve the blanket and the Bible – which looks old enough for Jesus himself to have handed it to Grandma fresh off the presses – Mom has taken a seat on the arm of the sofa and is looking out over the snowy back yard and frozen lake. She's holding her mother's hand and I feel I'm intruding on a very rare and private moment between mother and daughter, especially since I know my mother has issues with being touched, so this must mean something. I stop at the top of the den stairs and watch their backs in their silent state of connection. If I had a camera, I would take a picture of this serene moment – of the icicles hanging from the gutters above the large window; the leafless trees, looking like giant candelabras covered generously in powered sugar; my island, far out in the middle of the frozen lake, waiting for spring and for me.

Since this feels like one of those moments that I'm not supposed to interrupt, I stay behind them, up in our living room, behind the den doors in my eavesdropping place, waiting for the right time to enter. They are so still, as if suspended in time and the thought occurs to me that this could be the last time they will quietly sit together, looking out over the blanketed world, because Grandma is so very old and feels she's "stayed too long at the fair", as Mom puts it. So I stay where I am. It's so quiet I can hear my own heart beating.

Mr. Brinkley skates in front of our property. I can tell it's him, even from this high up, because of his pale green hat with the pom pom on top and matching scarf and because of his dog, Tim, who's chasing after him on the ice. They have broken the spell and my grandmother speaks.

"You're in trouble, my dear," she softly tells my mother.

"Trouble? What do you mean, Mom?"

"Pattie, it's Jack. He's changed. Your house has changed."

Mom sighs, looking out over the scene, as if she knows what Grandma is saying is true.

"There's a darkness here that wasn't here when you first came to Greenwich. I'm worried about you and Maggie."

"I know things seem different, Mom. Jack is never here and when he is, he's so preoccupied with business. We don't have a lot of fun anymore, that's for sure."

"That's not all of it, Patricia. It's his friends – those men – theirs is the work of the devil and it will bring dire consequences to you and your family. I promise you this."

"Well," Mom says, letting go of Grandma's hand and smoothing her hair away from her forehead, "what do you propose I do about that? You know he doesn't listen to me – well, to anyone, for that matter. He hasn't always been the most discerning when it comes to making friends, as you know."

"You, my dear, have married a peacock who thinks he's invincible. 'Like a muddied spring or a polluted fountain is a righteous man who gives way before the wicked.' Think the proverb over, Patricia. Please."

"I will, Mom. Please don't worry yourself about him anymore. We're going to have a great New Year's Eve tomorrow night and we're going to have fun," Mom says, trying to change the subject.

"I know it's none of my business, dear, but it's a mother's prerogative and her duty to warn her child to take cover when a storm is coming," Grandma says, reaching for Mom's hand and pulling it onto her lap.

"Well, I hope you're wrong, Mom."

"I do too, Pattie. I do too."

My mother turns to look at her mother and I can see her brow is worrying up into creases. She notices me standing behind the door, holding the blanket and Bible and she exchanges her furrows for a smile, so that, I assume, I don't notice the storm coming too.

"Oh, here's Maggie, Mom," she says, waving me over.

I deliver the blanket to Grandma's lap while Mom tucks it into each side of the wheelchair. I hand the Bible to Grandma as ceremoniously as possible, in my own version of trying to change the subject and she accepts it with a low bow of her head, smiling. My mother stands up, smoothes her pant legs with her palms and heads to the kitchen to check on some Hors d'oeuvres she's making for the party.

I take Mom's seat on the arm of the sofa beside my grandmother. She opens her Bible, fishes her reading glasses out of the bag that hangs on the side of her wheelchair, unfolds them, puts them on and gently turns the pages until she reaches her literary destination.

"An eye for an eye," she whispers into the Bible, pausing momentarily, "wound for a wound, stripe for a stripe."

She bows her head, closing her Bible and her eyes at the same time. Her shoulders drop and I can tell she's found the comfort she was looking for. I look out at the beautiful winter scene below us and wonder about *the storm coming*; the *work of the devil*; my *invincible* father.

Just as I'm attempting to manage these new things to

worry about, the front door flings open and a cold blast of air whips itself into the living room, down the steps and into the den, hitting the back of my neck. The peacock is home.

"God Damnit, it's cold out there!" Dad yells into the empty living room.

Grandma opens her eyes, sighs loudly and opens her Bible again.

#

It's snowing tonight and falling in large, festive chunks on the driveway. I watch headlights fanning out over our driveway through my lookout window, trying to make out who it is that's made it to the party first. I like that I no longer have to stand on my tiptoes to see out this window. My toes, when balancing on them, used to feel as if they'd set themselves on fire when I was small and staying out of the way was my only job.

It's a black car. It slowly pulls up, stops and sits with the engine running. Another car pulls up behind it and parks softly on the fresh snow. I can tell by the shape that this is Jimmy's Cadillac and I get excited. His headlights dim and both doors in front open at the same time, illuminating the interior. Jimmy and Lou step out. The first car is still idling, lights still on, plumes of exhaust sending up smoke signals – it must be Paul Castellano, waiting for the end of a song. Maybe Carlo is with him in the back seat, quietly wishing he'd turn the opera down.

"Mag, come in here," Mom calls from behind me, "I need your help in the kitchen, please."

She looks stunning in her false eye lashes, bright red lipstick and gold evening gown with large silver, sparkling swirls running wildly through the shimmering material, like a fireworks show. Gold bracelets jingle as she tries to hurry me with a wave.

Grandma is wheeled up to the kitchen table, placing cheese balls stuffed with green olives onto a baking sheet as I enter the room. She's dolled up too, well, as dolled up as my Grandma will tolerate, anyway. She's wearing the creamy, lavender cashmere sweater and black velvet skirt Mom and I picked out for her at Bloomingdale's after the Thanksgiving parade had ended. Her outfit makes her look more glamorous than I'm sure she's comfortable with as she's not too keen on vanity and makes it known by quoting the Bible if anyone stays in the bathroom too long. I notice her everyday terry cloth slippers resting on the footrests of the wheelchair beneath her skirt. I guess she's wearing those to even things out.

I'm wearing a new black velvet dress, with, I'm sorry to say, black tights, which are bound up and wrapped around my legs in some sort of diagonally torturous fashion because I put them on too quickly and most likely, backwards. I'm too busy now to correct the situation.

Mom hands me a plate of cheese and crackers and instructs me to take it to the den and place it on the bar. When I return to the kitchen, she's gone. Grandma pats the empty chair next to her, inviting me to sit.

"I have something for you. Remember the package I told you I brought with me?"

I nod at her, suddenly a little giddy. She reaches under her blanket, pulls out a small clump of white tissue paper, tied with a red length of thick yarn and hands it to me. It's very light in my hand. I pull on the yarn to untie the bow slowly to make the final remnants of Christmas last just a second longer. The tissue opens like a blooming flower in my palm, revealing a cream colored brooch the size of a prune.

"It was my mother's, dear," Grandma says, touching it with her index finger, "Her name was Sarah Hughes. It's ivory."

I lift the feather-light brooch from the tissue. It's intricately carved in the shape of an oval. An open flower sits in the middle surrounded by delicate flourishes and carved all the way through, so that if someone put it up close to their eye, they'd be able to see through the spaces between the carvings – like looking through the bars of a tiny and beautiful ivory prison cell.

"Thank you," I whisper, only because this feels like an important moment where whispering is required, like entering the New York Public Library.

I've never been given a piece of jewelry before and know nothing of this Sarah Hughes except that I've heard my mother mention her name a couple of times when she's taken me and my father on grave rubbing expeditions through New England.

Grave rubbing is, not surprisingly, just as creepy as it sounds. I'm in charge of taping the rice paper to the face of the head stone – nice and flat. Mom, wearing a wide brimmed sun hat to protect her freckles, kneels down on top of the grave and takes one of her three large crayon bricks (green, black or maroon, depending on her mood) out of her grave rubbing tote and gently, patiently rubs the tomb stone until the epitaph rises up and onto the rice paper. She's in charge of all that. Dad is in charge of standing a safe distance away and slapping the back of his neck saying, "For Christ's sake, Patricia! When are you going to be done? Theses God damned mosquitoes are eating me alive!" and sometimes adds, "Why can't you take up mountain climbing or golf lessons or some other God damned thing that doesn't involve me? This is one pain-in-the-ass hobby you've got here." And then he looks at me and rolls his eyes.

Back in the old days, when they were trying witches and the world was crazier and they had no electricity, they would sometimes put more than just the vital information on the grave marker, such as, *Bartholomew Winstead ~ Loving Husband and Father ~ 1865-1904*. Sometimes they'd include the details of the person's death: *Elton McNabb ~ Died in prison while serving 7 years for horse thievery ~ April 5, 1694* or once, *Beatrice Dunn ~ Stabbed in the head by her husband, Hubert Dunn, for committing adultery ~ 1636-1656*. I've even seen tomb stones with whole groups of people listed and underneath the list of names, simply etched in all caps, *HANGED,* as if they just dug a pit and flung dead guys into it to save time. It's hard to watch Mom kneeling directly on top of the graves but she's fascinated by this hobby and says she plans to frame each and every rubbing to hang in the dining room so we can see them when we eat.

So, this is where I've heard the name Sarah Hughes, as we search through New England cemeteries for Mom's dead ancestors. Creepy, yes, but much better than piano lessons or going to summer camp with people I don't know, so I don't complain.

"Your Great Grandmother was an extraordinary woman, Maggie. A pioneer, really. Brave as you can imagine and she was very much like you are, my dear. She was an adventurer."

This perks me up, falling into the category of adventurer. She takes the brooch from me and pins it to my dress near the collar. I place my fingers over it to make sure it's secure.

"My mother, Sarah, travelled – all alone, mind you, which was a very unusual thing for a woman in those – ,"

Mom hurries into the kitchen and opens the refrigerator door. She's fishing around in one of the drawers.

"You talking about Grandma Hughes, Mom?"

"We certainly are."

"Didn't she befriend the Indians during the massacres somehow?"

"Yes, she did, in fact."

"Didn't she ride on the train that carried Lincoln's body?"

This statement makes my skin prickle a little and I give Grandma a worried look.

"She certainly did, Pattie. We were just getting to that," she winks at me.

"Well, c'mon, Maggie, I need you to carry some ice to the den. You can visit with Grandma later," and with that, obviously not knowing how important this conversation was to me, Mom closes the fridge door, grabs the ice bucket from the counter and waits for me to come to the freezer with one eye brow raised.

I suspect this interruption will freeze the Sarah Hughes story in time and no ending (or middle, for that matter) will ever materialize because I'll forget to ask for the rest of the story and Grandma will die, taking the story with her. Then, years from now, when I'm trying to remember, I will only have a vague image of my great grandmother sitting on a train seat next to Lincoln's casket (and maybe by that time, as the story gains a ridiculous momentum in my head, her button-up boots are splattered with the President's blood because she was at the theater with Abe and his wife – maybe she was having an affair with Abe and that's why she escorted his casket to the plains – she snuck onto the train as it chugged out of the station because she just couldn't bring herself to leave his side) and then possibly another image of her stepping out of a cabin on some lonesome prairie in a long skirt, same blood-splattered boots on, carrying a basket of bran muffins out to the Cherokee Nation. And I won't understand why this is all I can muster. Thanks Mom.

#

We still have two hours to go before the ball drops and our house is already more crowded than I've ever seen it. Even so, the front door keeps opening with new people: women wrapped in diamonds and mink; men polished up in expensive suits and tuxedos. Some are hauling in cases of champagne; some have those silly paper New Year's hats and extremely bloodshot eyes – sure signs this isn't the first party they've hit tonight. This is a mad house.

I'm glad I took my seat on the stairs when I did. From the fifth step, I can clearly see the front door and my lookout window at the same time; will be able to hear Grandma (who went to bed thirty minutes ago to avoid the crowd and read her Bible) call from her room at the top of the stairs if she needs me and I've somehow – by sheer geographical luck, maybe – been assigned the job of coat check girl just like the girl who works at

Patsy's Restaurant (the one Dad calls a Tomato when Mom's out of earshot). A fresh fur or cashmere coat is launched over the crowd in my direction with each new guest and I catch it, scramble up the stairs, toss it on Mom's bed and I return to my perch before somebody decides it looks like a good place to sit. Being in charge of coats just might buy me a ticket to stay up until 1975 is rung in. Each time that door opens a fresh blast of cold, refreshing air hits me and everyone turns their attention towards the entrance to see who's arriving and welcoming cheers usher them deeper into the house. The volume of the cheers is in direct proportion to the popularity of the arriving person.

Lou has been in charge of music tonight and there's been a lot of Frank Sinatra and Dean Martin filling the already full house. VCV hasn't shown up, Carlo never materialized from the back of Paul's car and no family members besides Grandma are here. Even with all those folks missing, this house is packed and the volume swells.

My mother's laugh cuts through the party. She's standing by Lou's wife, Ruthie, who is wearing a deep red evening gown. I wonder when she got here and how she got by me and also why Lou keeps her at home so much. She has a spotted fur stole draped over one shoulder. It looks like something Wilma Flintstone would wear. Mom laughs again and it makes me smile.

A blast of cold rushes into the house and for some reason, this wind lacks the refreshing qualities of previous winds wrapping around my legs – this one feels insulting, different. The noise level quiets momentarily while guests survey the entrance and then a smattering of cheers – much more subdued than previous cheers, but luckily, whoever is walking through our door won't have anything to compare it to and hopefully won't be offended by the obviously unpopular vote that's just been handed down. From my step, I can see two very handsome, tall men – one is wearing a city hat and the other has thick, luscious dark hair and obviously doesn't see the need for a hat. The one with the hat looks familiar and like the sort of man who should be sitting behind a news desk or tanning himself at a café on Rodeo Drive or Hollywood Boulevard. Maybe I've seen him on TV. I stand to get a better look at these newcomers.

Panic overtakes me for a moment and I try to decide what to do and then I realize I'm fairly helpless on my step as it's too crowded to go anywhere even if I needed to, so I scan the room for possible trouble. Maybe this was the storm Grandma felt coming. I search for my father to see if he's realized what's going on at our front door. I don't see him. I look at my mother on the other side of the house – still talking with Ruthie, smiling, looking stunning and gracious, and then, turning her head towards the door in an almost slow-motion-y kind of way (or maybe that's just how it's happening in my head because I'm freaking out a little bit), her smile seems slapped from her face by some rude and invisible force. Mom's eyes narrow and she looks over her shoulder, turning her attention to the fireplace. I follow her gaze and find my father leaning on the mantle with a scotch in his hand, chatting up some neighbors. Dad doesn't seem to be aware of the front door or our most recent arrival. He places his glass on the mantle and lights a cigarette, nodding in agreement with something a neighbor is saying. Mom returns to her conversation with Ruthie, keeping a tentative eye on the weather. The incoming storm is all cashmere, cleavage, eyelashes and curves. Beth Gilleys is here.

#

Confetti and streamers litter the carpeting and the temperature drops slightly with each exiting guest. Ruthie Capalbo collects lipstick stained martini glasses and empties ashtrays in an attempt to save my mother some work tomorrow. Someone has turned on an extra bright light, ruining the mood by ending the already-nearly-finished party too abruptly – it's like skipping to the very last page of a book when you're half way through the last chapter. Unnecessary.

The end of New Year's Eve isn't sad like the end of Christmas with its naked trees and discarded wrappings. When Christmas is over and the last package opened, it's just over, and unceremoniously over at that. Dad goes upstairs to take a shower, Mom goes to the kitchen to do the dishes in hopes of ruining his shower by using all the hot water and I end up watching someone pack their luggage to be taken to LaGuardia in a shorter period of time than I'm happy with. New Year's Eve – even after the party is over and the carpet is littered with Auld Lang Syne – is a beginning, like springtime. I suppose the difference between the two is hope.

I was certainly doing a lot of hoping near the end of the party. Hoping Dad would ignore Beth Gilleys and her two dates; hoping Mom wouldn't walk gracefully across the party in her evening gown and scratch Beth's eyes out (as I suspect she might be on to them and I'm not sure what to do about it or which parent to be loyal to just yet); hoping Mom would be the gal Dad would kiss at midnight and not mix his women up because of too much scotch; and a great big whopping hope that VCV wouldn't show up in her fur boots and come up with a new and stupid reason for me to go to her house. I won the lottery in terms of those hopes tonight and even got to ring in the new year with the grown ups.

Mom makes eye contact with me and points towards the ceiling, giving me one quick, all-business sort of nod, chin to chest – the exact opposite of the Italian Chin Wave – and I take to the stairs to go to bed.

Wrestling these tights off is much more challenging than I'd imagined and much more freeing when I finally roll them up in a ball and throw them to the floor. Before slinging my party clothes in the same place, I remember and carefully remove the brooch before getting in my pajamas.

Opening the lid of my jewelry box, the tiny ballerina spins slowly as she needs some winding. The music tinks out, notes halting as if gasping for air like a fish just caught and placed on shore. I place the ivory brooch softly, ceremoniously inside. Someday

I'll show Jimmy Bruno that I finally have something worthwhile to keep in it.

#

1975 is already bringing adventure, as I'd hoped, but this adventure will require some courage on my part. I hold very still as the prissy, old woman with dyed jet-black hair holds the green wool skirt up to my body to gauge if it will fit.

My mother sits in the corner of the room, legs crossed at the ankles, hands folded neatly on her lap. She's smiling, so this is good. I need her to be in good spirits today so she can help me feel less shy. On our way here, I wasn't feeling shy at all; I was feeling brave, in fact, possibly like Sarah Hughes might have been – but, of course, I'll never know just how brave Sarah Hughes was because Mom deprived me of the end of that story before Grandma got to finish it – but, during the ride over, as we entered the long driveway and past the majestic maple tree and parked by the stern-looking Administrative Building with its intimidating columns and strictly organized bricks, my courage leaked out of me, onto the pavement and deep into the impressive, pristine grounds as I opened the car door.

I watch students rushing to class – giggling together, waving at each other in their uniforms – through the window as I hold very still. They all seem so happy to be here and I hope some of them become my friends because Mom says I'm becoming *something of a recluse and I need to get out more and socialize.* Nothing that great ever came from getting out more and socializing, from my experience, but I'll give it a go.

An ancient woman with perfectly combed, white hair enters the room. The people milling about, assisting the incoming students with paperwork and uniform fittings, immediately become hushed and more formal – their postures improve right away. Two students rise from their chairs for no reason. She stands in the doorway, hands cupped together and resting against her pale blue, Chanel suit. (I know it's Chanel because Mom makes a big deal out of Chanel when we shop at Loehmann's and because all Chanel looks exactly the same to me – stuffy and thick.) Her posture tells me she runs the joint, as does the change in everyone's demeanor.

My palms are sweating now. This woman makes me nervous and as soon as I notice this, she locks eyes with me and quickly makes a b-line in my direction.

She gives me the once-over, pursing her lips, as if I'm another Chanel suit she's considering adding to her probable collection. Okay, I don't like her. I've decided. And as soon as I think she's about to say something insulting to me, my mother rises from her chair in the corner and introduces herself to this serious woman in an equally serious, but polite manner.

"Patricia Dahlstrom," Mom says, extending her hand, "and my daughter, Maggie."

The ancient woman softens and takes my mother's hand gently, "Mrs. Dahlstrom, so very pleased. I'm Katherine Zierland, Head Mistress of Greenwich Academy," then she turns her attention back to me, "Maggie, I assume you will be one of our new students starting classes in the fall."

I nod and smile, trying to disguise my distaste for her, feeling certain that she knows my palms are sweating and would probably be disappointed if they weren't. I want to get out of here and apparently, so does the black haired woman holding my new skirt, as she silently backs away – as one would back away from a wild animal with a bad reputation – and heads towards the rack of wool skirts and matching blazers hanging by the window.

"Very well, then. I expect to hear good things about you," she curtly says to me, then, turning stiffly towards my mother, "Mrs. Dahlstrom, I think you should be pleased with our new Dean of Middle School, Mrs. Tippens – she's strict, but handles the girls well; they all seem to like her. She'll be contacting you about Orientation and tour of our campus. Have a lovely summer."

"You too," Mom says, watching the Head Mistress turn quickly and precisely on her heel and make her way to the exit to go make someone else uncomfortable.

Exiting the grounds of Greenwich Academy, my mother puts the windows down in the car and smiles over at me in the passenger seat. The spring air carries the fresh scent of beginnings and I lean my head out the window, taking it in.

"The daffodils should be coming up on Putnam Hill soon," Mom says, "I love that hill in the springtime."

This is her two-cocktail smile – the one I can trust – even though she has only had coffee and a piece of toast this morning, and no cocktails that I'm aware of. This smile is a natural one and a rare thing to behold, like Chinese purple carrots or a unicorn. There's also the three-cocktail smile, which is messier, where her eyes turn glassy and that one, I don't trust. Then there's the four-cocktail smile, which is the one where her mouth smiles but her eyes – which will be bloodshot and teary at this point – threaten the recipient in just the right way – the way in which they know they've been threatened but they can't put their finger on exactly how and if they confronted her about it, would be immediately discredited and then promptly villainized, so they keep their mouths shut but suffer from low self-esteem for a very long time afterwards. Anything after the third is just time to get out of the room and find a safe place to be until it's over.

"We'll have to go into the City and buy the rest of your new school clothes. The woman helping us gave me a list. You'll need yellow or green knee socks; sweaters, white blouses, brown Oxford shoes. We have a lot to do."

Mom and I discuss egg salad sandwiches as a possibility for lunch as she slowly navigates through the shady streets of Milbrook and I relish her mood, imagining that it will last at least through our upcoming trip to The City and back home again, which could mean weeks.

We pull up into our driveway and my stomach growls about lunch. Mom slows the car down sooner than she normally does when we notice a large, lone steamer trunk sitting in our driveway in front of the slate stairway that leads up to the front door.

"What in the world?" Mom says, glancing at me as if I should have an explanation for it.

I shrug my shoulders at her. She stops the car and throws it in park.

"How about you hop out and open the garage door for me? Then we'll find out what's going on here." she says.

Hop out? She's got to be kidding. Dad is always telling me to be suspicious of packages left by the door, so I can't imagine just how suspicious I'm supposed to be about a steamer trunk sitting by itself in the driveway. When I don't make a move for the door handle, she glances over at me with her eyebrows raised. This tells me her good mood is about to end if I don't do as she says and I feel as if I'm being sacrificed, and that if we were walking in the woods together and a pack of wolves emerged from the shadows to circle us with heads lowered, she might quickly tuck some lunch meat in my pocket and run in the opposite direction. But, since I'm more afraid of my mother than I am the trunk, I get out.

I make my way slowly around it, eyeing it. It's old, battered and banged up, with stickers slapped randomly on the sides and top that I have no time to read right now, but wish I did, so I'd have some clues. As I reach the garage door, bend down and grab the handle, I look at my mother, safe in her car with the windows now rolled up (and the doors probably securely locked by this point). Heaving the door open makes a racket, as usual – conveniently announcing to any bad guys lurking around, that I'm here now, fully exposed, out in the driveway, precisely in front of the garage. I wait for her to pull the car inside, feeling naked. She's just sitting there.

I jump, startled, as I hear a cough I don't recognize and just as I'm about to make a run for it, a hunched over old man wearing overalls and a newsboy cap shuffles out from the side of the house and I immediately worry that he's been in our back yard, casing the place, or worse, casing my boat. And then the thought occurs to me that he's come here to kill us with something sinister he's tucked safely away in his trunk. My flight instinct that had such power a moment ago – the instinct that made me feel as if I was powered by rocket fuel and could tear off in the direction of VCV's house, leaping over the steamer trunk as I head for the street, run down the path in the woods that runs along the lake, make it to Greenwich Station in under a minute and by the time I got there, would have enough momentum going that I could latch onto the back of a commuter train (as it's racing through town, of course) and easily, effortlessly, cling to it until it pulled into Grand Central, where I would jump off, run past the clock, up to street level and arrive at Jimmy's garage in Midtown where I would live with the goombahs and their mirrors on poles and with the cats that Jimmy saves from winter – well, that power is now gone and has been replaced with paralyzing fear. I literally can't move one muscle in my body. This makes no sense. It's as if some mysterious force is holding me here. Nothing moves other than my heart trying to pound its way out of my chest. I'm going to pass out.

He's looking down at the ground, carefully navigating his path, when he, himself, suddenly startles, seeing Mom's car idling in front of him. He doesn't see me yet, so I stay still (as if I had a choice), trying to make myself invisible.

Mom rolls her window down two inches. The old man smiles and waves at her and then claps his hands loudly, once. Out from the side of the house, a small brownish-black blur races in the old man's direction and sails effortlessly up and onto his shoulder.

Mom looks bewildered when she sees the recognition and delight on my face. Mac lifts his cap in my direction while Babbo Natale takes a small bow on his shoulder.

Afternoon shadows stripe the den carpeting, telling me Dad will be home soon and I can't wait to see his reaction. Mom's mood is even better than before we had a monkey in the house. She and Mac are drinking red wine at the table by the large picture window as Mac tells Mom about their travels, the carnival and something about Mac's sister, Louise and her brain hemorrhage in New Jersey last month. Mr. Natale squats in the middle of the table, eating cashews from a small basket and eyeing me as I take the seat nearest to him.

We've had to leave the trunk in the driveway until Dad gets home because, even with the three of us trying, and the monkey jumping up and down, chattering at the top of the steps as if cheering us on, we couldn't manage to get it anywhere near the front door. I wonder how Mac got it here in the first place.

I watch Mr. Natale's miniature hands selecting cashews, turning them over, examining each one carefully, bringing them up to his mouth and savoring every bite. He has soulful, wise old eyes like my Grandma. This has got to be the very best visitor we've ever had and too bad it's spring break because I'd take him to school regardless of Show N Tell being deemed obsolete by our new teacher and regardless of how much trouble I'd be in at the end of the day. The monkey pauses, looks at me and shows me his teeth.

"Well, you'll have to stay for dinner even if you won't let us put you up for the night."

"We would be delighted, Mrs. Dahlstrom," Mac says, bowing his head softly, "if it's not too much trouble."

"No trouble at all," she says, rising from her chair and heading to the kitchen, "I'll just go check on the pot roast. Mag, come help me, would you?"

Reluctantly, I follow my mother. The monkey taps the top of his head then flips his little hand up in the air, as if he's tipping an invisible hat to me. I enter the kitchen anxious to return to the den. The pot roast's bubbling gravy wraps its scent around me like a familiar and savory cloak, making my anxiousness simmer as Mom returns the cover to the roasting pot and closes the oven door.

"I don't think he has any money, Maggie, or anywhere to go," Mom says in a hushed tone, slipping her oven mitts off and setting them on the counter, "and I'd like you to be a little more selective when it comes to giving our address out in the future."

"But he was going to mail an autographed picture of Mr. Natale to me," my voice comes out much more whiny than I'd planned.

"I'm sure he was, but now he's sitting in our den with no place to go and with a monkey, no less, so we're going to have to figure something out."

Just as guilt starts tapping me on the shoulder, the back door opens, letting a fresh, green-smelling breeze into the kitchen in an attempt to chase away the smell of pot roast.

"Come on in, Paul. Sorry about all those steps, there," Dad says.

"Jack? Why are you using that door? You didn't knock my tomato plants off the railing, I hope," Mom warns.

"Jesus, Patricia, I'm using this door because the front walkway is barricaded by some old trunk, that's why! What the hell is going on here, anyway? Whose trunk is that out there?"

Mom sighs and leans against the counter, glaring at my father. Paul Castellano enters the kitchen looking sullen, as usual. I take a seat at the table, feeling certain this conversation isn't going to be over any time soon and I don't think Mom's finished trying to make me worry about Mac's future.

"Hello, Paul," Mom says, ignoring Dad's question.

Before Paul can acknowledge my mother, Dad pipes up again.

"Patricia, what is that trunk doing in the God damned driveway?"

Dad glances over at me as if he senses some of this is about to be my fault and I feel a bad mood creeping up behind me, trying to sour my afternoon completely and worse than that, Dad doesn't realize that Mom was in one of her rare and wonderful happy moods, which he's now managing to blow to smithereens in a single moment. Paul looks at me too now, with those large, brooding eyes of his; mouth turned downward, standing there like Lurch from the Addams Family. I suddenly find myself wanting to roll my eyes at him. I'm so sick of this guy.

"Jack, keep your voice down. We have company," Mom snips.

Dad's fists rise to rest on his hips, widening his eyes at my mother. He's probably thinking about what he's going to yell next. Paul stands there in his black sports jacket and beige slacks, like some kind of dismal mannequin somebody propped up next to my father. I can't explain my new and down right aggressive distaste for Paul, other than Mom's explanation that when a girl begins to grow older, we exchange the *age of innocence* for the *age of insolence.* If this is what turning thirteen feels like – like something ill-fitting that's about to boil over for no good reason – I'd rather stay twelve. I look down at my hands in my lap, trying to become small so they'll all stop taking turns looking at me. I can't think this way.

Then I hear Mom let out a squeak. I look up to see her covering her mouth, watching the floor behind me. When I turn in my seat I see Babbo Natale standing in the doorway, little fists on his hips, legs bowed, staring at my father in the exact same mimicking position as his. Paul lets out a gasp and the monkey turns his attention on Paul now. Mr. Natale brings his little hands up to his chest, clasps them together and scowls. He sticks his tiny pink tongue out and loudly – even by monkey standards, I guess – delivers to Paul, a very deliberate raspberry. I hear a loud clap coming from the den and the monkey dashes away.

"What in the Hell. Was. That?" Dad demands, looking at me, then my mother.

Paul looks confused. Mom has now buckled on her knees

and is holding her stomach, laughing so hard her eyes are watering and no sound is coming out except for a little wheezing sound every few seconds. She tries to explain and catch her breath at the same time. Dad isn't laughing. I have to get out of here. I return to the den knowing I won't be helping matters if I lose my composure as Mom just has. She should spend more time with Mrs. Zierland so she can learn to keep it together when I need her to.

After only a few minutes, Mom, still wiping the tears from her face, ushers Dad and Paul into the den to formally, calmly introduce Mac and his monkey. Things seem to be going well as soon as Dad gets to the Drambuie behind the bar and starts pouring drinks. Paul takes a seat next to Mac at the table. Mr. Natale perches on Mac's shoulder, carefully watching Paul and making funny little chattering noises. Mom grabs the wine bottle and tops off Mac's glass.

I move to the sofa by the window so Mom and Dad can sit at the table. It's awkward and quiet in here and just as I'm getting really uncomfortable, the front door flies open and Jimmy and Lou fill the doorway. As they come down the steps to the den, I can see Jimmy trying to place the old man sitting next to Paul, as if he's seen so many men with monkeys on their shoulders at our house that it takes a while for him to recall which one he's dealing with. Lou heads directly to the bar, not noticing anything unusual until he's clunked a few cubes of ice into a glass. He surveys the guests at the table, then looks at me, sitting on the sofa with my legs tucked underneath me. A sly smile emerges and he gives me a quick wink. I return the wink. He focuses on pouring the booze into his glass, smiling, shaking his head.

Paul's attention is on the guys so he hasn't noticed that Mr. Natale has nimbly, without making a sound, moved to the back of his chair and is squatting behind him, quietly inspecting the back of Paul's head. Mom notices and bows her head, covering her eyes with her hand, trying not to laugh again. Her shoulders begin to shake.

"Hey Jack," Lou says, "ya know you have a steamer trunk sitting in your driveway? We had to move it out of the way to get Bruno up the stairs. It's over by the garage."

"Yeah, I noticed," Dad says, taking the seat between Mom and Paul.

Mr. Natale balances on his hind legs on the back of Paul's chair and leans over to get a good look at Paul's right ear and then sticks his tiny index finger directly into the ear canal. Paul's head snaps to look at the monkey and swats him away.

"Mr. Natale, please," Mac says, "My apologies, Mr. Castellano. He does that on occasion, but only to people he's very interested in."

The monkey returns to Mac's shoulder and takes a quiet squat, feeling dismissed, I'm sure. He and Paul eye each other. I sense disdain on both parts.

The guys ooh and ahh over the pot roast as Mom sets it on the table. My parents take their usual places at either end; Lou and Paul sit across from Jimmy, Mac and me. Mr. Natale sits in Mac's lap, resting his chin on the table. Paul is scowling at him.

"Mac!" Dad says too loudly, making my mother jump in her seat slightly, "You mentioned you're from the Midwest. Patricia and I were raised in Minnesota, just four blocks away from each other."

"Sounds like a lovely case of fate," Mac says, scooping a potato onto his fork.

"Or the curse of geography, depending on how you look at things," Mom says, winking at Lou.

"He's a capuchin, right?" Jimmy says, pointing his fork at Mr. Natale.

"He is, Mr. Bruno. Formerly with the rodeo circuit, working with a once very famous rodeo clown, in fact."

"Hmm, interesting. I don't know much about the rodeo

circuit," Jimmy says, chewing loudly.

"That's a shock, Mr. Britannica," Lou says, chuckling "you know about everything else. How'd the rodeo slip past ya?"

I watch Jimmy stop chewing long enough to glare across the table at Lou. The monkey chirps a funny sound in Lou's direction as if he's laughing with him. Jimmy gives Mr. Natale a look of warning.

"So, Mac!" Dad says, making Mom jump again.

"Jack! For God's sake! Why are you talking so loudly? We're all right here," Mom snips.

Dad, ignoring my mother, continues, "Lou tells me you all met at the carnival over in Cos Cob. Guess it's back in town again?"

"I'm afraid not, Mr. Dahlstrom. My boss was under the impression that Mr. Natale and I had run out things to offer his enterprise and suggested it might be time for us to retire."

"Well, retirement can be a good thing, Mac. What are your plans now?" Mom says, trying to be cheerful.

"Our initial plan was to be with my sister – God rest her soul – but circumstances changed with her parting, of course. I have an old friend in Harlem. I thought about looking him up after stopping to visit you fine folks in Greenwich, but I can't seem to locate him. He's moved without leaving a forwarding address, so we're a bit, well…adrift, as it were."

Dad looks down the table at my mother with a look that says, *don't even think about inviting this guy and his monkey to live with us* and I hope she ignores him. I can only guess he feels safe giving her this look because he thinks Mom is only on her second glass of vodka. What he doesn't know is that she has a good undercoat of red wine curing beneath the two drinks he poured for her and this two-cocktail smile she's been wearing all through dinner is actually a four-cocktail smile, disguised as a two-cocktail smile, all because we have a monkey at the table that she's grown quite fond of and this smile is riding the coattails of the exceptionally good mood she's been in since this morning's uniform fitting. Dad's teetering on the brink of disaster here. When it comes to reading my mother's emotional stability and using it as a compass on how to proceed, I would think that by this time he should be like an air traffic controller – keenly tuned in to all things around him or like those old crab fishermen who can still steer their ships by the stars. Instead, he reminds me of a big wet dog who has wandered into an elegant party and then stops dead in the middle of it; he splays his front paws, just to get a little traction and then, before anyone can stop him, he begins to shake off, building momentum as he goes, from nose to tail, until every last drop of water is dispersed, drenching everything and everyone around him. And then he wonders why no one is happy he's shown up. Maybe this is what Grandma means when she shakes her head and says, "Pattie, you had fair warning when I told you never to marry your intellectual inferior. I should know; I was married to an idiot – God rest your father's soul – and the only thing that kept me from murdering him in his sleep was the good Lord himself."

I'm counting on this monkey to keep things light. Paul and Lou are glancing from Dad to Mom as if watching a dangerous tennis match. Mr. Natale is staring at my dinner. I don't think the cashews were enough for him, so I lift a crouton from my plate in a sneaky way so no one will notice and I slip it to him under the table. He accepts it in his small, leathery hand and makes a kissing noise at me.

"Well, Mac, we have plenty of room here if you don't feel up to moving on tonight," Mom says, keeping her eyes on my father, provoking him.

"Thank you, Mrs. Dahlstrom. That's very kind of you but we will have to be moving on. We're going to look for work in New York for now and see where that takes us."

"Well, I'm sure Jack can help you with that. He knows a lot of people in The City," Mom says, still staring my father down.

He gives in, probably recognizing that he's miscalculated

the number of cocktails fueling her insistence and says, "I'll see what I can do, Mac," taking a bite of potato and sighing loudly enough for all of us to hear.

"I might be able to help with that, Jack" Jimmy announces with a mouth full of food, holding his knife in the air.

"Yeah? Good," Dad says.

"Yeah. I got a guy. He might even be able to give that monkey somethin to do. Well, as long as he behaves himself," Jimmy turns his attention to Mac, swallowing his food down hard, now pointing his knife at Mac, "He doesn't throw his own shit at people, does he? Monkeys are known to do that to display dominance."

Before Mac can respond Lou pipes up, "Bruno, you should do that when you're doing collections. Ya know, to display your dominance."

Dad laughs. Paul stares at the monkey. Mom gives Mac an apologetic glance. Mr. Natale leaps up on top of the dining table, races over to my mother and stands before her plate on his hind legs, holding the crouton I gave him out to Mom with his left hand as if he's offering it to her in a gesture of friendship. Her face softens. She is clearly in love with him. I like seeing her this way – gentle, sentimental, soft. The monkey pulls back and slaps my mother hard and clean across the face. The sound of the slap hangs in the air over our table. He shows her his teeth quickly and hurries back to Mac's lap.

"Oh, dear. Oh, no. Mrs. Dahlstrom. I am so sorry…" Mac says, voice quivering.

I notice my hand has involuntarily flown up to cover my mouth. Jimmy has dropped his fork. Mom looks downright stunned and her eyes are watering. The room is silent as we all watch a very small, red hand print rising up on Mom's cheek. I'm paralyzed for the second time today. But then the unexpected happens – even more unexpected than a monkey accosting someone during dinner – my mother smiles, still looking confused, but it's a smile just the same and then slowly, like a refreshing rain rumbling in our direction, she begins to laugh and soon she's howling and tossing her head back so that I can see the gold crowns that cover her molars, tears rolling down over the tiny hand print.

"Well, Mr. Natale, I can only assume this means my homemade croutons are not up to par," Mom says, wiping her tears with her napkin.

And with that, the entire table cracks up and I come out of my paralysis, relieved.

We say goodbye in the driveway, well, everyone but Paul, who's busy glaring into a glass of scotch in the den like a big baby. Lou and Jimmy are loading Mac's trunk into the back seat of the Caddy when he asks them to pause so he can get something important out of it. He digs around inside, Mr. Natale balances on his shoulder, peering into the trunk. Mac pulls out a large envelope and walks over to me.

"I believe Mr. Natale promised you this, my dear," Mac says, presenting me with the envelope.

I thank him and open it, not being able to wait. I slide out the 8 X 10 glossy of Mr. Natale wearing a tuxedo and a top hat. He has a serene, angelic smile on his little face, looking like the last monkey on earth that would ever smack someone, and in black magic marker, inscribed in the bottom right corner it reads: *To Maggie, my best girl. Forever your greatest admirer, Mr. Babbo Natale.*

I feel a lump forming in my throat as Mac takes my mother's hand and kisses it.

"Thank you, gracious lady, for your hospitality and kindness."

My mother beams at him and bows her head in a dramatic fashion. The monkey reaches out to Mom from Mac's shoulder and leaps onto her chest, surprising her. He wraps his furry arms around her shoulders and nuzzles his forehead into her neck. Then he pulls back, looking up at her face and gently, sweetly places a soft kiss on her cheek. Now I'm really choked up. I hate all goodbyes – especially sweet ones – and sweet goodbyes as the sun is setting are the worst.

Lou hurries them into the back seat of the car as if he's late for something and closes the door. Mac waves at my parents and me through the window.

"Thanks for taking care of this, Jimmy," Dad says, rocking back on his heels.

"No problem. My guy owes me one. I'll get them sorted out tonight. I kinda like that monkey."

Lou's standing at the locked passenger door, trying the handle, looking impatient.

"Bruno! The door?"

Jimmy ignores him, giving me a hug goodbye.

"And I swear, if your friend, Babbo here, starts slinging shit in the car, I'm gonna shoot you," Lou continues.

"That's Mr. Natale to you, Capalbo. Babbo, by itself, without the *Natale* after it, means *idiot* and I'm a little surprised and disappointed you didn't know that. I thought you were fluent in Italian. Who will I look up to now?" Jimmy teases.

"Oh, I'm fluent alright. Open the friggin door, Babbo."

As we watch Jimmy's taillights leaving our driveway, I catch a glimpse of Mr. Natale in the back window. He lifts his little hand and presses it up against the glass.

CHAPTER FOURTEEN

*In Which Treasured Memories and Coveted Secrets
Are Wrapped in Paper and Packed in Boxes,
Greenwich, Connecticut, 1977*

Ripples on Milbrook Lake are moving south this afternoon. As I lean an elbow on the window frame, I notice years of childhood dust have gathered at the corners around the glass panes. I wish I had noticed it before; I would have cleaned it, would have taken better care of things here in my red room. I no longer have to stand on tiptoes to see my island in the middle of the lake. I haven't had to do that in quite a while.

I won't be taking my boat out on the water again. I can't bear to say goodbye. I'd rather not look back.

My soul sits on my bed with shoulders drooped and head hanging down, surrounded by moving boxes. It's in despair and I do nothing to comfort it.

I try not to think about why I didn't run with the neighborhood kids more often, or play kick the can on autumn nights, or join them when they cleaned out the Gibson's pond every spring. I could have had more fun. I could have walked to the edge of Milbrook every Fourth of July, with a folded blanket and a picnic basket, the way they all did, to find a flat spot with open sky and watch the Greenwich fireworks show, but I didn't do that either. I guess I always thought there would be a better time for all that. But now I think if I had done all those things, this goodbye would be even harder. Maybe the cowering recluse in me had been a good thing.

All of this is my father's fault. He stepped through the front door three weeks ago, called my mother and me to the den, ushered us to the table by the window that looks out over the old dogwood tree, and announced we would be leaving Greenwich because of an opportunity he couldn't afford to pass up. Mom had a cocktail in her hand when this happened. I wish I'd had one myself.

She did her best to argue him out of it.

"Jack, honestly! All our friends are here, and we can't possibly remove Maggie from Greenwich Academy now. She's doing so well. This is our home! You cannot do this to our family again."

My father employed his finely tuned negotiating skills for what seemed a very long and torturous time until finally, my soul rose up from my chair and left the den without so much as a glance back at me. I could hear it going up the staircase, pausing at my old lookout window, before heading up to my room to, I can only assume, start sorting through my things to prepare for a move halfway across country.

I stayed in my chair, feeling the familiar cracked-open feeling that comes from never being in control of things; from always being surprised when a decision has been made that affects your life so entirely; from my soul always needing to leave the room.

I said nothing as Dad continued to persuade my mother to accede to his plans.

Just when Mom seemed to have run out of ammunition and hot tears began to singe my lids, she issued an ultimatum. She raised her glass to her lips and her eyebrows into stubborn, foreboding arches, and told him that if he was determined to destroy our lives, then he would buy her the house of her dreams and that it should have a lake, a good sized piece of land, tennis courts, a two-car garage (three would be better) and an indoor pool. If he could not acquire that sort of house, she and I would not be going with him. Anywhere. And then she said it. She dealt her final card.

"And quite honestly, Jack, I find it unfathomable that you'd consider leaving this place with absolutely no regard for your family, but what surprises me the most is that you would be willing to leave your lover down at 53 Orchard Drive. How will Beth survive without you?"

There it was. She knew. I suddenly felt caught in some devious act myself. Dad's eyes darted at me, searching for traces of betrayal. I felt my face flush even though I was innocent on that count. Mom stayed cool and took another sip of her cocktail.

"I'll *get* you your house, Patricia," Dad hissed, and with that, he rose from the table and stiffly, defiantly went out the front door, slamming it as he made his exit.

I didn't know which terrified me more: leaving my lake, my woods, Dad's friends; being left in Greenwich alone with my mother; or realizing that she knew about Dad and Beth's affair and had kept it under her hat, as a secret stash of ammunition brought out at precisely the right moment, or the worst possibility – that my father might blame me, suspecting I'd seen or heard something during all my years of espionage and that I'd ratted him out. It was as if someone had tossed butcher knives up in the air, over my head and I was waiting to see which one would deliver the fiercest slice. I worried at a consistent 24-hour-a-day clip for nearly a week.

I didn't have to worry for long.

When Dad returned from a five-day house hunting expedition in Minnesota with Lou Capalbo, he handed my mother a brochure with a proud smile. Lou sloughed off his leather shoulder harness, gun nestled in its cradle, and slung it over the chair by the fireplace. The urge to grab the gun, whip it out of its holster, spin it a few times like a gun slinger, point it confidently at my father and threaten to shoot his knee caps off was overwhelming at that moment. Instead, I watched helplessly as my mother switched sides and began batting for Dad's team. No mention of Beth Gilleys whatsoever – from either one of them. I was dumbfounded by his cunning agility in the art of bribery.

Mom's right; Greenwich Academy has been good for me. I like that it's an all-girls College Prep school where the curriculum includes mastering the required curtsy, remembering never to cross my legs at the knee (because apparently that leads to a life of turning tricks), and holding my fork in the British fashion – upside down. Uncle Jim would be proud.

Limousines and the occasional Rolls Royce drop my classmates off in the impressive circular drive with the equally impressive and ancient maple tree standing at its center. I'll be fifteen years old soon and feel a blossoming has occurred inside me and I've made good friends. Friends I can invite over and take to the woods on weekends when my mother is tucked away in her room and my father is out of town or perhaps moving Beth Gilleys' heavy things down the street at 53 Orchard Drive. Things have been looking up. Well, they *had* been looking up.

And then the brochure entered the house and announced a dreadful shift in my universe. The house is called White Oaks and sits on the shore of Sunfish Lake in St. Paul. The house has its own name. Pillars and columns, the lighted tennis court at the edge of a stand of birch trees, and the indoor pool sparkles beneath a sixteen-foot ceiling. It even has a convenient cocktail table set in the shallow end so our swimming guests won't have to make the trip to the edge of the pool for their drinks or the ashtray. All of this sits dead in the center of a glorious nine-acre lot. And if there is any question of its grandeur, Dad would like us to look over the brochure again and read about the private pond near the lake and the three-room guest cabin at its shore. He has described it as a magnificent fortress and assures us it will bring us happiness.

He's employed his negotiating skills on the current owner, gently persuading him to sell. I wonder if the current residents had this brochure lying around or if Dad had it printed up in order to impress my mother further and solidify his position. So now we are packing up our lives. My father has placed a carefully printed *For Sale* sign on my boat because, as he puts it, why go to the trouble of hauling it half way across the country when you're moving to a place that has it all?

I lift my *Winnie The Pooh* book from the shelf and turn it over in my hands. It's worn and tattered like I am at the moment. I gently place it at the bottom of an empty moving box and decide I need an ally to talk this nightmare over so that I won't shatter in two and I head to my mother's room.

She's in her bed with the blanket pulled up to her chest, her head sunken down in her pillows. A damp cloth is folded over her eyes. The door is open and I knock on the door frame, waiting to be granted access onto the cream-colored carpeting. She lifts the cloth and smiles meekly at me, waving me in.

"I had to take a break after going through the attic and coming across some memories that had been tucked away since Dallas. I'd forgotten about those things entirely," her voice sounds weak.

She pats the side of her bed, inviting me to sit beside her. I do, being careful not to land too heavily as the damp cloth is an indicator of a migraine.

"I remember how inconsolable you were when we first arrived here in Greenwich. It was 1963…the moving truck pulled in and the men started to unload our furniture and all the boxes. Jack had you in his arms in the driveway and you craned your neck and peered into the empty trailer with those huge, hopeful eyes and lifted your little palms up and asked, 'Where's everybody?' You'd been expecting all of our Dallas neighbors and friends to walk out of the truck because I'd told you not to worry as we packed up your toys and your books – that everything would arrive in Greenwich safe and sound at our new home. I always regretted not remembering how literal children can be. It seemed to be your first real disappointment."

Mom refolds her cloth and places it on her forehead. Her eyes are puffed up from crying.

"I hadn't known exactly what to expect when we came to New England, but that was a different time when I accepted change more readily, and would follow your father anywhere. Overall, it has been one great adventure. So, I suppose we're on to the next."

I look down at the carpet, feeling myself choke up, knowing she's trying her hardest to give me some hope. I imagine it's not going to be easy for her to return to her childhood home with Grandma gone. We lost her right in the middle of a game of gin rummy. She, according to nurses, was being charitable and had invited my grandmother, Ruth, to play cards with her in the sun room of their nursing home. An hour into the game, Grandma suddenly slumped over in her wheelchair, her cards falling to the laminate floor like leaves in autumn. Three queens, three aces and the four of spades. I guess her patience for Grandmother finally gave out. Dad's mother died five months later in her bed. I'm sure her last breath came out as a sigh and not as a breath at all.

"The winters will be cold there, honey," Mom says softly, "I remember being so small and left alone so often in that horrible basement turned into a make-shift house. Your father's parents owned that place, you know. My mother would go *Out West* for months at a time, leaving me and my siblings to fend for ourselves. I still wonder where it was that Mom went all those times. I hope it was a place that brought her some peace. I'd hate to think we went through all that for nothing."

Mom's eyes begin to water and I snatch a tissue from the box on her night table and hand it to her.

"At the time, I didn't realize just how traumatic all of it was. It was just life. But my father was the real problem," she squeezes her eyes shut against the memory.

"Any time I was down – which was often – he would say,

'Oh, my darling little Pattie – life ain't all ya want, but it's all ya got. So stick a feather in yer arse and 'ave at it!' He was such a bastard."

I feel myself wanting to touch her, hold her hand, but not wanting to break this spell – this very first truthful, adult conversation we've had – I stay quiet.

"Then I met your father – which wasn't so great at first. We were so young then…not even teenagers yet and he and his friends used to hang around at the druggist on the corner and I had to pass them on my way to school in the mornings. I can still feel my sagging stockings and worn winter coat and the way it made my skin itch. Jack's friends made such fun of me for being so obviously poor, cat-calling, snickering, but sometimes he protected me from them – well, as much as he could without losing face, I guess. With a simple wave of his hand, the fellows would quiet, granting me passage. Bernie Botts was one of his friends. He was the cruelest."

Now I'm the one to squeeze my eyes shut at just the mention of his name.

"And I would hug my books close to my heart as if they were my guardians. I loved books so much, Maggie. Much like you always have. Do you remember you used to sleep in your crib surrounded by your books?"

"No," I say, laughing quietly, "surrounded by books?"

"Oh yes. Your books, my books, Jane's high school English book – it didn't matter, as long as you had books in your crib, you'd be alright, but if someone dared put a teddy bear or stuffed animal in there with you, you'd hurl them out and demand to have those books back, calling out, 'No! Book.' It was the oddest thing. But, anyway, yes, books were my only friends as a child. The words were the wings that carried me away to places I couldn't be hurt, where I could live the life I dreamed of."

Her eyes mist up again and she dabs the corners of her eyes with the tissue.

She suddenly looks so small in her large bed, like a frightened child. An unwelcome memory creeps up and nestles in my mind. Mom, sitting in a Minneapolis hotel room in front of the mirror, trying to apply mascara that was running in a steady stream down her cheeks, blending effortlessly with the tears. I sat on the bed watching her, not knowing what to say. She'd already re-applied her makeup three times and by then had become an irredeemable mess. Dad was slipping his suit coat on when he finally noticed Mom was crying. I felt she wanted so desperately for him to come to her, to hold her, to tell her it would all be all right, that this too would pass and that he was sorry she was sad.

"Patricia, what in the hell are you crying about?" is what he said instead.

Rage instantly replaced grief, stopping her tears and making it possible to wipe the black from her cheeks one last time. As Dad waited by the door, exasperation emanating from him in angry waves, I realized how selfish he was – abominable, really – and took note of how rage often disguises itself as a hero when our worlds have darkened. Mom coldly collected herself as she replaced the mascara wand into the tube and was somehow able to slap her dark sunglasses on, slip her purse over her arm, walk out of the hotel room and get to her mother's funeral by 1:00 without killing my father.

I see her shudder as she pulls the blanket up higher, near her chin.

"Then your father and I fell in love...and as they say, the rest is history and here we are – going right back to the scene of the crime. Full circle and all. Some things turn out to be for the best, Maggie, and hopefully this is one of them."

"The goodbye party will be tomorrow night," I say, "when we say goodbye. I don't know if I can stomach it, Mom."

"I don't know if I can either but we have no choice, do we?"

I'm hesitant to mention it, but if this isn't the perfect

time to become her confidant, I don't know what is, so I brave this new found solidarity with, "Are you and Dad going to be alright, Mom?"

She stops breathing and looks past me, out the window, then down at the tissue in her hand. I sense shame.

"I married a peacock, Maggie. And fidelity was never his strongest virtue. Even when we were young. Beth's not the first he's fooled around with. There were others back in Dallas and I'm sure some I don't know about, and don't want to know about. Sometimes you just have to become resigned to what your life has become – otherwise, it kills you."

I can do nothing but nod my head and focus on the carpet beneath my bare feet. I'm embarrassed for her, for my father's behavior and for keeping this secret for as long as I have. I wonder why she's kept Beth as such a close friend all these years, knowing all the while what was really going on. They did everything together. The lunches, the night classes, shopping in Manhattan, tennis lessons, vacations, the private jokes that take years to cultivate between two best friends. Beth has cried on her shoulder more times than I can count. Her divorce from Dr. Gillcys was messy and long, and she gained the reputation as a flirt. Women whispered cruel things behind her back, but Mom stayed loyal to her. It could be keeping her enemies closest but it makes no sense to me other than some misguided notion that she thinks she deserves this betrayal somehow.

"Are you going to tell her that you know?"

"No, Maggie. I will not."

A floorboard creaks in the hallway outside Mom's bedroom door.

Dad's standing there with his head cocked, probably trying to figure out why we're sitting together on Mom's bed with the obviously intimate air circulating around us. I feel protective of her suddenly and I sit a bit taller, lifting my chin at him, silently daring him to intrude. I lift an eyebrow in his direction making sure my usual delight in his presence is, in no way, detectable this time.

"You two all packed up?"

I ignore him and redirect my focus on the floor. Mom places the cloth back over her eyes and sighs.

"Okay, then, I guess I'll go make myself a drink," he says.

As I watch him make his way down the hallway and turn the corner for the stairs, I feel a pang of guilt for being rude to him. I pat Mom's arm and return to my room to finish packing my things. My soul is standing in the corner with its hands on its hips, surveying the room, looking lost.

"What's up?" I ask it.

How are we ever going to get all this packed? Our whole world is here.

"We're just going to do it, is all. What choice do we have?"

We could run away.

"You're being silly now."

We could go live with Jimmy in his garage.

I notice the small green bowl on my book shelf near the window. I will have to wrap it securely in a section of the *New York Times* so it makes the trip.

Well, what are we going to do about this? You're not just going to let this happen, are you?

"You know, a wise woman once told me that sometimes you just have to become resigned to what your life has become – otherwise, it kills you. Let's get packing."

CHAPTER FIFTEEN

*In Which We Grow Into Something Quite Different,
St. Paul, Minnesota, 1978*

My stubborn insistence on attempting the impossible has taught me that trying to get a straight answer from a Mafioso is as futile an endeavor as dressing a tiger in a bowler hat and spats in an attempt to change what he is. You can prod and coax, come at him from various angles, but in the end, despite all your tactical efforts, the mobster's words have not become reliable truths any more than the tiger has become a gentleman.

Even so, I continue my fruitless inquisition. I'm such a fool.

I don't know when things shifted, but they did. It could have been spring or summer. It could have been when I turned sixteen and found myself riding a tidal wave of choppy rebellion and had decided the best way to deal with things was to buy some tight jeans, befriend boys that my father ironically deemed "a motley crew," wear far too much mascara and listen to far too much Aerosmith. It could have been when my mother's behavior needed more steady consideration; as our beloved home at 88 Orchard Drive filled up with moving boxes and we discovered her crouching in one. Or it could have been later, a year or so after our move to Minnesota, when I found blood smeared across the trunk of my father's car.

Maybe I'd become so desensitized by my surroundings and by my father's associates, that I merely came to a crossroads where I stood for a short while, considering which way I should go, and finally decided to drop my bags and stop walking, stop wondering, quit hiding and just start asking questions. I felt entitled to some truths.

Dad and I have entered into a fresh, new world with fewer secrets. It has camaraderie, communion and an unexpected pinch of honesty, but ironically I now trust him less. He has begun to feel too comfortable, and he has started spilling the beans. He lets these miniature grenades of corruption and blackened greed roll quietly off the arm of his chair by the fire at night or out of his coat sleeve while we walk in the woods together, and I pick them up, one by one, and slip them into my pocket, adding to my collection. They gather together, bursting my seams, and become a living thing that wants to break free.

This new world of ours may be a less lonely place for him since I'm here to pal around with but it is far more dangerous than anything I've ever envisioned.

Every now and then I long for the good old days when I knew very little.

Carlo Gambino has died and there's a sadness in my father that he can't shake. He's lost the spring in his step. Now he walks the way Paul Castellano always did, with determination and worry, his body following his furrowed brow from place to place. He rarely wears his fedoras and city hats; now it's old captain's hats or woolen newsboys, old man Levi's that sag in the seat. I get the sense that he's gone into hiding, although this has never been said out loud.

But this hiding is good news for my mother. In our new house, she has many more places to slip away and not be discovered, no matter how many are in the hunting party. She's lost interest in squirrels, although we occasionally catch her out in the backyard with a wide-mouthed jar of Vaseline at the birdhouse, which my father has fixed to a metal pole high above the ground. She dips her hand in and brings out a glob of thick petroleum jelly and slaps it onto the pole, coating it slowly from top to bottom.

Living in a mansion is not what most people would expect. It's certainly not what I expected. It's how I imagine living in the Museum of Modern Art after closing time might be. Twenty-eight large rooms, one attached to the next in a spooky labyrinth, twelve thousand square feet in the main section alone. I move through these rooms, sometimes losing my sense of direction, and listen to the quiet, the absence of parties, of cocktails being served, of glasses clinking and the Italian cheers ringing out. This mansion is the worst kind of super model; beautiful in appearance, but lacking soul and character.

I live on the fourth level at the top of a Gone With The Wind sort of staircase by myself. My mother stays at the far end of the west wing in a suite with floor to ceiling windows that look out over Sunfish Lake. In her bathroom there's a sunken tub where she sits submerged in bubbles most of the time, drinking martinis and mourning Greenwich. Dad calls it her sulking tub. I imagine he'd like one of his own, but he's been issued a smaller bedroom down the hallway from my mother's suite with just a walk-in shower.

My mother is reluctant to admit that money has not bought the happiness she had been guaranteed as soon as the moving trucks unloaded our belongings. Now she orders my father to wash his hands before touching her in any way. Perhaps it's because she's almost always clean these days.

No matter; he's rarely here. Most of his meetings are now held in Castellano's house in Todt Hill on Staten Island, Las Vegas, or the newest addition to his itinerary, Miami Beach. At least these are the places he admits going. Last month he arrived from the airport with packages of Givenchy perfume, a marionette and a miniature Eiffel Tower. He claimed to have just come back from Phoenix. The receipt I found underneath one of the gifts was in French and from a shop in Paris. I haven't asked him about this omitted itinerary yet. I'm waiting until he's good and liquored up.

Paul has taken over the family and Carlo's place. Now

men hold umbrellas over *his* head when the rains fall.

The story of how my father procured this house is still a mystery, and he likes it that way. I imagine he thinks it makes the place more valuable.

I can imagine how it all happened: Lou and my father decide to stake out the best house in the city. They've been skulking around the place for two days, peeking in windows, shaking gutter drains, bringing in surveying equipment when the owners step out for groceries. They sit in their rented Caddy in the dark driveway, chain smoking and doing shots of Drambuie while they wait to make their move. Lou points out the lit tennis court on the side of the property.

"Yeah, that's a nice touch, isn't it? Patricia would like having a tennis court," Dad says.

"But she doesn't play tennis, does she?"

"That's not the point."

"I think it might come in handy to know how to play tennis if you own an actual court to play tennis on. I mean, it's stupid not to use it."

"You ever play tennis?"

"No. I can't pull off the white shorts."

"Oh, I think you could. You have very sexy legs, Capalbo."

"Fuck you."

Dad laughs out loud. "What? You do. Very sexy. C'mon, let's see 'em."

"Fuck you."

Lou passes Dad the Drambuie for a final swig and they exit the car. Lou hikes his pants up, tucking his golf shirt in. A lit cigarette hangs from his lips. Dad takes a final drag from his smoke and flicks it onto the driveway like he already owns the place. They approach the front door. Dad straightens his tie and buttons up his suit coat. Lou rings the bell. Dad rocks back on his heels, admiring the massive white columns flanking the large porch.

The owner, a man named Cliff Johnson, appears, letting the screen door act like a barrier between him and these suspicious characters. They introduce themselves. Cliff looks nervous.

Dad tells him, "I'd like to make you an offer on your lovely home here, Cliff."

"There must be some mistake. This house isn't for sale."

"It's about to be," Lou says.

Lou reaches for the screen door handle and pulls it open. "Go on in, Jack. We can't do business on the front porch like a bunch of hillbillies."

"Thank you, Lou."

Dad steps into the foyer, surveying the curving staircase as Cliff Johnson takes a step back. He notices the hand gun resting in Lou's shoulder holster.

"Cliff," Dad says, "Where do you keep the booze in this place? What do you say we have a drink and talk things over?"

As sweat beads up on Cliff Johnson's forehead and he knocks back a few shots of Johnnie Walker, a deal is finally made.

"Thank you, Cliff. It's been nice doing business with you, my man."

Cliff accepts Dad's hand shake and sees them to the door in stunned silence.

As Dad and Lou make their way back to the Caddy, Dad calls over his shoulder, "I'll have the paperwork sent over in the morning, Cliff! Make sure you're home."

Dad starts up the car, admiring his new house through the windshield.

"Got a good deal, Jack," Lou says. "A fine deal."

"I could've gotten a better deal if you'd shown a little leg in there."

"Fuck you."

And they drive away laughing and congratulating themselves.

I have tried to act as my mother's advocate concerning Dad's indiscretions. I mean, somebody needs to do something.

She's really losing it. This morning I caught him in his bathroom with no way to escape.

"Dad, Mom got a birthday card from Beth Gilleys yesterday. It made her cry for two hours."

He was shaving, getting ready to go someplace he'd probably have to lie about later. The razor paused at his chin for a moment. He looked at me briefly, then ran the blade under the running water.

"And?" he asked, looking at himself in the mirror again.

"C'mon, Dad," I realized I was being too loud and quickly lowered my voice, "have you seen her lately? You have to do something! You keep going out of town and who's left to clean up the mess, huh? Me, that's who. This has gotten out of hand."

He turned off the water and sighed in my direction.

"What do you want me to do? Have her locked up?"

"I don't know what I want you to –"

And then, as if on cue, I heard her. I followed Dad's eyes to the hallway behind me. And there she was, walking slowly by his room, the Hibachi grill from the basement balanced on top of her head, her hands steadying it in place and one of her bed sheets tied around her neck like a cape. I stood frozen. She moved down the hallway and as she moved out of sight, I saw she was dragging a large mound of charcoal piled up on the sheet that trailed behind her. Some of the coals glowed crimson and were beginning to burn holes through the cotton sheet.

Somehow the house didn't burn down and we were able to lure her back to her bed with a glass of vodka and a cup of chicken broth and she's been in there ever since, doing God knows what. I woke up this morning wishing this place had burned to the ground and we could just go back home, return to Greenwich and turn our world right-side-up again.

This house – this fortress – is yet another mystery I feel determined to unravel.

What the brochure for this house hadn't noted, which I

so desperately wish it had, was that among the fine hand carved moldings, the imported Italian and Moroccan tiles, the nine bathrooms of marble and stone, was that it also has ghosts.

The house is cold and the rules are now stitched together with paranoia-colored thread, far more strict than they were at 88 Orchard Drive. This leads me to believe that our sudden move from Greenwich could be more accurately described as our sudden fleeing from Greenwich. All packages delivered are to be left untouched; doorbells are not to be answered by anyone but my father. If a car pulls up in the drive, we are ushered to the basement and ordered to stay underground rather than peer out of windows. Telephones are left to ring through the echoing halls until Dad can "deal with things." Anything out of the ordinary is suspect, which doesn't leave much because everything in our lives seems out of the ordinary. With the natural defiance that comes with being a teenager, I ignore these rules as often as I can and go about my business of trying to avoid this new other-worldly realm we've moved into.

Sometimes I forget about the spooky feelings here. I'll be reading a book, doing my homework, or applying an appalling amount of eyeliner, when I feel electricity rising up my spine. I can sense when one saunters into the room, chilling the air so much it is as if a freezer door has been flung open directly behind me.

The one thing I now rely upon is my internal alarm system. I know which men are dangerous. I can tell if someone is concealing a gun from four blocks away. I'm aware when a fellow has spent time in prison, even if he's wearing a good suit. I know when a father is planning on molesting his young child after they leave a playground hand in hand. I can tell if a man can keep a dark secret. All of these so-called talents rob the mystery from life somehow but they're my protection just the same.

I suppose this is where the ghosts have decided to inject a little mystery of their own and target me. Maybe they know I can sense things others sometimes miss. My mother has noticed them also, but refuses to say it out loud. We've been together in the hallways at night – when she's stable and I'm not feeling especially obstinate and we can tolerate each other's company – and footsteps will emerge from the shadows and follow behind. We stop and listen as they come up to our backs and then stop after a beat or two. I grab onto her arm, ignoring her stiffening at my touch, and pull her out of the frigid current until we feel that we are alone again. I often fight the urge to turn around and scream at these things to go somewhere else, to explain to them that this world is scary enough without having to deal with some spectral creeps playing their haunting games. But I know they'd only laugh, that I would be playing into their phantom hands. I haven't mentioned to either of my parents that there are times in the middle of the night when I'm awakened by a strong breath sweeping the back of my neck or a deep guttural moan coming from the corner of my room. I have not spoken of the times I have seen a smoky gray apparition take a step back from a doorway and slink out of sight as I approach. We all have enough to worry about already. And so I just worry.

I also worry that I've become a bona fide mental case because I'm getting used to crazy. Dad says it's hereditary, which doesn't help. We don't belong here, there's no doubt in my mind. Just when I thought Mom couldn't get any worse, she has. Between her stashing herself away in the linen closet (just last week, I passed the closed double doors and paused when I heard her singing the National Anthem from within, surrounded by the folded towels and guest soaps, and I kept right on going), and her attempts to curl up in the fetal position under assorted furniture, she's really losing it. She's taken to swilling booze at the edge of the pool, forgetting her fear of water. I'm sure I will find her floating face down in the deep end under the diving board before the year is out.

To make matters worse, Minnesota is the coldest place imaginable. Nobody here is having any fun except the ice fishermen and bundled children who make snowmen and don't know any better. I long for the mobsters and cocktail parties and quirky piano teachers and geisha. I long for four seasons of similar duration and not nine months of winter, three of spring and then immediately back to blizzards. I want normalcy and I'm not getting it.

Along with homesickness comes embarrassment. My father has decided to embrace his Scandinavian heritage more fully now that we're surrounded by Swedes. He's bought himself a pair of personalized license plates for his new silver Mercedes sedan that says, "UFFDA." He likes people to ask him what it means so he can lean back on his heels and say, "It's Swedish for Holy Shit!" He cracks himself up. It wasn't funny the first time, and I worry that he's lost his edge.

So now the questions. I'm older and a little less naïve than my father thinks. I really can read a newspaper. I'm onto my father, have become certain he's in the Mafia.

At first, he was cagey and avoided giving me direct answers. While we stood in a snow bank and he smoked his cigarette (my mother no longer allows him to smoke in the house, no matter the square footage), I told him he looked ridiculous. I said it to break the ice because I wanted to interrogate him, but it was also true. He was wearing his puffy snowmobile suit and one of those Russian fur hats with the ear flaps. We don't even own a snowmobile. After he had warmed up a little, I asked him, point blank if he was in the Mafia.

He shot me a sideways glance and expelled a smoky puff of air. But then I saw him soften.

After reminding me that that word is not *acceptable* in our house – and adding that "there is no such thing anyhow" – I reminded him that only people in the Mafia say there's no such thing as the Mafia. I pushed him to tell me if he was a true card-carrying member.

"You can't be made if you're Swedish," he said. "If your

roots can't be traced back to Italy, you're suspect."

When I told him that wasn't an answer, he chuckled, as he often does when he's trying to avoid something uncomfortable.

"I don't think you'd like it very much if I told you I was, would you?"

Again, not an answer.

So I watched him smoke his cigarette down to the nub and I waited, staring at the side of his head, at the ear flap, trying to unnerve him. He was making a big decision. I saw it, so I could be patient. He seemed lonely without his crew around him, without the parties, without the power he'd had back in New England. If I waited long enough, he would tell me something.

"So how many do I know, Dad?" I said.

And the standoff ended. He turned stiffly toward me, in his puffy suit.

"I don't know, Mag. Eleven or twelve, I guess."

The number surprised me, as well as how easily his confession slipped from his tongue. I mentally counted back, knowing I must be missing a few Italians somewhere along the line.

I wondered why he was now so suddenly willing to surrender them to me. Although this was what I wanted, it made me doubt his loyalty. A quiet sorrow had burrowed down inside of me as I realized I'd lost respect for this hero of mine, and all because he simply answered my question. In a half-assed Mafia sort of way, yes, but an answer just the same. Just because I'd stared at the ear flap and asked.

"Things are different now. Everyone likes their privacy, but they have to worry about wire-tapping and surveillance. You have FBI agents sitting in vans wearing headphones, listening in on you, so new language had to be developed. The FBI guy might think he's listening in on a normal conversation. He might hear, 'Hey Louie, you got tickets to the Yankees game on Saturday? I heard Nick put down six hundred dollars on that game. Yeah...

he and that guy Patsy are gonna take a dive on that one, ya know what I mean?' But what has actually been said is, 'Hey Louie. Go to New York City on Saturday. Kill Nick at 6:00. He'll be having dinner at Patsy's Restaurant. Guys will be waiting by the river – get rid of the body there.' Details can be changed, such as if Nick will be in Miami on Saturday, then it's a Dolphins game they talk about. If the hit is to take place at 11:00, then the bet is said to be eleven hundred dollars. If a distinction between 11:00 am and 11:00 pm needs to be made, then the guy issuing the order will mention the word *dark* for pm. Bottom line is, you can't be indicted for talking with Louie about a baseball game. But that's not for public consumption, you understand? There are things you don't need to know, Mag." And then he lit another cigarette. "Where's your mother? Any idea?"

I ignored the question, trying to digest what I'd just heard. I licked my lips and shook my head. I wasn't up to discussing my mother.

"When I came out here earlier," he continued, "I passed her in the kitchen. She was wearing a raincoat over her nightgown and yelling ingredients into the incinerator shoot: 'Baking soda! Half cup all purpose flour! Eggs! Granny smith apples! Diced!' – God, it was horrible."

I closed my eyes and remained silent. Minnesota was going to take some getting used to. I decided at that moment, I needed to embrace it as fully as I could, bone up on my Garrison Keillor and local polka bands, get one of those ear flap hats like Dad's before I completely and utterly go insane from not belonging anywhere but 88 Orchard Drive, high up in a tree, hanging over the driveway and eavesdropping on the mob.

I long for the times when the most hazardous thing in the room was Uncle Lou's gun resting in the shoulder harness slung across the back of a chair by the fireplace, or jeopardizing the welfare of a handful of geisha and being sent to that small chair to face the red wall, or trying to convince that old imp, Carlo

Gambino, that he'd be a hit at Show and Tell at Julian Curtiss Elementary School.

Lately, as if all that wasn't enough, there's a new and disturbing variety of madness in our house. Take the garage incident of last week. The one with the blood.

Dad had gotten liquored up after we discovered my mother, coiled into a rather tight fetal position, under a bench in one of the dressing rooms by the swimming pool, vying for space with the silverfish. I'd found him in the back of the garage shortly afterward, cussing softly to himself. He couldn't find the bocce ball set and he was getting pissed. He was tossing things aside, kicking boxes around, chain smoking. I helped, even though it is the dead of winter and would still be for at least six more months. I saw no need to find the bocce ball set on that particular day when we had so many other things we could be occupied with, such as locating a good source of lithium for my mother or coming up with a triple suicide pact. But no, he had to find it – he wanted to play in the snow. So I helped him look through the garage.

The balls rolled a lot faster on packed snow then we'd anticipated, so we spent most of our time chasing after them. Chasing one after it ricocheted into the open three-car garage, I stopped short. There, smeared across the back side of the Mercedes' trunk, was a wide streak of blood. And fairly fresh blood at that. Now, the way I see it, unless you've just been in some horrific accident, or you work in a slaughterhouse, or you've just come back from a lunch date with Charles Manson, there should never be any reason whatsoever for fresh blood to be smeared on anything. Worse, it goes completely unnoticed all the afternoon. Exactly how much blood does a person need to be exposed to in life, to make a large streak of it – say, twelve inches long by eight inches wide – glistening against a car's silver paint job, something they'd overlook? I turned to my father, who was standing in his snowmobile suit and rubber boots like he was a normal guy and I pointed a thumb at the trunk of his car.

"What?"

And so I sighed. He only lifted his eyebrows at me.

"Why is there blood on your car?"

He cocked his head, as if trying to see it more clearly. "What blood?"

I stared at him silently until he had no choice but to approach the car. He bent down (as much as one can while wearing a snowmobile suit), surveyed the bloody smear, took a greasy rag out of his pocket and began wiping it clean.

"Oh, c'mon! You're not going to tell me you have some guy's body in the trunk of your car, are you?"

He laughed. Nervously.

This reminded me of the old family joke when we were shopping for cars. Dad would pop the trunk open and ask, "So ya think that's a two-body trunk or a three-body trunk?"

Somewhere deep in my shallow reserves of hope, I thought he'd actually have a normal explanation for the blood. I prayed for it, really.

After some accusing glances and Italian hand gestures and a lot of, "Boy oh boy, you sure ask a lot of questions, don't you?" he opened the trunk of the car to reveal something large and wrapped in plastic, duct taped at the ends. More blood had run down and coagulated inside of the plastic sheet. It was a hulking form, thick in the middle. I closed my eyes, even though I knew that no amount of shutting myself off would make my life go away. I waited for an answer.

"It's a shark," he said, and closed the trunk.

It has not been lost on me that we are landlocked in St. Paul, Minnesota, far from any shark infested waters, and that my father had not, as far as I know, been deep sea fishing in at least a decade. But from what my father prefers to tell me, his new buddy, Milo Masters, had given him the fish that morning as a gift.

Milo is most certainly gangster material – half Greek,

half Italian. He carries a gun in his glove compartment and talks incessantly about his interests in Vegas casinos and his plan to feel up Frank Sinatra's wife at least once in his lifetime. I have no idea where this guy came from – he's one of the new guys, thugs that appear from nowhere for dinner, only one or two at a time. They seem more like caricatures of mobsters than the real thing. Anyway, I wish Milo would stop coming around. He brags about his affiliates, wears flashy jewelry and tells tales about having this guy whacked and that guy taken care of. He's decidedly uncouth.

Milo presented my father with a large book, a leather bound thing with newspaper articles and pictures from various coroners' vaults, pressed and glued carefully in place. The souvenirs in this book must be some sort of homage to the mob, with articles written about Carlo Gambino, Paul Castellano, Sam Giancana, going back to Al Capone and Joe Kennedy's bootlegging days. Dad seemed overjoyed and honored when the Greek first gave it to him, but after he turned the pages, scanned the print and thanked Milo for the gift, the light in his eyes dimmed. He closed the book and, as far as I know, never opened it again. I've looked through it twice, and the only thing I can think is this: Why does the press print pictures of these men after they've been slaughtered by rivals or, worse, by once close friends? The press withholds discretion when it comes to these situations. Black and white photos of a sprawled body on the curb in front of a New Jersey club, an Armani suit still hugging the gangster's frame in impeccable style; a boss sliding off a sofa on his back, as if he'd been overcome with laughter and couldn't stay upright – only his right eye is now a gaping, bloody hole. There's a photo of two goombahs in the front seat of a Lincoln Continental – the driver is devouring the bloody steering wheel; his passenger is missing most of his head.

If your neighbor, Mrs. Livingston – head of the PTA and long time member of the Junior League – met an untimely demise, there surely would be no snapshots of the empty prescription bottles scattered on the bathroom floor, a shattered bottle of gin next to her curled up body, a trail of soupy shit oozing through the back of her nightgown. That would be disrespectful and would probably instigate a nasty lawsuit, but a Consiglieri cradling his own brains in his lap? *Perfect! Let's go to print.* Truly, I don't know how they get away with it. No matter what their professions, prison records or misdeeds, they still have families, friends. These men were once babies bouncing on their mothers' laps. I do not condone their line of "work," but they are still human beings and deserve a little more consideration than that. I don't care for this Milo Masters' gift very much. I think he's a nut job and should stop scrapbooking.

I have chosen to believe that the thing in the trunk may very well be an overweight great white. But I've been back in the garage a few times since. I have popped the trunk and have found no evidence of blood, plastic, fish or man back there. I have checked the freezer for packets labeled "shark" and have found none. Giving my father the benefit of the doubt is something I rarely do anymore, but while I'm still stranded on this shaky ground, I sit by, pay attention and take careful notes.

I made one final observation after he closed the trunk. "That's a lot of blood."

"It's a big fish," he said.

#

Just when I think things can't get any weirder, I arrive home from school and walk in on my Uncle Jim – the scoundrel with the phony British accent who is not above hiding under furniture himself, who sells life insurance out of the back of his Buick in Mendota Heights, who seems to resent his younger brother's prestige in Washington and because of this resentment has started wearing berets for some reason – pinning my mother, his sister, up against the side of the pool and French-kissing her hard on the mouth. His thinning gray hair is damp, his head tilted at a cobra-like angle.

Why hadn't I just gone about my business, gone up to my room and done a little homework, or got on the horn with an "undesirable boy who'd never amount to anything," or mounted a paranormal investigation with some slick recording devices and a Ouija Board? There are a million things I could have done to keep myself occupied; instead, I wandered into the wrong part of the house. It could have been the Buick that sent me to find my mother without changing out of my school clothes, or it could have been a gut feeling that overtook me. Perhaps it was just some very unlucky timing.

The day was like any other spring day in Minnesota – thirty degrees, robins hopping on the lawn, feathers coated in frost. I'd returned home from school, taken a large chunk of cheese from the fridge and began a casual and unenthusiastic search for my mother. I'd called out to her and got the usual silence in return, but something lifted the delicate hairs from my forearms.

A spiral staircase leading downstairs from the main foyer reflects light from the glass walls in the pool area. On a normal afternoon, the reflections are shining and still, like crystals pasted on the wall. But on this day they danced a waltz. The cedar door to the pool room is five inches thick to keep the humidity from the rest of the house, and it sticks. It's become my habit to turn the knob and give the door a hip check when entering the room. As my hip rammed the door and it opened with a heavy, lumbering swing, I spotted them chest deep in the water. Her back was against the side, his arms caging her in place, his freckled hands grasping the cement lip of the pool. They continued to kiss for a second or two longer – his tongue glistened wet and searching in her mouth – before they turned in unison to look up at me standing on the landing with my piece of sharp cheddar frozen in mid air. Sirens blared, shards of thick ice cracked and peeled off inside me and raced to my bowels; a meat grinder churned in my brain, spilling tendrils of matter out my ears.

Uncle Jim backed away only slightly from my mother. They both continued to stare at me with a look one might have if interrupted while weeding the garden or chopping celery for an upcoming tuna fish sandwich. It was their casual surprise that would stay with me. The image so indelible, so staining and inky – a Rorschach of two phantom siblings intertwined in a chlorinated pool. I felt I'd just barged in on 1925 and had been met by the same vacant gaze I'd seen in the faces of nursing home residents who'd returned to their childhoods and believed they were once again setting up tea parties or being rocked by a parent dead forty years. And I am the nurse who places a hand on their shoulders and pulls them back to the present so they can be wheeled into the social room for a bland and soft lunch.

My mother's eyes were those of a prisoner who'd just been pulled back from a daydream so deep that she hadn't noticed the clanking bars have slid open and the guard has been calling her name. In that moment I recognized that we were the same. I'd seen that same look in the mirror in a hotel room in Austria just after God had left the room.

I turned, my movements jerky and robotic, brains leaking out and reaching for my jeans. I opened the mammoth door and somehow managed to walk away. I decided that something had to be done, but what? Every option I came up with was sticky and dire. I could try to talk to my mother but shame and embarrassment (for both of us) snuffed the idea. I could do nothing and feel the craggy edges of guilt stabbing me for years to come, wondering if I was making her life worse by pretending I'd never seen what I'd seen.

I had no sympathy for my uncle. He had made his position clear. He had not only violated my mother but had betrayed my father as well – and in our own home at that. He'd taken liberties that you didn't take with men like my father, or any man for that matter. He needed to be punished.

Dad arrived back at the house an hour after Uncle Jim's Buick rattled out of our driveway. I quickly and cryptically told him what I'd seen.

"You go outside. Now. I'll come get you when I've taken care of this," he said.

Telling my father could have been a mistake. I see that now. Mom and I now sail on a turbulent and suspicious sea together. I feel as if I'm the one who has betrayed her. One minute she acts as if I've skipped Algebra class or spilled grape juice on the rug, passing me in our haunted hallways with an irritated, forced smile or a nod of her head. The next time we meet, she narrows her eyes and threatens something deadly and silent. I don't know if I've saved her or killed her. I don't know whose secret I've exposed, hers or my uncle's, or if there's a possibility that I've just signed Jim Scott's death warrant. I wish I could rewind my entire life. Her entire life. I am beginning to understand her fragility.

We continue to sail under charred and threatening skies, going about our days, my father avoiding us both. I'm sick of surprises and feeling that I am now the enemy. I bide my time until a rogue bully wave pushes my legs out from under me yet again. And then, just when I'm sure I'm going under for the last time, the always unexpected brief calm comes and I drag myself limp, up over the railing and flop onto the deck of the ship, exhausted and grateful for the sun and dry air. And there she is in her captain's hat, gripping the ship's wheel in her freckled hands, smiling that cold smile at me as I gasp on the deck, as if nothing has just happened.

"Oh, there you are," she says. "You've gotten your lederhosen wet. Well, they're ruined now. Great."

Five weeks after the pool incident, she stops hating me for an afternoon. Uncle Jim comes to visit with his horsey wife, Carol, whose gums show when she smiles. We all gather for dinner to partake of Mom's famous gazpacho soup and discuss how the Vikings did last season. I wonder if this dinner is a new form of punishment for me. I find it impossible to look anyone in the eye for too long. Dad tends bar, giving me a wink. I wonder if his wink is telling me he's mixing a little anti-freeze into Jim's Tom Collins. This must be one of those times when we're all supposed to pretend that nothing out of the ordinary has occurred. I wish someone had let me look over the script before we went on stage.

CHAPTER SIXTEEN

*In Which Wolves Line Their Cozy Den With the Soft,
Trusting Down of the General Public,
Dallas, Texas, November 22, 1963 ~ 11:40 am*

The President's plane touches down at Love Field at 11:40 a.m. By noon it is far too late to abort the operation should anyone decide to do so. Too many people are involved for Jack Dahlstrom's taste, but they are all essential in the hit. A public hit. A televised hit. With so many people needed to pull something of this magnitude off, there will be casualties, no doubt. Some might be detained or questioned by the Dallas Police, there could be witnesses to the men moving the rifles through the downtown area, innocent people could be shot, but this is all in a crucial day's work.

This will be a day of warning, the bullets a message: You don't go back on your word and you don't gnaw on the hand that serves you the sirloin. After today, finally, everyone can get back to business.

Jack stands on the hill behind the fence near a maintenance shed with his city hat cocked over his brow to shield his eyes from the sun. Civilian crowds are thickening along the curb and on the grass below him. He glances at a sewer slit in the curb, then scans the overpass at the railroad tracks, then up and to his left at the open windows of the buildings surrounding the new motorcade route.

Ruby had delivered Jack's envelope after the *Dallas Morning News* had prematurely printed the original map on the front page. Scrambling editors and print men decided to repair the mistake in the most economical way possible, before the bundles of papers were lobbed out onto city sidewalks for circulation, they ran the front page through the presses another time, quickly blacking out the original route.

Jack scans the crowd for friends and neighbors and sees none. The family is tucked safely away, back at home, except for his daughter, Jane, who is being held captive in math class by her teacher, the young widow, Mrs. Jean Tucker. Mrs. Tucker has been slipped a much needed envelope of cash, has been appropriately threatened, and will most likely need to be shot in the back of the head should she decide to tell what little she knows. The safeguard is that her four year old son, Scottie, has been scooped up from the playground of his nursery school and driven in a rented pickup truck to Kip's Big Boy, where right now he is in a booth enjoying a cheeseburger with his new friend Jimmy Bruno. Insurance.

Three buzzards circle overhead like guests too early for dinner; their scraggy bodies block the sun, casting shadows on Elm Street and the grassy knoll.

The guys should be moving into place now. Each person only knows his own particular instruction and placement. Very few of them know every detail from beginning to end. It will all come together in the end if everyone follows direction. This is the way to get things done, with strategic timing and small, well orchestrated moves. There is little reason to think it won't go off as planned. These are professionals he's working with.

Jack doesn't know the shooters personally. These aren't his running buddies who are good with a pistol or snaring a man's throat with piano wire; these are sharp shooters. Experts. There are five, possibly six shooters, according to Jack's superiors, spread out across the area, which leaves little to no possibility of error. Dozens of men have arrived in Dallas at different times for different fractions of the job. Some are dressed as construction workers, some as tourists, a few as cops. Some have come in on the train and hang around the tracks smoking cigarettes and drinking whiskey from bottles wrapped in paper sacks.

Three decoy rifles are placed in buildings downtown and one instrumental rifle lies one hundred yards to his right under a hedge of bushes. The decoy rifles, as well as the ones that will be used in the hit, move through the city unnoticed as they pass local shopkeepers sweeping their entryways, businessmen weaving through traffic, maids bustling in rubber-soled shoes and throngs of school children gathering for the event. They are high-powered rifles tucked in their soft cases, taped to short flag poles and loosely wrapped in the American flag by a man dressed as a janitor. They are camouflaged among hoses and equipment being lowered into the city's sewer system by men wearing hard hats. One comes nestled beneath tissue in a long box coming off the train labeled *Long Stemmed Roses*.

His son's accident has slowed Jack's business dealings down to a molasses-slow drip. He has spent so much of his time at Parkland Memorial over the past couple of months, he's had no time to concentrate on much else. His throat thickens as he thinks of Sid and wonders if he will ever fully recover. He needs this job to come off with no problems. He's been assured he will be paid handsomely but finds it difficult to imagine never having to worry about money again. The hospital bills are mounting. Comas cost a damn fortune.

He lights a cigarette behind the fence and watches the people mingle. Women smooth their hair with their palms, wipe children's snotty faces clean; police officers stand in pairs on corners. He'd thought changing the motorcade route would be the most difficult aspect of the job, having Jack Ruby convince guys up at City Hall and the Police Department. His brother-in-law was right about one thing: the guy's squirrelly. But everything seems to be going smoothly from what he can see from his perch.

Jack adjusts his hat and takes a pull from his smoke, thinking how the original route wouldn't have afforded them enough of the preferred angles for the guys down in the sewers.

They needed hills. They also needed the curves that this new route affords in order to slow the motorcade down. The sound of gun shots should echo and ricochet, distorting wildly in this area. A bonus. The shooters below ground are the more valued members and have a lesser chance of being spotted. The ones in the buildings and down the road past the underpass could be more vulnerable as far as public exposure is concerned, but they've positioned the men according to worth in the organization. He doubts the men farther down the road will even be necessary; they are just extra insurance.

Patricia hadn't asked any questions but he suspects she knows something is coming. A look had passed between them this morning as he left the house. Surely, at some point, she will ask him who could have benefited from Kennedy's death, and his answer will be, "Who doesn't?" The simple fact is, they will have everyone looking in every direction, at every group who has ever had a beef with the guy: the CIA, the Mob, there's the Cuban group, LBJ and every anti-Kennedy nut job out there who is able to procure a gun in Texas.

There will surely be mayhem in the aftermath, but they're ready for it. Everyone will accuse everyone else, and everyone will be right. No one is going down for it entirely, although some are sure to be sacrificed. There will be speculation and people will wonder if it was Giancana's crew, Gambino's crew or perhaps even the heads of the good old U.S. of A. Today Jack takes comfort in the fact there's only one difference between the Mafia and the U.S. Government: geography. They are all the same breed; their respective headquarters are just in different locations.

He reaches into the pocket of his slacks and pulls out a small cotton ball and slowly begins pulling it apart. He balls up a section and tucks it in his right ear. He does the same with his left, pushing the cotton in with his pinkie. He leaves a little bit of the cotton showing at the opening of the ear canal. He's not trying to block out noise.

Jack has been waiting for this day for over two months and is ready to get it wrapped up.

A man in a mechanic's jumpsuit sidles up one hundred yards away and to his right. He's standing directly above the hidden rifle in the bush. Jack and the man swivel their heads towards each other in a casual fashion. Jack notices a tuft of cotton in the man's left ear and gives him a shallow nod. The man in the jumpsuit glances at Jack's ear, nods back. He takes a short step closer to the bushes and surveys the scene on the street.

CHAPTER SEVENTEEN

*In Which Family Comes to Stay and a Package
Arrives from Hoboken,
St. Paul, Minnesota, 1979*

As my father pushes the large envelope slowly across the table with his tan hand, his ruby pinkie ring catches the afternoon light coming in through the windows of the Garden Room.

"We have a problem," he says to me.

This could mean anything. Problems in our house have proven to be, as a rule, of a much larger magnitude than in the average American household, but of course my only idea of what normality is comes from what I've learned from TV. Our kinds of problems never happened to Ricky and Lucy. If Mike Brady said, "We have a problem," it usually meant that Jan Brady had pilfered a couple of bucks from the Girl Scout cookie fund she'd collected from unsuspecting neighbors or she'd lost her retainer again.

This could have something to do with Dad being concerned about my new attitude, which he has deemed to be belligerent. He has made it clear that he believes the fault lies squarely on the shoulders of Keith Richards, Steven Tyler and Ozzy Osbourne, and on how much time I spend in my room listening to "that crap they call music." Or this could be the result of my being chased through the lunchroom at high speed, on foot, by my algebra teacher, Mr. Callahan, who'd spotted me skipping class this past Thursday. I hadn't meant to run. It was sheer instinct that had overtaken me. Unfortunately, a massive food fight broke out amongst my fellow students, in an attempt to create a diversion in my defense. As I raced through the tables, the smell of institutional hamburgers joined Mr. Callahan close at my heels.

Later that day, sitting in an unwelcoming metal chair in the school office awaiting my sentencing, I knew this episode would eventually land me in hot water at home. Mr. Callahan came out of the Vice-Principal's office, picking bits of iceberg lettuce from his hair.

I stare at the envelope, not wanting to touch it. Dad waits. Mom sets her cocktail down on the table and takes a seat next to my father. She's glaring at me. The look is not unusual these days. After the incestuous pool incident with Uncle Jim, and that one inexplicable afternoon when she temporarily didn't despise me and we all had a disturbingly nice meal together, I've become more of an enemy than ever before. She has been suggesting that I start seeing a shrink because I've "been acting erratic and frankly she's a little concerned." This is an obvious attempt to discredit me and blacken my reputation in the house. Who can blame her, really? Anyone clever enough would do the same.

The envelope is addressed to my father. It is postmarked Hoboken, NJ. No return address. I want to ask what this is about before I reach for it, but from the look on Dad's face, I can see the answer is stuffed inside this mysterious mailer and no one's going to give me any clues or make this easy on me.

I lift it from the table with two fingers as if it's something dead I've found behind the washing machine. Its weight is substantial considering how flat it is. I give my father a final glance before turning it over in my hands to lift the already opened flap and peek inside. He's worried, I can tell. Mom sips her cocktail, dusty rose lipstick staining the rim, marking her territory.

A door opens and closes again in the east wing of the house and two sets of footsteps – one steady, one hurried and sugared-up – move towards us. I swivel my chair around with the envelope clutched in my hands to see my sister, Jane, carrying her sleeping toddler, Molly, into the room. Her six year old son, Adam, bounces with vigor in our direction.

"Hey, Mag! What's up?" she says.

I toss her a smile as my nephew, now bouncing in place beside my chair, eyes the envelope and gives me a hopeful look with his massive blue eyes. His page boy bangs jump and slap against his brow with every landing on the hard tile floor. Jane sets Molly down on the sofa by the fireplace and approaches us, placing a calming hand on Adam's shoulder. He simmers.

My sister and her two children have come to stay with us for an indefinite amount of time. I hope indefinitely turns into forever, but I already see she feels out of place and wants to flee. My mother greeted them with an unusually caustic chill when they arrived three weeks ago, as if Jane were a mongrel stray followed by her two mangy pups, wandering up to our door looking for a meal and not three of our desperate loved ones in search of a safe place to land.

#

Size sixteen; a shoe to be taken seriously. This is what first comes to mind when I think of my sister's husband, John, along with his height, which matches his soaring IQ. Then what comes to mind is the way I've seen him look at my sister: as if she is the very oil that fuels his heart. He loves her in a boundless and infinite fashion.

Jane met him while she was studying drama and he was mastering film making at Southern Methodist University. Their curriculum interlaced together in perfect fluidity like a pair dancing a steamy tango; they'd wasted no time falling in love. They fit together despite her tiny frame and delicate little hands, and his lanky, soaring build. Jane, with her vivid, imaginative mind, and John, with his sparkling dreams effortlessly fueled by his genius. They shared their souls like a couple sharing warm bunches of burgundy grapes on a summer blanket. Mutual muses.

In a dim and musty basement on the SMU campus, the university janitor – who'd become an ordained minister through an ad found in an issue of *Rolling Stone* – married the two. Jane wore a thrift store mini-dress slathered in white lace and carried an unruly cluster of wild violets. *Hey Jude* played from a portable record player on a folding metal chair in the corner while John Peyton Hayes sweetly became my sister's husband.

John had already achieved a certain greatness that his fellow students would be hard-pressed to achieve. He'd won a Merit Scholarship, was earning recognition for his film work and was sharing tightly rolled joints with Dennis Hopper and Jack Nicholson – two stormy, up and coming actors who'd come through Dallas to sit in on a class. They'd all quickly become friends. Jane liked to sit and bask in Dennis' warmth as he pondered life's riddles and told generous, elaborate tales of adventure. Nicholson was another story. He made her skin crawl with his wild eyes and tendency to become over-exuberant in the passes he made at her in front of John. But they were all heading in the same exciting direction and riding the same shooting stars towards lives of fame and accolades.

Drama class was packed tight with talent. Jane could spot the ones, as they read their lines and sharpened their craft, who were most likely to succeed. A cantankerous and foul-mouthed classmate named Kathy Bates rehearsed for long intervals as Jane prodded her in the art of acting crazy. Kathy was steady and stoic and didn't have the fragile, quivering mind that could easily pull off madness at a moment's notice the way Jane did. Insanity was easy for Jane to emulate. All she had to do was mimic our mother. She schooled Kathy with ease, feeling sure that somewhere down the road it would come in handy for her friend.

Even within the excitement and wonder of the hopeful, pregnant era of the late 1960s, Jane suspected John was becoming tenderly unhinged. It began with a look in her direction that felt foreign; a look one might receive from a suspicious stranger. His eyes would suddenly turn oily and black, as if his soul had just stepped out for a smoke, leaving something ethereal and foreboding in the room. There were moments when she entered a room to find him standing – his face only inches from a wall – whispering secrets into a nail hole. Jane was busy raising their son, Adam, nursing their newborn daughter and determined to make the marriage work, despite the lunacy that was swelling with symphonic steadiness.

While Jane was digging for frozen peas in the freezer one evening, she discovered thick cakes of angel dust wrapped in plastic wrap. Things went south from there.

John had apparently learned to channel voices from another realm in between making movies, and one day she walked in on him. He sat cross-legged in the middle of the floor, surrounded by lit candles dripping wax down their sides and onto the wood floor. John was smiling wide-eyed at the ceiling. And he was speaking Chinese.

After a ginger interrogation, he admitted that he was sure he'd been channeling the ox-riding Lao Tzu, author of the twenty-five-hundred-year-old Book of Tao. Not only did John not speak Chinese and never had, he'd also never studied Taoism and knew very little about the legendary Chinese profit, but a message was being delivered to him in any case; a message he contemplated for more than a year before it set sail.

Later that month, Lao Tzu was of the opinion that John should stop on his way home to pick up a bag of corn on the cob for dinner and then swing by the hardware store and purchase a large ax with a red handle. So he did.

The baby, Molly, was curled up on her side in her crib, tiny thumb still resting at the tip of her sleeping lips, ready, in case something stirred her from sleep, while Adam stacked wooden blocks on the living room floor in front of the TV, Elmer Fudd and Bugs Bunny trading wisecracks at a volume much too high.

Jane was wiping a frying pan dry when John came through the screen door at the back of the house. He lowered the large bag of corn from his shoulder and set it down at the base of a cupboard. He stood still for a moment, admiring Jane, then bent to kiss her softly on the nape of her neck. She smiled and set the pan down and turned towards her husband to thank him for the corn when she noticed the ax. He leaned on it like a cane, palming the butt of the red handle. He smiled so sweetly that she almost didn't notice the liquid darkness pass over his irises. A chill swarmed up her backside despite the stifling heat in the Dallas kitchen, and she quickly employed her dramatic skills, took a deep breath and camouflaged her fear in some casual batting of her long lashes. A dense cloud passed over the sun, turning the kitchen gray as she fought her flight instinct back down with silent force.

"How about some pork chops to go with that nice corn there? I think we have enough left over in the fridge," she said, keeping her casual air steady.

"Yes. Let's do that," he said. His smile faded just enough to alarm her heart into a rapid drumming, which she was sure was visible through her faded Bob Dylan T-shirt.

Jane's mind scrambled to route her escape. Adam was only ten or twelve yards away and still busy on the floor in front of his cartoons; he hadn't heard his father enter the house because of the volume. Molly was down the hall in the first bedroom. If she went down the hallway and John came after her there, she would have no way out other than going through a window, and she couldn't remember which ones she'd left open. Grabbing the baby from her crib, making it to the window, shifting the latch to unlock it, lifting it (the one in the baby's room had a tendency to stick) and getting both of them out could take more than thirty seconds. Even if she did manage to get the baby out safely, what about Adam? She couldn't count on his following her direction and ignoring the father he adored.

John tilted his head at her and narrowed his eyes as if he'd just read her mind.

"Wait. Let me make sure we have enough," she said, her voice trembling slightly as she turned away from him and opened the door to the fridge. She bent down to eye the meat on the metal shelf and closed her eyes in frantic prayer.

"Jane," John said to her back.

She composed herself and stood straight, closing the door and turning to face him again.

He moved closer to her, dragging the ax over the grimy kitchen floor. She couldn't fake it anymore and felt hot tears creeping up. A soft whimper escaped from her mouth.

"Janey, now I want you to listen to me. Listen carefully. Are you listening to me?"

She forced the corners of her mouth to rise, nodding her head. She glanced through the open doorway at Adam, who was mesmerized by the colorful images bouncing across the TV screen.

"A prophet spoke," John said softly. "You know this already though, don't you? And when he gave me the message, it became a duty. An honorable duty. Some might call it a commandment."

A river of sweat escaped from beneath her long brown hair and ran down her spine. She couldn't speak.

"Now here's the thing." He leaned over her small frame and lowered his voice to a haunting whisper. "I'm going to have to take this ax and chop up the kids with it, and then I'll have to do the same to you. But there's nothing to worry about, Janey, really. This is nothing but deliverance. Something we wait our entire lives to experience."

Jane's survival skills spoke for her as she met his calm gaze. There was only one possible way out of this.

"Yes, I do see it, John. First, though, would you please take that corn out to the garage and open it there? It's leaking dirt and I think it'll make too much of a mess if you open it in here."

He cocked his head and smiled. "That's a very good idea." He rested the ax handle against the cupboard below the kitchen sink, picked up the bag of corn and walked in a long, sure stride out the back door.

Jane's eyes darted around the kitchen searching for her purse and car keys. They weren't in the room. She raced to the living room and spotted them on the couch by the front door. She passed the TV, slapped the power knob, silencing the cartoons and hissed at her son, "Adam! Go get in the car. Now!" and with what could only be the grace of God, he sprang to a standing position and tore out the front door in the direction of her pale blue VW bug parked out at the curb.

She ran down the hall, scooped her sleeping baby out of her crib, ran back to the living room, picked up her purse and car keys and was out the door, running faster than she'd ever run. Her son was sitting in the passenger seat of the VW, waiting with a worried brow.

As she peeled away from the curb, grinding the gears between first and second, she stole a final glance at their home. Something moved in the front window just before her mother-in-law's old china hutch came sailing through the window sending arrows of glass out onto the front lawn.

She pulled into the corner 7-11. She found a crumpled dollar bill and three quarters at the bottom of her purse – not even enough to buy one package of diapers. So she drove across town to beg some spare change and one long distance phone call from an old college friend.

Dad instructed her to drive to the airport and get on a plane bound for St. Paul. He'd call the airlines and arrange the tickets over the phone. He would pick them up at their gate when they arrived in Minnesota.

While she was buckling Adam into his seat next to hers on the plane, five muscular members of the Dallas Police Force used every ounce of their strength and training to wrestle John Peyton Hayes out of the nearly destroyed interior of the home and into a squad car.

This is how my sister and her children have managed to come to White Oaks to live for a while. My fear is that she will soon discover that this house is only slightly saner than the one she's just fled.

#

"Jane, we need a minute alone with Mag," Dad tells her.

Her eyes move to me and the envelope in my hand before she steers Adam out of the room, leaving Molly sacked out by the fireplace.

As I slide the contents out, my father shifts in his chair. Black and white 8 X 10 photographs – seven or eight of them. The first is of me standing in a group of my friends, Tim Gilcrease, Joe Schmidt and Arnie Stanger, at the edge of the football field in back of our high school. I'm wearing my newest jeans with the white embroidery on the back pockets and a thin peasant blouse. I'm looking in the direction of the camera lens. I slide the photo and shuffle it behind the others, exposing the next. I'm in this one also, walking with the same friends across the parking lot; I have my head tossed back and I'm laughing in Joe's direction. I remember this day; it wasn't long ago...maybe a week or two. I shoot Dad a curious look and he nods to the photos as if I should continue. The next one is a vertical shot. I turn the stack clockwise. In this one, the wind has blown my long blond hair up into the air and across my face as I lean into Tim's car to tell him something. I'm wearing different clothes in this one. Old jeans and a Bob Seger T-shirt.

"What is this? Who took these?"

"Now listen to me, "Dad says, "this probably is nothing to worry about, but there have been kidnapping threats coming in."

My breath catches. I look at Mom but her eyes register nothing but maybe a little disdain or warning. I can't tell which.

"Coming in? From where?" I flip the envelope over, noting

the postmark again. "From Hoboken?"

"This is just some guys throwing their weight around. This happens all the time and nothing ever comes from it and most likely nothing will come from this, but I just want you to be aware."

"They're threatening to kidnap me? What would they want with me?"

Panic has swallowed me whole. I struggle to lift the envelope to the table. My arms feel weighted down with leaden sleeves. My father has managed to detonate some Cosa Nostra bomb and I am now the one about to be tweezing the repercussions from my backside. A million questions that I know will never be answered (not as long as my mother is present anyway) are whipping through my mind. I could very well still be trying to unravel this puzzle from the trunk of some guy's car before the week is out.

"It's just a threat. They do this. They take pictures to let us know that they know what you look like, where you go to school, who your friends are. Then they issue a threat and a day later, photos arrive just to drive the point home." My father is trying to look calm but his nerves are making his eyes water slightly.

His face blurs as I feel my wits rise from my chair and make their way towards the front door.

"This happened with Carlo's nephew back in '72, and he didn't panic. He didn't pay a ransom, because he knew if he did, it would never end. The kid was returned – no problem. Just be aware, that's all. Stay with your friends, don't hang out in the parking lot – you shouldn't be out there hanging around those losers anyway – and watch for men in suits, dark cars. You know, people that don't fit in. Listen, Mag, this will all be taken care of in a few days. There's nothing to worry..."

Before he can finish his sentence, I feel my neck muscles give, a black cloud bubbles up from below me and everything goes dark.

CHAPTER EIGHTEEN

*In Which We Reach an Emotional Summit,
St. Paul, Minnesota, 1979*

The sorrowful call of a loon pulls me out of a deep sleep. I try to slip back into the luxurious dream that I've just been peeled away from. I force my eyes shut again and will my mind to latch onto the remnants of what I remember. There had been swaying. And the sound of water lapping up against something beneath my head. A gentle breeze moved through my hair and I was safe. Safe in my old boat on the lake behind 88 Orchard Drive.

It's no good. I'm awake and Greenwich is gone. I hear the loon again. Such a mournful, spooky cry. It makes early dawn seem darker than it is.

I cannot say exactly what has happened to my sister's husband, John. Not with any conviction anyway. He is just dead. Poof. Gone. I recall my father's words to Jane, *All it takes is a phone call, Jane.* I wonder if he has ever stopped to consider alternative methods of solving problems. I'm beginning to believe he has not.

John was released from the state mental hospital after a very long stay and stepped out into the Texas dust in his size sixteen shoes and somehow made his way to our doorstep to pay my sister and their children a visit.

Two weeks later my father announced that John had been killed. Shot between the eyes. Then Dad had a few cocktails and retold the story to me. Somewhere he slipped. My mother always says, if you're a liar, you'd better have a damned good memory. Maybe he hadn't had time to come up with a good story or maybe he just didn't care that much about accuracy in this instance. But when I asked him to explain it all to me again, he told me that John had killed himself in a hotel room and that the police had called Dad to let him know. When I asked why the police would call him and not Jane, why John hadn't left a note, why he'd first said John had been killed and now it was suicide and why he'd patiently told Jane that all it takes is a phone call to get rid of people who need to be gotten rid of, he quietly ordered me to stop asking questions and dismissed me from the room.

I don't know exactly what has happened and probably never will, but after careful consideration, I only know that I can no longer stay here.

Every time my mother passes me in one of the common areas, she gives me a threatening sneer that rattles my heart and will forever mystify me. I know she will never tell me why she now despises me so much – more now than after the pool incident – and maybe even she doesn't know. But it has exhausted me fully.

My sister has moved back to her beloved Texas and has left me here in this ghostly palace alone and haunted. I understand her needing to escape. Before her cab left to take her away, she pulled me close to her and wrapped her arms around my neck and said, "As soon as I get settled, I'll send for you. We can start over."

For months, I felt like one of those women, standing by the window in her corset, looking out at the Civil War going on in the back yard, long before they had phones, waiting for a man on a horse to deliver word from a loved one. Her letter finally came with an airline ticket tucked between the pages. Now it's my turn to go.

I sit up on my bed and look out the tall glass windows at the pond where the loon must live. My clothes are packed in a bag on the creamy carpeting.

My brother, Sid, has not been back home to visit in many years. I wish he had come around more often. He has his own life and lives with his wife in Oregon at the edge of a thick forest of pines. I wonder if he knows everything that I have learned about our family. When I was wrestling with this decision of leaving, with how I would make it on my own, how I could find happiness, Sid's words echoed back to me from many years ago. He'd said, "I find that any time I have ever had to make a big decision, the decision always makes itself for me." Now I know what he meant. This decision had made itself.

My taxi will be arriving soon. I take one final look around the room, searching for something I'm going to miss, for something that should touch my heart and pull me into some nostalgic puddle of tears, but nothing does. I anticipate my new life, one that will bring only normal problems. I want to be worried about things like a guy not calling me back after a first date, about whether I left the coffee pot on before leaving my apartment, or if I'm ever going to get that stain out of my new white blouse. What a life that will be.

I slip on my jeans and sweater. I bend to collect my bag from the floor and sense someone behind me. When I turn, there is no one there, of course. The spirits that roam these twelve thousand square feet have helped me pack quickly, and I'm relieved to be rid of them.

The decision was made all the easier when my parents invited someone to dinner. A pre-prison term dinner – the obligatory Mafia send-off for old chums going to do some time. The guest of honor was Bernie Botts.

I did not faint. I didn't stomp my foot or freak out in any way. I simply and calmly told my parents that I would not be joining them and I told them why. In as scant and cryptic detail as possible, I told them what Bernie had done to me in that room in Austria on New Year's Eve, 1969.

"He hurt me that night – in the most horrific way you can imagine – and he threatened to do more than hurt the two of you, actually. That's why I couldn't speak for so long; I was protecting you. You might want to think about getting some new friends, Dad."

After so many years of silence, it was like coming down

out of screamingly high altitude and finally being able to breathe again. My father said nothing, but his face paled severely and I saw a blood-thirsty desire to kill cross his face. My mother narrowed her eyes in my direction and stormed out of the room. Not the reactions one would expect from normal parents. I don't think this is love. It has left me so hollow that if someone detonated a bomb in a seat next to me, I doubt I'd even flinch.

I heard a car arrive and muffled voices that night, so I have to assume my rape was not reason enough to cancel a perfectly good dinner. I stayed in my room with the music turned up.

It should be no surprise to me that a few weeks after my confession, I found my father in his workshop repainting a cupboard door, a cigarette smoldering in the ashtray beside him, and he casually mentioned that there had been an accident. A little mishap, I believe he called it. Bernie Botts was dead. My visceral reaction was one of skepticism. I wanted some photographic evidence. I gave Dad a bored and belligerent look, waiting for the rest.

"He was climbing over a fence in the middle of the night. On his ranch, and he slipped. Broke his neck in two places. Poor bastard lay there screaming in agony, covered in horse shit for three hours before somebody found him, but by then he was dead," Dad said, concentrating on dabbing extra paint onto the raw underside of the wood.

"If they found him dead, then how do you know he screamed for three hours?" I asked him, folding my arms in front of my chest.

His brush stopped mid-dab a beat too late. He stood up straight and reached for his cigarette, flicking the ash into the tray. He turned his head slowly in my direction, studying me in the doorway. Then he gave me a wink, took a final drag and put his cigarette out with a crush.

The sun comes up over the pond, spraying the landscape in gold as I slip out between the heavy front doors of White Oaks while my parents sleep. I walk through the exhaust fumes coming from the taxi's tailpipe and drop my bag into the open trunk. I notice it's a two-body trunk before I shut it. I slide into the back seat and ignore the stale stench of the taxi. The driver flips the meter on and looks at me through his rearview mirror expectantly.

"The airport, please," I say, watching the mansion roll out of sight as I leave my parents alone with their ghosts.

CHAPTER NINETEEN

In Which the Tiger Has Peeled Off His Fancy Clothes and Stands Naked in His Stripes, Present Day

There's a Portuguese word, *saudade*, which, although often described as untranslatable, means having nostalgia for something you never knew and something you will never know. This is the word I think of when I stir up the past and realize just how much I still don't know.

My father died just before my thirty-ninth birthday. After the massive stroke that rendered him virtually irredeemable and wheelchair-bound, my mother tried to care for him in their home. He often became combative and insolent and Mom would occasionally ask me to fly up, pay him a visit and talk some sense into him. Have a sit down. Negotiate. After my unceremonious departure, my relationship with my parents took some time to repair, but things smoothed over the phone lines and the occasional Christmas gathering and with maturity came an acceptance and forgiveness – on everyone's part.

It's unnerving to see a man who was once so powerful and full of vigor sitting in a wheelchair with a knitted blanket across his lap, staring out the window at his past.

"You're the only one who can talk to him, Maggie. I just can't deal with him anymore. He's a monster," Mom would say.

A veterinarian once told me that a dog will wag his tail for his owner even as it lay dying, so I didn't hold much hope when he brightened up and smiled as I walked into his bedroom the last time. I sat down on his bed and spun his wheelchair around so he could face me.

"How ya doing, Dad?"

"Not so great, kiddo. This life is hell. This is no way for anyone to live," he said. "You know your mother's trying to kill me, don't you?"

I took his hand in mine and patted it softly, hoping it didn't come across as too condescending.

"Yes, Dad, I imagine she is," I teased. "I'd expect nothing less."

I gave him a wink and he offered me a quiet, unenthusiastic chuckle before his steely blue eyes misted up with tears.

"I've done a lot of terrible things, Mag," he said.

I'd never seen my father this fragile before. Unnerved, I tried to calm him in order to bring back some version of the man who had raised me. I wanted to know him beyond the suits, beyond the swagger and flippant responses. I wanted to know what made this man tick, what made this man cry. I wanted to know what was in that paper sack back in Verona, Italy, and where and when my father had learned to tame the Italian language so beautifully, yet keep this knowledge such a secret. I wanted to know everything.

After a while, he opened up. I'm not ashamed to say that I took full advantage of the opportunity. Feeling my time was running out, I prodded him gently, as a priest in a confessional might do with someone reluctant to begin a shameful admission, trying to get some answers out of the old boy. In his weakened state, the tiger willingly offered his paws and allowed me to slip on the spats. He bowed his head down so I could set the bowler hat on his head, just so, at a dapper angle.

He began by listing the friends he'd lost along the way, as the elderly are prone to do. Paul Castellano, for one, gunned down in front of Spark's Steak House in Manhattan.

"It was that punk, John Gotti," Dad said. "Had Paulie

shot in the street like some stray dog. And they took pictures! For the whole world to see! That's the part that would have pissed Paulie off the most – the pictures. They stripped him of his dignity that night.

"You know, that's what began the feud between me and Gotti. Of course, I never liked him to begin with. He was nothing but a small time thug in a good suit."

I thought about this word, *feud*.

"Sometimes I wonder if his men were the ones who threatened to kidnap me back in high school," I held my breath waiting for the answer, knowing I may have just stepped over a line.

He became silent for a long time, wiping the corners of his mouth with a tissue.

"Yeah, I know. Pull that shade down a little more, would ya, Mag?"

I pulled the shade down until a band of sunlight only draped across his blanketed lap. He closed his eyes and sighed loudly, letting me know the subject would be better off dead. I let it go.

I wanted to talk about so many things. I wanted to ask about Jimmy Bruno but just the mention of his name was enough to make my father's face contort into a grimace of sorrow. My memories of Jimmy were ones of feeling protected, music boxes and grilled cheese sandwiches in the back of the Woolworth's, of lighting candles in the Catholic church. I can still hear Lou Capalbo razzing Jimmy about his pottery after coming home from our trip to Dr. O'Leary's office.

"You should open a pottery shop, Jimmy. You could call it *The Dago Potter*," Lou said.

"You know what I think? I think you should change the name of your bakery. How 'bout you call it *The Rotund Ginny's House of Inedible Crap*. How 'bout you try that?"

Watching them go after each other – in that best friend

sort of way — was some of my best childhood entertainment. They loved each other deeply and I loved them — as well you can love people you know so little about.

Jane told me Jimmy had disappeared one night after descending a subway entrance beneath the sidewalk near his parking garage and was not heard from again. But something told me that Jimmy had met up with something that even Jack Dahlstrom could not bring himself to face.

Maybe Dad had just lost too much and too many. I still only knew snippets — bullet points.

- Lou Capalbo died of lung cancer in a New York hospital a few years after Jimmy vanished.
- Uncle Budd contracted cancer of the jaw and refused to have it removed, opting instead for going out all in one piece.
- Virginia Coopersmith Vanderoth was moved to a nursing home in upstate New York where, I assume, she sat surrounded by her many harps until she died sitting upright, in meticulous posture, in an easy chair by the window, wearing her black horn rimmed glasses and her rubber boots. I imagine the Hellman's jar containing her late husband's remains cradled between her huge hands on her lap.

Dad only remained calm when he spoke of how he'd helped people get ahead. I suppose he was trying to make himself feel a bit better about his life. After retirement, and losing a substantial amount of power, he joined various organizations in a meager attempt to recapture some version of running things: the local zoning commission, the library committee, and he volunteered as the County Santa Claus — arriving via fire truck at the Courthouse to sit in an elaborate throne where children would perch on his lap and whisper their secret wishes in his ear. I imagined his reply being, "All it takes is a phone call, kid." I wonder what they would have thought had they known whose lap they were really sitting in.

He took some pride in assisting his buddy Sam Giancana set up casinos in Cuba and Mexico back in the sixties or seventies; he couldn't remember. He felt Giancana had been misunderstood and championed the man whenever he spoke of him.

"It's not that Sam killed more guys than anyone else, he just enjoyed it more," Dad said. "So he got a nasty reputation for being a maniacal killer. Really, he was just a business man."

It was Jack Ruby that he felt he'd helped the most. He'd gotten him into the business as a hit man so that he could vent his uncontrollable temper in a more organized fashion than slinging wrenches through airplane hangars for the rest of his life. But things had backfired in the end, and my father seemed to feel responsible for some of it. Henry Wade was part of what went wrong after Ruby shot Lee Harvey Oswald. As District Attorney, Henry was to be sent in to prosecute Ruby and steer the verdict in the direction of murder without malicious intent, which carried a prison sentence of five years at the most. Ruby would serve maybe three of those years – with good behavior – and then be released, handed a substantial amount of money and would purchase a nice plot of land he'd been eyeing on Oahu. Something went wrong. The verdict came back as murder with malicious intent and he was sentenced to life. Henry Wade shrugged his shoulders and went outside and lit a fat cigar.

Dad kept in contact with Ruby when the prison phone lines and letters allowed. He agreed to help him with one final request. Ruby's cancer was eating away at his insides and he had little time left, so he asked my father to contact John Connally – then, the Governor of Texas – to arrange a pardon for Candy Barr, his best dancer and loyal friend who'd been imprisoned for marijuana back in Dallas and whose life was deeply stunted by her parole restrictions. No dancing, being part of those restrictions. The pardon came quickly. Candy Barr, in a later interview, would say that she'd never met John Connally and was puzzled by his pardon, but that perhaps the Governor had seen how unfair her treatment had been all those years ago and had wanted to do the right thing. My father never took the credit.

I waited a moment and then I asked him the question I knew I wasn't supposed to ask – the one about the big Presidential elephant that had been sitting in his lap for half a century.

"Will you tell me about Kennedy? About what happened back in Dallas?"

His blue eyes, cloudy with cataracts, squinted as clouds parted and allowed harsh sunlight to stream in through his bedroom window, illuminating his slippered feet. I rose and pulled the shade down a bit farther, making the room dark. He dabbed the corners of his mouth with the tissue again

"Dallas. Jesus Christ. It was a mess up at Parkland. Everyone was screwing up. It was so easy, really, just toss some brain and bullet fragments into the big metal sink in the corner and that's it!" He made the gesture with his right arm, of lobbing something underhand, into the air, "They tell you to do it and you do it. No fuss, no muss, no questions why. All the guys got out okay though. They were hidden, tucked away. Well, except Ruby, of course. He was such a hot head. I couldn't get him out of prison. I tried," He stopped, dabbing his mouth with the tissue again and then said, "Get me a glass of Drambuie, would you, Mag?"

When I rose from his bed to sneak out to the bar in search of some truth serum, I noticed my mother standing in the doorway of Dad's bedroom with her arms crossed over her chest. She narrowed her eyes at my father. He waved her away in a dismissive manner. I knew the confessional was closed. My mother had become the gatekeeper of the liquor cabinet and, possibly, of his secrets now that he was nearly incapable of keeping his mouth shut if caught in the right moment. I saw there was no getting past her guard.

I imagine that I could have sat with the man for a hundred days and never feel I'd gotten the whole story. My father's history involved such a vast cast of characters and their interactions were such a delicately intertwined web that perhaps even Jack

Dahlstrom couldn't keep it all straight himself. His story was jumbled and ragged, skipping vital elements along the way. *Toss part of the brain? What the hell was he talking about?* I was stunned and mesmerized by the sheer gravity of the secrets he must still be keeping. I suppose that's the way it always is with these men. They travel with as many secrets as they can, hauling them to their graves. In the interim, if they become senile and restless and spill a few on their way out, they like to think they have kept their pledge to be buried still honoring the code of *Omerta.* As much as they are able.

Before I left his room that final day and I rose from his bed to leave, he softly grabbed my arm and pulled me lower so that we were eye to eye.

"What is it, Dad?"

"Hang on a minute," he said.

He began twisting and pulling on his ruby pinkie ring until he was able to pry it off his finger. He placed it in my hand, closed my fingers around it and then turned his head to stare out the window at the street.

CHAPTER TWENTY

*In Which Camelot Crumbles and a Phone Call Is Made,
Dallas, Texas, November 22, 1963 ~ 12:27 pm*

Faint cheers sail out into the Dallas sky from a few blocks away. The President must be approaching. Jack checks his coat pocket one more time for his extra key to the Carousel Lounge. He keeps it as a favor in case Ruby is called away and someone has to close up for him.

The man in the mechanic's gear looks in the direction of the sounds coming from the crowded streets and clenches his fists, then splays his fingers wide, then clenches again and then cracks his knuckles. He's warming up.

Ruby's not keeping his cool lately. It reminds Jack of when he first met him at Hollywood Park Racetrack where they were both stationed during the war. He'd been covered in grease and had just slung a large wrench through the air that nearly caught the side of Jack's head as he approached the B-24 Ruby was working on. The guy couldn't fix a lawn mower, much less an airplane engine, which fueled his hourly temper tantrums. Ruby had become a joke around the base. The more the fly boys laughed at him, the more unstable his temperament became. Jack had felt sorry for the guy back then when he was just a short, little Jewish mechanic named Rubenstein, so he'd prodded his pal, Lou Capalbo, to hook him up with some influential friends so he'd have a chance at earning some kind of a living after the war was over. It turned out Ruby had one talent: killing. Ruby did odd jobs for Sam Giancana for a number of years after the war, earning respect and the reputation of being just unhinged enough to take pride in his work while carrying out orders. He didn't get creative the way Lou and Jimmy did. He was blatant and literal in his hits. If a guy had to go down, he walked up to the man, shot him in the face and took him down. No nonsense.

With his new career under way, he'd gained a small confidence that Jack felt solely responsible for. But now the guy's nerves were showing again. He could become a liability before the afternoon was over.

The key is lying deep within the pocket next to Jack's good luck coin. He rubs them together, trying not to feel fidgety. The coin had been shiny and new, fresh off the mint press, the day he'd caught it in the air from his drug store stoop back in1929. He can still see the scene in his mind. Capone's doggish, determined face, emerging from his green bulletproof car, as little Jackie Dahlstrom receives his first official mob order. *Watch the car for me, kid.*

Excited roars gather and roll like waves in his direction. He sees the motorcade bank the corner and head slowly down the hill.

A man in a business suit and sunglasses strolls along the grass opposite Jack's spot behind the fence. He can tell by the man's gait that it's his brother-in-law, Budd. He watches him move against a river of late-comers rushing to get a glimpse of Kennedy and then he vanishes, most likely not wanting to get clipped by a stray bullet before he has a chance to take his early government retirement in Morocco with Betty.

The black Presidential convertible is moving slowly in the center of the motorcade. Security is thinner than Jack had anticipated. A flicker of bright pink moves at the back of the car like an unexpected wild flower blooming from a pile of coal.

The man in the mechanic's clothes bends down and reaches for the hidden rifle. Jack turns his head one final time to scan the area. Nobody sees anything but JFK and his entourage. The shooter lifts the rifle and nestles it on top of the hedge, resting both hands on it. Jack's eyes light on the sewer slit between the street and the curb. It's too far for him to see the rifle's nose moving into position, but he knows it's there.

The limousine halts momentarily, slowing their progress and Jack waits. He has a clear shot of the President and his wife in her pink hat. The mechanic hunches over the hedge, grips the rifle, and takes aim as the limousine starts to pass in front of him. Jack holds his breath waiting for the first shot. Nothing happens. They're late. They should have taken a shot by now. A deep, worried line creases between his eyes. He takes another look at the sewer opening across the street.

Then he hears it. One pop. Just loud enough for a few people in the crowd to turn their attention away from the President for a brief moment. Kennedy's head turns towards the sound. Another shot, this one louder, closer, rings out and echoes off the surrounding stand of buildings. The President's head bends down and his arms come up, as if an invisible puppeteer has yanked on strings tied to his elbows and wrists. His fists clench and meet under his chin. John Connally, sitting in the seat directly in front of Kennedy, turns his head – he's yelling something.

The motorcade continues to roll on Elm Street. The mechanic carefully aligns his right eye with the sight of the rifle, his chin settles steadily into the leaves on top of the hedge.

Jack palms the coin in his pocket. The rifle next to him fires, emitting a plume of metallic smoke into the air. He thinks he hears another shot sounding off to his left. A man in a black captain's hat and grimy blue jeans pushes a wheeled cart stacked with brush and tree limbs behind them.

The President's head snaps up and back. A massive chunk of his skull is obliterated. The First Lady leans into her husband briefly, and then is suddenly scrambling up and out of her seat, crawling on hands and knees over the freshly-waxed trunk of the Lincoln, towards a Secret Service man running up behind the car.

The shooter next to Jack wheels around and buries the rifle in the brush of the rolling cart in a quick, fluid movement. The man pauses just long enough to place two leafy branches over the gun and then continues to roll the cart calmly and quickly away from them. Jack turns away from the man with the cart and notices the mechanic is now gone. Wails of horror begin to ring out over Dealey Plaza as he adjusts the top of his hat with the palm of his hand and walks away.

#

The key fits snugly into the lock. The club smells of stale cigarettes and desperation, as usual. Jack waits for his eyes to adjust after coming in from the mid-day sun. Ruby's greed and constant worrying presence cling to the sticky floor, creating a slight suction as Jack flicks the light switch on the wall and strolls to the bar across the room, making his way around the still hazy silhouettes of tables and chairs.

He pulls the black phone from a shelf below and sets it on top of the bar. Lifting the receiver, he dials the memorized long distance number and listens to the tinny ring on the other end. After the third ring, someone picks up and says nothing.

"Good news at the races today," Jack says, placing a steady hand on the edge of the bar.

"Our horse won then," the man says.

"By a neck."

"Good. I'll tell them." The man on the other end sounds as if he's smiling. "So you'll be coming to town on Sunday."

"Sure thing. See you then," Jack says. A click on the line, followed by a steady hum, tells him the conversation is over.

The man on the other end will deliver the news to another, then it will be delivered to another and another, until it has rippled into the ears of the appropriate parties. By the time Jack replaces the phone back on the shelf, walks over the sticky floor, flicks the light switch off and has locked up the Carousel Lounge, the message will have made final delivery. He can feel his life shifting as he walks across the street to his Pontiac Bonneville parked at the curb. He rehearses the speech in his head, how he will announce to his wife and children that things are about to change, how life will be easier from this day forward.

This is fate; he knows it. It was going to happen with or without him. *With* him was much more appealing to all involved; he wonders if he'd ever really had a choice. Destiny is funny that way; it snares you around the ankles and drags you where it needs to go. You can let the force direct you or you can fight it and remain in constant struggle against the tide. He simply chose to let it carry him away in the direction he was always intended to go.

He checks his watch. 12:45. Making good time. Jack settles into the leather seat behind the wheel and turns the ignition over. He steers the car in the opposite direction. The pleasant November air feels like a new life introducing itself as it wraps around and over the upholstery. He delights in how palpable his future now suddenly feels. The future that is paved by the past. If he'd never met Jack Ruby or Lou Capalbo during the war, if he hadn't married the sister of a Secret Service Agent, if he'd never met Al Capone and witnessed that powerful essence he might never have become such a vital link in this deal.

The added bonus is having spent so much miserable time up at Parkland Hospital, worrying over his son and insisting the team of brain specialists work around the clock to pull Sid through his injuries and out of his coma. He shouldn't have trouble getting into the hospital, since he knows every employee and doctor in the place by now. Once he's inside, he'll be able to complete his final part of the assignment.

It's been a while since he's been in the presence of a corpse, not since the end of the war, when he returned home, married Patricia and worked in his Uncle Joe's funeral parlor below their first dingy, dark, one bedroom apartment with the bad plumbing.

Parkland is humming with news cameras, reporters, cops and emergency vehicles. The black convertible limousine sits empty under the overhang at the Emergency Room Entrance. Jack snakes by the people outside and walks through the hospital doors. Chaotic, urgent arguing rumbles and echoes the crowded corridors. He keeps his gait steady, authoritative, while searching the faces for his brother-in-law. Two men, embraced in a maniacal dance, grasping each other's throats, hit the wall together in front of Jack.

As he nears the entrance to Trauma Room One, a dark suited figure steps in his path, making him come to an abrupt stop. They lock eyes momentarily. Jack shifts his stare to the man's lapel and then turns his head slowly to the right, making sure the cotton in his ear is clearly visible. The man steps aside letting him enter the room.

Dr. Clark looks up from where he stands at the head of the gurney and nods to Jack.

By 1:17, according to the clock on the wall of Trauma Room One, Jack is rinsing off his hands at the metal sink. The attendees in the room are deciding on an official time of death somewhere between 12:38 – when the President's body arrived at Parkland – and now. It has all taken far too long in Jack's opinion. He's glad he'd been deemed the "fixer" and stepped in when he had.

A pea-sized piece of twisted brain matter fights the pull of the water descending the drain. He cups his hands together, collecting enough water to force it down with one final splash. As he towels off his palms, he thinks how the brain's weight is equal to that of a coconut, and how easily what was left of it had sailed across the small room and into the metal surgical sink with a resounding thud. He'd heard one of the men in the room gasp, as if to comment on the uncustomary way he'd disposed of it; clearly the guy doesn't understand that Jack is only trying to be efficient. A body is just a body after all. A shell. Whether you're a President or a hobo. It's been four minutes since the orderly unknowingly carried it out of the room in a sack of garbage, through the noisy corridor and down to the basement incinerator.

The Bonneville accelerates up the entrance ramp and merges with traffic on Stemmons. Jack pulls the tuft of cotton from his right ear and lets it loose out the window to ride the rush of air. He pulls the piece from his left and holds it out the window a second before letting go and releasing it along with all his worries, about the mounting hospital bills and the secrets of the past few months that have kept him up at night.

The men in the sewers will remain underground for a couple hours more, traveling on foot through the sewer system and will eventually come out on another side of town where cars will be waiting. The decoy rifles may or may not be recovered. They could be left as false evidence to further jumble the day's trail of events.

Some things had gone wrong; Connally, for one thing. Jack hadn't known John had been hit until he'd arrived at Parkland. A civilian standing near the motorcade had also been hit but was only grazed by the passing bullet. He's somewhat amazed at how the operation has been pulled off, despite how often he'd been assured that every detail would be handled and there would be nothing to worry about. He'd still had his doubts.

Thin wisps of cotton kiss the warm pavement, dancing with every passing car.

CHAPTER TWENTY-ONE

*In Which Most of the World Weeps While Others
Simply Have Cocktails,
Dallas, Texas, November 22, 1963 ~ 2:58 pm*

Lou Capalbo's white sedan waits in the driveway of 806 Classen Drive. Jack pulls in behind it. The AM/FM radio announces businesses and schools are closing for the rest of the afternoon. Jane should be on her way home soon. He shuts the engine down and takes a deep breath before opening the car door and stepping out onto the driveway. He takes in their modest home with its red front door. This house has been good to them for more than ten years, but he won't be sorry to say goodbye. They need a fresh start. All of them.

Patricia is filling Lou's glass with ice when Jack steps through the doorway. The smell of something beefy reminds him he hasn't eaten today. The baby wears nothing but a diaper, struggling to rise to a standing position, gripping Lou's pant leg with determined Dahlstrom grit. The low drone of an anchorman streams from the television in the corner of the living room. Jack meets his wife's glance with little expression. She's been a bit better since Sid came home from the hospital; no more hysterics, restraints haven't been necessary for weeks now. She's been almost pleasant. Patricia quickly looks away from her husband and wipes her hands on a dish towel before slinging it over her shoulder to return to the stove to doctor whatever she's cooking. Jack loosens his tie and takes a seat at the table across from Lou.

"I noticed you took down that wall...looks good. Opens

the place up," Lou says.

"Yeah, we did that about six months ago. Pat wanted to be able to see the living room while she's in the kitchen," Jack says, "Makes the place look bigger, doesn't it?"

The phone on the kitchen wall rings.

"Gaaad, this phone has been going non-stop for the last hour, Jack," Patricia says, clicking off the burner and going to answer it.

"And that's my fault?" he says.

"Hello?" She turns her back to the living room, leaning against the white refrigerator. "Hi... Yes, I know...No, they've closed the schools down. Jane should be on her way home now...I know...it's just awful."

Jimmy Bruno swings the front door open without ringing the bell. He wipes his feet on the welcome mat before entering the house.

"Where ya been, Bruno?" Lou says.

"Baby sitting," Jimmy says. "I tell ya, that kid's a Nazi."

He steps over the threshold, removing his jacket and closes the door behind him.

"The kid don't like pickles. What sort of kid don't want a good pickle on his burger? He had a big snit about it. I think there's somethin' wrong with him. I liked pickles when I was four," Jimmy says, taking a seat on the long, olive green couch, making the frame squeak.

"Bruno, your mother was still nursing you when you were four, what did you know about pickles?" Lou says, jabbing Jack in the arm.

"Everything go okay, then?" Jack asks Jimmy.

Jimmy lights a cigarette, takes a deep drag and sinks into the back of the couch, blowing smoke out slowly.

"Except for the pickle thing, yeah. Dropped him back off at the fence and watched him walk back inside. I don't even think they knew he'd been gone. Maybe they were glad to get rid of him for a while. I gotta tell ya, that kid must have asked me three thousand questions. 'Do you have a car? What kind of car? Do you like kangaroos? How much money do you have? Have you ever been on a boat? Did you know my grandfather only has eight fingers?' Jesus. I wanted to pull my friggin' hair out."

Jack shakes his head, chuckling, watching Jimmy slick his black hair back with the palm of his hand.

Patricia says goodbye to the caller and turns to give Jack a roll of her eyes. A low groan sounds from Sid's bedroom down the long hallway.

"I think Sid needs you, Pat," Jack says.

"Yes, Jack. I hear him," she snips.

She tosses the dish towel into the sink with a slap and leaves to tend to their son.

Jimmy rises from the couch and stretches his fists into the air. He watches the baby wobble on chubby legs in front of Lou. She drops to the floor on her bottom and watches Jimmy approach with expectant blue eyes.

"Give me that baby," he says to Lou, securing his cigarette between his lips and scooping Maggie up by her armpits.

He raises her high above his head and shimmies her back and forth. A clear droplet of spit falls to the carpet from her wide-mouthed smile. Her rumbling belly-laugh fills the room, making the men chuckle.

"Jesus, Jimmy, you're gonna break her friggin' neck shaking her that way," Lou says.

"She likes it," Jimmy says. "What a happy baby you are." He tosses her gently toward the ceiling, making her laugh even harder. "You're happy I rescued you from that bad old Uncle Lou, aren't you? He's a smelly bastard, isn't he?"

"There's nothing more disgusting than hearing a big, dumb Wop talking baby talk," Lou says, smiling at Jack.

Jimmy brings Maggie down to straddle his hip and carries her to the kitchen. He bounces her gently with one arm as she smiles up at him, a lavender ribbon tied in a bow around the thin tuft of hair at the crown of her head bounces in time.

"Hey, Mary Poppins! Bring me that bottle of scotch on the counter while you're over there, will ya?" Lou calls out.

Jimmy ignores him, extinguishing his cigarette in an ashtray on the kitchen counter, then kissing the baby's forehead.

Jimmy coos in her ear, "He's a mean old son of a bitch. Let's stay away from him."

Maggie giggles, opens her mouth wide and clamps down on Jimmy's shoulder with tiny teeth.

Henry Wade flings the front door open and enters the house with a scowl. The nub of his lit cigar clenched tightly between his teeth.

"God damnit, I need a drink," Henry says, as he makes his way to the bottle of scotch on the kitchen counter and begins searching the cupboards for a glass.

"I propose a toast, fellas," Lou calls out.

As Henry fills a glass with ice, Jack and Jimmy raise their cocktails.

"Let's hear it," Jack says.

Lou clears his throat, "To a job well done, new beginnings and bigger bank accounts."

"To the hope that Dahlstrom here, will one day soon, be able to start buying some decent booze instead of serving this pathetic and vile swill he calls scotch," Henry says, filling his glass.

"I have an announcement," Jimmy says, shifting the baby to his other hip, "I'm thinking of taking up pottery."

The men laugh. Lou and Jack clink their glasses together. Jimmy, not bothered by their snickers, clears his throat to continue, "Gentlemen, you laugh, but please remember these words of wisdom: The greatest danger is not that we set our aims too high and don't achieve them; it is that we set our aims too low – and we do."

Patricia has returned from the hallway and leans against the doorway next to Henry. The room has become silent as the men stare at Jimmy with mouths hanging open.

"Henry, did Jimmy Bruno just quote Michelangelo?" she asks.

"I believe he did, Patricia. I believe he did."

A FINAL THOUGHT

In Which We Fold The Tiger's Fancy Clothes and Put Them In A Box, and Finally, Ceremoniously, Place His Bowler Hat and Spats Inside And Close The Lid

The surprising thing about losing your hair after chemo is what no one tells you. You expect it to fall out gradually, letting everyone, including yourself, get used to the idea over a period of weeks; maybe you get a chance to try on different hats, have a wig or two made, become practiced in the art of wrapping your skull in European scarves so that you look like Joan Crawford, but that's not how it goes. You wake up ten days after your first round of chemo and most of your hair is on your pillow.

When this happened to me, I raced my hands up to my head that first balding morning and found vacant lots of scalp amidst some very long tendrils of blond patches that were reluctant to let go. I pulled gently on a remaining chunk to find that it came out loose and painless in my hand. I got up from the bed and went to the bathroom mirror. Nothing can prepare a person for this. I stared at my reflection, mouth gaping – and it was in that moment, I noticed my soul close its eyes slowly; it shook its head at me, sighed loudly and walked directly out the front door, to my car, opened the back door, climbed inside and locked the doors. Some things never change.

I'd imagined losing my hair. I'd even once put on a baseball cap and tucked my hair up inside to see what I was going to look like bald. I hadn't even come close. My head still retained the obnoxious Tweety Bird shape I'd been teased about as a kid.

Long, freakish tufts of hair sprouted sporadically from the top of my head. The sides and back were completely bald except at the very base where more long strands still clung. I looked like I'd just come from a hair appointment at Three Mile Island.

Mom hadn't known anything about my diagnosis for about a month. I think I was too terrified of her saying something cruel or scoffing at me or maybe saying, "You think you've got problems? Let me tell you what happened to me yesterday down in the basement while I was looking for the Haviland china."

But none of that happened. She boarded a flight for Austin to accompany me to my next chemo appointment and stayed by my side, holding her aged, freckled hand over mine with misty eyes as the oncology nurse inserted the needle into the port in my chest. She watched the medicine drip steadily from the bag into my body. I noticed she was trembling. I smiled at her, wondering what it must be like to watch your child go through something like that.

She was warm and funny, brave and supportive. She returned to Portland but called every day. In one particular phone call, an astonishing admission came.

"Mag, I've started seeing a therapist here. I've learned a lot, Honey, even as long in the tooth as I am, and I owe you an apology," she said.

"An apology? For what, Mom?"

"When you told me what Bernie Botts did to you in Austria, I reacted cruelly and I don't yet know why, but I'm trying to figure it out."

"I think I know why," I paused, waiting for her to say something. When she didn't, I continued. "I think it's because your father did the same thing to you; I think Uncle Jim did too and I imagine it sent you back to your own traumatic childhood."

She was quiet for a moment and then said, "I think you're probably right."

After that, at the end of each phone call she told me she

loved me, a thing I'd never heard her say. It reminded me of hearing someone you've known for years suddenly speak a foreign language fluently.

The final casualty by the end of the year was my breast; it had to be removed, but with that removal came a healing with Mom, so let's call it even. Perhaps in Dad's absence, she'd found a freedom in learning how to love and connect, because it was only after he died that she began to unfurl, to relax – maybe for the very first time – like the waters of a river breaking loose and free after a thaw.

I have always been grateful that my father wasn't around for my year of cancer. Knowing him, he would have taken out a hit on the tumor. Sending a band of beefy Italians, wearing black leather gloves, to my house to sneak up behind me while I did the dishes. One, the most ballsy of the bunch, would pull a stretch of piano wire out of his coat pocket, wrap it quickly around my right boob, holding it tightly, while one of his pals would take careful aim with his hand gun – silencer screwed securely in place – and blow a jagged tunnel through the tumor. Then they'd hacksaw the rest of it off, stuff the remains in a black plastic bag and toss it in their glove compartment. They would cart it off to the New Jersey woods in the dead of night, where they'd bury it deep in a hole in the ground, all the while illuminated by the headlights of a black Town Car. As they tossed their shovels into the trunk, ready to leave the scene, one (the ballsy one, no doubt) would narrow his eyes, threatening the fresh mound of soil and point his gloved finger at it in final warning before driving off through the fog. I mean, really, who needs all that drama?

#

I've heard that a moment before death, the dying will sometimes raise their hands in supplication, palms up, and hold them there briefly with eyes closed before going on to the other side. Are they saying, "Okay, I give, take me with you"? I wonder. This, I'm told, is what my mother did just before she died a few months shy of her ninety-second birthday. I wasn't there, so I'll have to take my brother's word for it.

I keep imagining that this was just a repeat performance; that Mom had just slowed her heart rate down to an indecipherable rhythm like some ancient Indian guru, playing a big joke on us all. I keep expecting to get a call from Sid saying, "Well, Mag, turns out Mom was just messing around. She's not dead after all. We found her lying on her back underneath the dining table, clutching a bouquet of daffodils and we fell for it."

But that call hasn't come. For the past several months, I have kept an ear open for the phone, expecting it to ring. When I answer, I will hear my mother's trembling, ancient voice croak out my name as we begin one of our regularly scheduled Saturday morning chats. That call hasn't come either. I think she might actually be dead this time.

I'm getting tired of losing people – especially the ones I'm just now beginning to truly understand – and the older I get, the more people I seem to lose lately. Death is relentless.

Jane and I don't discuss those tumultuous years very often. She feels it's best to only move forward, while I still seem to be able to slip back into the past and try to figure things out, forever determined to squeeze that tiger into some pants. But she says I'm better than I used to be about all that. Maybe I am.

Truth be told, I still don't know if this is how the story really goes. I don't know exactly who shot Kennedy on that November day, or why; I don't know what was in that package my father had in Italy or when he learned to speak Italian or who was out to kidnap me and I don't know what the links between the Mafia, the Oval Office and my loved ones were all about, but if I had all of those answers I'd have my own talk show.

But this story is what I have come to believe is as close to the truth as I can get after trying to get the puzzles pieces to fit together. This is how we survive things. We make the most sense of them in the best way we know how, with what little information we're given.

Maybe life isn't about finding all the answers. Maybe it's about the experience which leads us to learn about love and forgiveness, listening to one's heart and trying our damnedest to live in peace regardless of what's going on around us or who's hiding under the furniture. Perhaps it's about appreciating the little things, like the fact that I can now pass a can of Aqua Net in the drug store without needing to book an emergency appointment with my therapist. Maybe it's about *allowing* oneself to pack up the things that keep us awake at night – the flying monkeys, tornados that send folks to the asylum, sharks stashed in trunks, mothers in linen closets, visits to the dentist and all the Je Ne Sais Quoi we encounter along the way– and willingly, ceremoniously put these things in a secret box and close the lid. Perhaps in the end, if we've learned anything at all, we just allow tigers to run naked and we accept and embrace the great *Saudade*, because it is there, in that longing, untranslatable place where the magic lies and our stories write themselves. And maybe that's enough.

Acknowledgments

First off, let's start with a big, fat disclaimer so as not to ruffle any feathers or land me in the trunk of someone's black Town Car secured with rope and duct tape. Some names, places and events were changed to protect some people's privacy, but mostly (if we're being honest here) to cover my own ass. Some of the dialog would have been impossible for me to remember verbatim from such a very young age, so I reconstructed conversations in the way I remember, imagined, or in some cases, hoped them to be. The events that take place before my birth have some fictional elements to them for the obvious reasons. I made one guy up completely. Don't ask. You'll ruin it.

That being said, most of the events in this book, did, in fact, happen. (Yes, even the geisha. I actually did take them for Show N Tell and have photos to prove this but I left this out as I was leaning towards overkill with the whole Show N Tell thing and believe it or not, there is such a thing as too much Show N Tell mentioned in one book.) And one note: My mother was bitten by a llama at the Bronx Zoo but was never slapped by an actual monkey at the dinner table – that part was written to break up any potential monotony that can occur while eating roast beef.

One might be wondering, why, if my father was a Teamster Negotiator, I would leave out any mention of Jimmy Hoffa. Easy: Because they were friends, the Teamsters are still a really big deal and Dad asked me to. (And if more explanation is necessary, please refer to the black Town Car scenario mentioned above.)

Big thanks to my editor, Liz Stein in New Jersey. A genius at taking this book to the next level while making me laugh and talking me off the ledge at the same time throughout the editing process and agent-related fiascos – not an easy feat.

Thanks to Marie Carter, www.mariewritesandedits.com, of Gotham Writers Workshop in NYC and author of *The Trapeze Diaries* for the book layout design, cover design, for mentoring me and offering an avalanche of advice along the way.

Thank you to all my patient friends and family for reading various versions of the manuscript and for not telling me I sucked. That kind of support is what keeps a writer writing. I appreciate all of you.

To my son, Sage – Thank you for believing in your mother so endlessly. I love you madly. I hope this book helps you understand your family history a little better and that you don't wind up in therapy because of it. And…you owe me $221,785.43 for cell phone charges, excessive date usage, vet bills for that dog you picked up on the highway and other various "loans". (Just a reminder)

The Great Ernest Hemingway – thank you for teaching me it's alright to toss a little fiction into a memoir as long as it empowers the story. P.S. You were a hottie.

Elizabeth Gilbert – for taking the time to reply to my weepy FB message during the query process and saying, "Maggie, don't you dare give up." You've been an incredible inspiration on this journey.

To my very best friend on the planet, Sheryl (last name left out due to her being a Scorpio and prone to excessive bouts of secrecy for undisclosed reasons that only Scorpios understand), for being my champion on this journey; for pulling me out of the dark holes that writers sometimes find themselves in when they wake up to yet another rejection slip from an agent or publisher; for traveling with me to New York City to find the man in the tiny sombrero and breakfast at Zabar's. My rock for over 30 years.

Steven Luna at Dapper Press – Thank you for the words of wisdom, tons of advice and for writing a book (Joe Vampire) that made me laugh out loud. It's genius.

To my publicist, Meryl Zegarek for guiding me so gently and professionally and for not letting me get on the plane without some fresh New York bagels and some great books.

To John Griffin, my friend and handyman, for finding

typos that escaped me (even after reading the manuscript 3400 times) and my bathroom sink is still dripping. Please call to book appointment.

To my parents, God love 'em, for giving me the tools to be self-sufficient, to forgive, to explore, to ask the big questions of life and to follow my instincts when it comes to all things shady. You two were something else.

I wrote this book in 150 hours. The editing took me 3 years until I found an actual real-life editor. So, with that, I must thank my loyal Shepherd/Coon Hound mix, Broozer, for patiently curling up under my feet while I worked – in dog years that would be the equivalent of about 22 years. Good boy.

On a more serious note: This is a portrayal of the softer side of the mob – the mob I knew. I realize these men did some horrible things and changed the world in some pretty disturbing ways and I don't mean to romanticize their life style. But, these men are/were people; they are human beings, good or bad. We are all multi-faceted and I think it's important to tell the other side of stories, the softer side, the vulnerable side, the human side – even though I, at various times, found myself in grave danger because of them and am forever mortified by their behavior. I am deeply sorry for everything the Kennedy family endured and it troubles me greatly to think my father could have had something to do with part of their pain. JFK is one of my greatest heroes. That being said, I did feel this story needed to be told before it was lost forever.

www.ingramcontent.com/pod-product-compliance
Lightning Source LLC
Chambersburg PA
CBHW051646040426
42446CB00009B/1003